JUST WAGES

High on the agenda for Canadian feminists in the 1990s, pay equity continues to be a controversial issue throughout all sectors of the economy. The essays in this collection analyse the past, present, and future of pay equity and its implications for women.

In the introduction the editors address the central political question of pay equity: who benefits from the legal imposition of pay equity programs? The papers which follow reflect three different disciplinary approaches (sociological, economic, and legal) and discuss the three sectors that pay equity legislation may be designed to work within (public service, public sector, and private sector). They also consider the implications of various legislative techniques in each sector.

The multi-disciplinary nature of this collection makes possible a comprehensive evaluation of pay equity initiatives as a strategy in the context of current economic restructuring.

JUDY FUDGE is Associate Professor, Osgoode Hall Law School.
PATRICIA MCDERMOTT is a member of the Faculty of Social Sciences, York University.

JUST WAGES

A Feminist Assessment of
Pay Equity

Edited by
JUDY FUDGE
PATRICIA MCDERMOTT

UNIVERSITY OF TORONTO PRESS
Toronto Buffalo London

© University of Toronto Press 1991
Toronto Buffalo London
Printed in Canada

ISBN 0-8020-5937-6 (cloth)
ISBN 0-8020-6878-2 (paper)

∞

Printed on acid free paper

Canadian Cataloguing in Publication Data

Main entry under title:

Just wages

Papers presented at the Pay Equity: Theory and Practice
Conference organized through York University's Centre
for Public Law and Public Policy, May 14–15, 1990.
ISBN 0-8020-5937-6 (bound) – ISBN 0-8020-6878-2 (pbk.)

1. Pay equity – Canada – Congresses.   2. Wages – Women – Canada –
Congresses.   I. Fudge, Judy.
II. McDermott, Patricia.   III. Pay Equity: Theory
and Practice Conference (1990 : Toronto, Ont.).

HD6061.2.C3J8 1991 331.4'21'0971 C91-094645-0   72223

This book is dedicated in loving memory to:

Margaret Lowe Benston (1937–1991) and

Jacqueline S. Greatbatch (1956–1991)

Contents

Acknowledgments

The papers in this volume were presented at the 'Pay Equity: Theory and Practice' Conference organized by the editors through York University's Centre for Public Law and Public Policy on 14 and 15 May 1990. Nicola Cunningham, Leanne M. MacMillan, and Mavis Morton provided invaluable assistance in organizing the conference, and special thanks are also due to Denise Boissoneau, Rose Della Rocco, and John Ferguson who stepped in to help with the conference when needed. We would also to like thank the following speakers and workshop leaders for their contributions in making the conference a success: Susan Colley, Mary Cornish, Paul Durber, Roberta Ellis-Grunfeld, Sonja Greckol, Irene Harris, Raymonde Leblanc, Joyce McKerrow, Brigid O'Reilly, Isla Peters, Cela Ramkhalawansingh, Elizabeth Shilton, Beth Symes, Joanne Toews, and Lawrence Walter.

The title for this collection, *Just Wages*, was originally used by a quarterly bulletin on wage discrimination and pay equity published by the Women's Resource Centre, in conjunction with the Trade Union Research Bureau. It brings news and critical analysis of the issues to a popular audience and is aimed at activists working to achieve more money for women. For information about the bulletin, write to Just Wages, Suite 101, 2245 West Broadway, Vancouver, BC, V6K 2E4.

We would like to thank Virgil Duff, of the University of Toronto Press, for his enthusiasm and support for the project. Early drafts of the manuscript were much improved by the skilled editorial guidance of Erika Krolman and the careful assistance of Jan Kainer. We would also like to thank Beverley Beetham Endersby for her detailed editorial work on the final manuscript.

Neither the conference nor this collection of essays would have been

x Acknowledgments

possible without the generous financial support of the following institutions: the Federal Department of Justice, Law Foundation of Ontario,
Labour Canada, and the Social Sciences and Humanities Research Council, Osgoode Hall Law School, and York University.

EDITORS

JUST WAGES:
A FEMINIST ASSESSMENT OF
PAY EQUITY

Introduction:
Putting Feminism to Work

Judy Fudge and Patricia McDermott

Pay Equity and Feminism

Pay equity is a global process. In the past two decades there have been literally tens of thousands of pay equity initiatives throughout the world. The debate over how pay equity should be implemented dates back to 1951, when the principle of equal pay for work of equal value was codified into the International Labour Organization Convention 100.[1] Pay equity depends on the ability to value jobs and, thus, is closely related to the growth and expansion of job-evaluation and related wage-classification schemes. Although, initially, job evaluation was a management tool used for wage administration, hiring, placement, and supervision, during the Second World War it was explicitly used in the United States to equalize the wage or salary rates paid to women with those paid to men for comparable quality and quantity of work (Evans and Nelson 1989a, 25–6). In fact, many of the job-evaluation systems developed by management-consulting firms in the 1940s continue to be used today in pay equity implementation (Elliott and Saxe 1987, 26). Job evaluation is a big business and is expanding with the increasing popularity of pay equity. This book assesses some of the recent history of pay equity in terms of its effectiveness in closing the gendered wage gap; one of the central concerns here is the relationship between pay equity and job evaluation.

Historically, women not only have earned significantly less money than men, but also have been employed in what have come to be understood to be women's jobs. Despite the fact that the post-1950 Canadian labour market has been characterized by a dramatic increase in the labour-force participation rates of women, whether single or married and with or without dependents, women have largely remained segregated in female-dominated occupations (Connelly and MacDonald 1990, 22–4; Gunderson, Muszynski, and Keck 1990, 76–8). Moreover, the gap between men and women's earnings has persisted and is particularly pronounced between female-dominated and male-dominated occupations (Ehrenberg 1989, 90; Gunderson 1989). And, although there continues to be a number of methodological problems in computing the wage gap (Gunderson 1989), in Canada empirical research aimed at estimating its magnitude has consistently confirmed that an overall differential of approximately 40 per cent exists (Robb 1988).

While the evidence of differential pay for male- and female-dominated jobs is strong, sharply divergent explanations of the wage gap have been offered. On the one hand, the wage gap is regarded as the result of a cumulative history of discrimination and bias; on the other, it is understood as the outcome of neutral market forces that reflect the different skills and education of women and men workers and their individual family and employment choices. In the recent past, the first explanation has gained ground, with the result that a number of policy initiatives have been introduced to end the wage gap. These have included equal-pay-for-equal-work legislation and some minimal, and mostly voluntary, affirmative-action schemes. These efforts have not, however, addressed the dramatic segregation of the modern labour market by sex and the consistent devaluation of work associated with women.

In the past two decades 'pay equity,' or 'comparable worth' as it is often termed in the United States, has become the main strategy for resolving this long-standing problem. While both terms refer to the same type of initiative, 'pay equity' emphasizes the *goal* of ending wage discrimination, whereas 'comparable worth' emphasizes the *process* by which wage discrimination is to be ended (Evans and Nelson 1989a, 11). But common to all such initiatives is 'the principle that jobs dissimilar in nature can be compared in terms of knowledge, skill, effort, responsibility, and working conditions, and that jobs equivalent in value in these terms should be paid equally' (American Association of University Women 1987, 5). Pay equity is, therefore, a strategy based on the acknowledgment that, despite efforts to move women into areas of work that are not traditionally identified as women's work, a gendered labour-market segmentation remains a prominent feature of modern industrial economies. Pay equity is also based on the assumption that women do valuable work – work that is, in most cases, as valuable to society and employers as work done by their male co-workers. The recognition of the widespread undervaluation of women's work has moved efforts to address the problem of the wage gap away from schemes involving individuals or groups who launch complaints about their unfair wages with commissions and tribunals, typical of the provisions in the Canadian and Quebec human rights acts, to legislatively based proactive models. Pay equity is proactive in that it requires employers to assess whether their pay practices are discriminatory and to develop wage-adjustment programs to end such discrimination. Although there are several methods for evaluating and correcting underpaid jobs, by the late 1970s most American and Canadian pay equity initiatives have involved the use of job-evaluation systems to measure the worth of male- and female-dominated jobs.

Pay equity has been placed on the policy agenda in Canada and the United States primarily as a result of the work of feminists, who have been at the forefront of the struggle both to have wage discrimination identified as a crucial and pressing political issue and to develop and implement strategies for ending such discrimination. This collection of essays adopts an explicitly feminist stance in evaluating pay equity as a feminist strategy to end wage discrimination.

Feminism is both an intellectual project and a political movement (Maroney and Luxton 1987). As an intellectual project, it is concerned with understanding how gender is constructed, identified, and valued in social relations characterized by a profound inequality between men and women. As a political movement, it is motivated by the desire to end the systemic inequality that women experience in relation to men. Thus, the theoretical and methodological debates that characterize feminist research also involve political and strategic questions that are crucial for feminist activists. However, it is important to recognize both that the wage gap is but one aspect of systemic discrimination against women and that pay equity is only one of many strategies for ending such discrimination.

Pay equity puts feminism to work in two senses. First, it puts the intellectual project of feminism to work in developing an understanding of how gender is expressed in economic relations. The relationship between gender and class in reproducing women's inferior position to men has generated a great deal of academic debate and has challenged our understanding of how subordination is reproduced (Hartmann 1981;

Armstrong and Armstrong 1990d). The wage is 'an essential component of the capitalist economic system and is *both* an aspect of production and a mechanism for distribution' (Acker 1988, 482). As the primary mechanism of distribution within capitalist economies, the wage is gendered in specific ways. Sex segregation of occupations and the wage gap are pervasive, and the family wage, with its assumption that women will be dependent upon men, is a frequently invoked ideal. Moreover, the sex segregation of jobs reinforces 'the association of masculinity with mechanical and technical skills and the association of feminity with patience and selfless dedication to repetitive tasks. The linkage of masculinity with skill can, in turn, be an ideological weapon in the exclusion of women in male-dominated jobs' (Acker 1988, 482, footnote omitted). Not only are jobs gendered, they are also organized on a gendered hierarchical basis – in organizations women work, disproportionately to men, at the bottom. According to Acker, 'gender is so deeply embedded in the hierarchical structure that alteration of the gender order tends to threaten the hierarchy itself' (Acker 1988, 482). Pay equity, which challenges the gender bias of the workplace hierarchy, consequently provides an opportunity to examine how the wage is shaped by gender as well as class relations.

Second, pay equity requires feminists who are active in the struggle to eliminate the gender wage gap to make political and strategic decisions about how this should be done. Some success having been achieved in influencing the legislative agenda in many jurisdictions, the struggle has shifted to the implementation stage. Pay equity implementation is a growing industry that engages large management-consulting firms, trade unions, government managers, and feminist advocates in negotiation and litigation. These localized struggles revolve around questions of technique – definitions, measurements, and systems. For this reason, it is important to understand the technical issues addressed in several of the essays in this volume. But since, as several of the contributors to this collection argue, the resolution of technical questions is essentially political, it is also necessary to look at the techniques of politics – the resources and strategies used both to implement and to resist pay equity's social vision.

Feminists are no longer content simply to achieve equality in the predominantly male-defined world of work; they want to examine how work has historically been valued in order to revalue it in a way that incorporates women's interests. Pay equity, therefore, expresses a larger social vision as much as it names a technique for rectifying gender-based wage differentials. Feminists who are working to revalue women's work can learn from the experiences of those who have participated in pay equity implementation. For this reason, we have included essays in this book that evaluate pay equity initiatives in a variety of jurisdictions across North America, which will enable the reader to compare them and identify whether there are common problems that feminist advocates of pay equity face.

With the exception of Acker's discussion of pay equity in the Nordic countries in Part IV, the essays in this volume focus on North American pay equity initiatives. There are two reasons for this. First, the proactive pay equity schemes that have been implemented across North America share a methodology premised on job evaluation (see chapter 1; Evans and Nelson 1989, 7–8). The fact that pay equity has become virtually synonymous with job evaluation is an issue that has concerned pay equity advocates. Is job evaluation an opportunity to challenge the undervaluation of women's work? Or is it simply a means of further entrenching hierarchical and managerial prerogatives? The manner in which job-evaluation techniques have been implemented – specifically with regard to the gender bias contained in traditional evaluation methodologies – is another area that has received much attention, indeed, from several of the authors in this volume. Some of these analyses ask fundamental questions about the way we perceive and measure such critical elements as 'skill' and 'responsibility,' which play such a key role in both pay equity legislation and job-evaluation systems.

Second, Canada and the United States have similar labour-relations and collective-bargaining systems. While there are important differences (Kettler, Struthers, and Huxley 1990), both have highly fragmented collective-bargaining structures based on similar legal principles. Bargaining tends to take place on a per-establishment basis, and there is little coordination across an industry or on a national basis. As a result, wage differentials between both sectors and establishments are firmly entrenched and reinforced by the bargaining structures. This situation contrasts profoundly with that in the Nordic countries, where, as Acker describes in her essay, bargaining is highly coordinated at the industry level and wage-solidarity bargaining proposals are directed at minimizing wage differentials. As McDermott's discussion of Canadian pay equity initiatives in Part I suggests, the common elements within North American pay equity endeavours may be explained in terms of a policy to disrupt as little as possible existing bargaining structures. Moreover, the structure of North American collective bargaining may make it difficult, if not impossible, to adopt and implement other strategies to end wage discrimination, which are based upon profoundly different collective-bargaining regimes.

Almost half of the essays in the collection focus on the Ontario Pay Equity Act, which came into force in January 1988. The reason that this legislation receives so much attention in this volume is that it goes beyond most other proactive pay equity initiatives in two crucial respects. First, the Ontario statute applies to both the broadly defined public sector and the private sector. It is the first proactive pay equity initiative in the world to apply to the private sector. The significance of this bold step cannot be overestimated. Since the wage gap between men and women workers is generally larger in the private sector than the public sector (Ontario Government 1985, 45), pay equity is likely to be quite costly to private-sector employers. But, perhaps just as important as the monetary gains for women workers, the extension of pay equity to the private sector symbolizes the government's willingness to encroach upon employers' traditional prerogatives by intervening in the market to ensure that 'neutral' market forces do not result in pay practices that discriminate against women.

Second, the Ontario legislation provides a mechanism for resolving disputes arising from the pay equity process that theoretically does not depend upon the bargaining strength of the parties. Parties may bring a complaint to the Pay Equity Commission – an independent commission charged with the responsibility of administering the act. Ultimately, such disputes may be referred to the Pay Equity Tribunal, a quasi-judicial body, for resolution. Of course, it is always possible for one of the parties to apply to the courts for review of the tribunal's decision. The process of judicial review slows down the entire pay equity procedure and can complicate it considerably. Thus, an important question will be whether this approach to dispute resolution encourages time-consuming and expensive litigation by those who oppose the push to end the wage gap.

Because of the path-breaking nature of the Ontario Pay Equity Act, the close examination of various aspects of its design and implementation offered in several of the essays in this collection will put feminists in a better position to evaluate the promise of pay equity initiatives. Moreover, as Cuneo's essay reveals, a close examination discloses that, despite the fact the Ontario legislation goes farther than the vast majority of other existing initiatives, serious shortcomings are embedded in its design. Although the act proposes to 'redress systemic discrimination in compensation' (Pay Equity Act, s. 4[1]) for those who work in jobs where women predominate, it, in fact, shifts 'focus from the gender based wage gap to a process whereby each individual group seeks its own equity' (McDermott 1990, 407).

Feminists at Work

Implementing a pay equity process involves negotiation, consultation, and litigation, each requiring a great deal of time, effort, and money. Employers, unions, feminist organizations, and women workers have substantially unequal resources to devote to the implementation process. Ultimately, these unequal resources may determine, to a large extent, the result of the pay equity process. Despite these qualifications, feminists have made pay equity the most visible answer to one of the most crucial questions asked by activists: What are the best strategies for achieving economic equality between men and women (Acker 1989, 3)? But now that we have moved to the implementation stage of pay equity, the most important question has become: Does it work?

To date, there has been strong disagreement among feminists over the answer to this question. Some have identified pay equity's radical potential in its challenge to the allocation of economic rewards on the basis of stereotypical gender traits, which thereby extends 'the notion of discrimination to include the systemic undervaluation and payment of the work women do' (Blum 1987, 383–4). By questioning conventional notions of the worth of women's work, supporters of pay equity argue that it undermines the ideology of the neutral market and contributes to the goal of ending gender stratification in compensation (Armstrong and Armstrong 1990a, 32; Steinberg 1987a, 470). Other feminists, by contrast, locate pay equity within liberal political discourse and emphasize its commitment to wage hierarchies and its reliance upon the managerial instrument known as job evaluation – a technique whereby different jobs within an organization are positioned in the hierarchy of wage rates according to their value to the employer (Brenner 1987, 447; Lewis 1988). Consequently, opponents of pay equity argue that it fails to bridge the race and class divisions among women and reinforces the separation of feminists from other subordinated groups (Brenner 1987). The fact that Canadian pay equity legislation tends to be both divorced from employment equity initiatives and directed exclusively at the gender wage gap at the expense of the race-based gap lends support to this view.

The resolution of the strategic question of whether pay equity works is urgent. This collection of essays is a feminist look at the different political considerations, theoretical perspectives, evaluative standards, and methodologies that a complete answer to the question requires. To say a particular pay equity initiative works depends upon how success is defined, which in turn depends on how interests are characterized and represented and on the universe of alternatives perceived to be available and possible to achieve. Such questions are explicitly political, for they require us to consider not only the capacity of the women's movement to influence the political agenda, but the ability of employers to modify and resist initiatives at both the policy-formation and the implementation stages. The government's commitment to increasing women's wages and the resources it provides to ensure implementation of pay equity must also be assessed, as must the responses of trade unions and male workers to initiatives designed to close the gender wage gap.

The strategic question of whether pay equity works is part of the larger theoretical and methodological debates central to a feminist understanding of women's work. These include: What is the relationship between gender and class and how does this relationship figure in shaping women's waged work? Is it possible to talk of women who share a common interest that can form the basis of progressive feminist strategies and politics? Can we construct a potentially transformative feminist strategy using techniques (job evaluation) and rhetoric (value, comparable worth) that have been employed to the detriment of women? It is impossible to consider the strategic question without, ultimately, addressing theoretical and methodological issues.

The essays in this volume illustrate feminism at work in both its intellectual and its political aspects. Strategic and political questions, as well as theoretical and methodological ones, are addressed in each of the four parts. However, from the outset it is important to define clearly the limits to the essays collected in this volume. First, none of the essays is concerned with measuring the size of the wage gap or debating its causes. Each essay assumes that a substantial gender-based wage gap exists and that it is caused by systemic discrimination against women. Second, the essays do not address pay equity as a mechanism for closing a race-based wage gap. In Canada, all of the existing pay equity initiatives are directed exclusively to the gender wage gap and the majority of comparable-worth initiatives in the United States have been similarly limited. Moreover, in Canada there do not exist at present adequate statistical data to demonstrate the existence or extent of a race-based wage gap, although casual observation suggests that visible-minority workers are crowded into low-paid occupations. However, the following evaluation of pay equity in closing the gender-based wage gap should provide a useful resource for activists and policy makers who are considering extending this strategy to redress race-based wage discrimination.

In Part I, 'Setting the Stage,' Patricia McDermott presents an overview of the proactive pay equity initiatives that have been introduced in Canada. She briefly outlines how Canadian pay equity statutes operate, emphasizing that the pay equity process looks easier than it actually is and warning pay equity advocates that the very complexity of the pay equity process is a cause for concern. By focusing on several key technical features shared by each of the Canadian statutes, she assesses the commitment of Canadian legislators to closing the wage gap. Her broader concern, that technical decisions are indeed political, is a theme that runs through many of the essays that follow.

In his essay Carl Cuneo examines how the Ontario state incorporated gender and class in its pay equity legislation by mediating the interests of lobby groups through the three political parties in the legislative committee. This case-study illuminates the political tactics used to construct a compromise that partially satisfied both feminist and labour demands while minimizing the disruption of key employer prerogatives. From his analysis of the legislative process, Cuneo concludes that devices were established in the legislation whereby pay equity would not cost employers more in terms of pay increases than they would otherwise have had to bear in its absence.

In 'Litigating Our Way to Gender Neutrality: Mission Impossible?' Judy Fudge focuses on one of the most contentious aspects of the implementation process in Ontario – the legislative requirement that a gender-neutral job-comparison system be used to compare the value of work performed by incumbents in female- and male-dominated jobs. The legal requirement of gender neutrality imposed by the Ontario statute is an important step towards 'true' pay equity, especially in light of the concern that traditional job-evaluation methodologies are gender-biased. But the problem is that the Ontario legislation does not give any guidance concerning what constitutes a gender-neutral job-comparison system. Instead, the Pay Equity Act provides a means for adjudicating disputes by the Hearings Tribunal. Fudge examines the tribunal's attempt to develop a legal standards for gender neutrality in order to resolve the challenges over the gender-neutral character of job-comparison systems brought before it. She concludes that the failure to provide guidelines in the legislation and the choice of an adjudicative mechanism to resolve key elements in the legislation results in a litigation nightmare, which is likely, ultimately, to undermine the attainment of true pay equity.

Part II also focuses on the Ontario legislation, but the concern in these essays is to illustrate the choices that can and must be made by feminists involved in implementing pay equity in light of the compromises and contradictions embedded in the Ontario legislation. In her essay, 'Making Sense of Pay Equity: Issues for a Feminist Political Practice,' Sue Findlay discusses a major weakness in the Ontario legislation – that almost 50 per cent of the women in establishments covered by the Pay Equity Act are unable to claim pay equity adjustments because these establishments have no appropriate male comparators. This flaw in the legislation was acknowledged at the time of its introduction, and an obligation was imposed upon the Pay Equity Commission, the bureaucracy charged with administering the legislation, to issue recommendations designed to remedy this problem. Through an examination of the Pay Equity Commission's recommendations for the female workers employed in the broader public sector, child-welfare agencies, libraries, day-care centres, and the like, Findlay develops an analysis of state reform as a particular form of strategy that cannot simply be explained as co-optation. The fact that the Pay Equity Commission was not able to challenge the Liberal government's commitment to limiting pay equity comparisons to an individual employer's establishment meant that it was unable to propose recommendations that addressed the needs of women workers in predominantly female establishments. However, she concludes on an optimistic note by suggesting that Ontario's first social-democratic government might well be prepared to implement policies that extend pay equity to women in the female-dominated sector. The New Democratic government did in fact announce that it would introduce legislation to broaden the scope of the Pay Equity Act in order to benefit another 420,000 Ontario women workers (*Financial Post*, 19 December 1990, 1).

The essay by Pat Armstrong and Hugh Armstrong draws out the contradictory implications of pay equity. To this end, they pose a series of questions that they attempt to answer: Does pay equity legitimate or delegitimate the market distribution of wages? Will job evaluation reinforce or undermine the hierarchy in job classification and compensation? Will pay equity promote division or unity either among women or between women and men? What is the role of the state in pay equity initiatives? Focusing on the experience with the Ontario legislation, they identify both the limited possibilities and the possible limits for pay equity. While recognizing that the Ontario Pay Equity Act is most likely to benefit women who already are in the best-paid jobs, they argue that the overall impact of pay equity need not necessarily foster greater divisions among women. According to them, 'the greater gains of women in strong unions may also be used to strengthen women in general. If these gains are used to help women outside unions understand that state legislation is not enough and that collective action is what leads to improvements, then the legislation can serve to extend the union movement. This requires coordination among women from different workplaces and efforts by union women to help those outside their membership.' Thus, they conclude that, through strategic action, women and unions may be able to keep pay equity's radical potential alive.

This part concludes with Patricia McDermott's examination of the potential challenges, both legal and political, that Ontario's Pay Equity Act presents to the established regime of collective bargaining. This essay claims that the Pay Equity Act in Ontario appears to have been drafted 'with little thought given to how it would operate, not only with current labour legislation, but indeed more importantly, with long-standing traditions and practices in collective bargaining.'

The essays in Part III broaden the focus of the collection by examining issues of concern to pay equity initiatives generally. This part examines some of the technical problems that arise in the process of pay equity implementation. Although there are non-technical ways of closing the wage gap, there are no non-technical ways of implementing pay equity initiatives (Evans and Nelson 1989b). These essays develop the theme, raised in earlier essays, that technical decisions have a larger political dimension that must be addressed. Even feminists opposed to pay equity strategies acknowledge that, as long as pay equity initiatives are around, it is best to develop the technical skills needed to exert influence over the outcomes of implementation (Lewis 1988). Consequently, these essays draw upon the experience of pay equity implementation in jurisdictions other than Ontario's in order to provide some guidance as to how to avoid some of the major pitfalls in the pay equity process.

The first essay in this part, Jane Gaskell's 'What Counts as Skill?,' questions the centrality of technique by examining the meaning and significance of skill. According to Gaskell, 'much of the ideological power of pay equity lies in its promise of a process that substitutes objectivity for politics, expertise for power relations.' But, she argues, the choice is not between buying into a politics that suggests there is some unbiased scale of values to which we can appeal or endorsing a politics that embraces the relativistic concept that we can see in the social processes we observe. She opts for accepting the notion of pay equity and tries to bring feminist politics to its implementation. She concludes that 'the data suggest pretty clearly that women have not been paid for the skills they have. But the question of how one recognizes a "skill," values it, and pays for it is more complicated than that. Regression analysis can never tell us. The answer lies in our political commitments.'

Lois Haignere's essay illustrates some of the political commitments that often arise to derail the pay equity process. She identifies six recurring problems that have impeded the full implementation of pay equity. By drawing on the experience of various implementation processes, Haignere argues that feminists will be better placed to use pay equity to minimize systemic wage discrimination against women workers.

In her essay, Rosemary Warskett adopts a historical and relational analysis in order to illuminate the strategic choices confronting women who are struggling for wage parity with men. To do this, she uses the example of the equal-pay-for-work-of-equal-value provisions of the Canadian Human Rights Code and how they were used by the union representing the majority of women workers in the federal public service. While the women workers represented by the union received a monetary settlement, the government, in its role as employer, acted unilaterally to keep wage costs to a minimum and maintain the hierarchy of the public service's classification system. On the basis of her study, Warskett concludes that 'it remains to be seen if the union can organize the power of its membership to contest the employer's decision through the grievance and collective-bargaining process.'

Although this case-study does not involve proactive pay equity legislation, it illustrates the sorts of dilemmas that a union must confront when it attempts to challenge traditional managerial prerogatives – which are also threatened by proactive pay equity legislation. The question is whether proactive legislation that improves the ability of unions representing women workers to challenge these prerogatives can be designed.

Ronnie J. Steinberg examines how competing political commitments influence the implementation of pay equity. She illustrates how employers have developed successful strategies of containment, rather than outright opposition, to limit the radical potential of pay equity. In this way, she is concerned, as was Haignere, to show how opponents of pay equity use technique to undermine its social goal. However, rather than abandoning pay equity, Steinberg urges feminists to enter the policy arena, with the awareness that administrators are there to contain and control. By participating fully in the reform's implementation, feminists can gain greater control of the debate, greater access to information, and greater control over political decisions. In other words, only by active engagement in the implementation process can pay equity's promise be realized.

Part IV of the collection considers the possibilities and limitations of pay equity as both a political and an economic strategy to end wage discrimination. How unequal power relations shape the design, implementation, and meaning of pay equity is a recurring theme throughout the contributions to this volume. In 'Pay Equity and the State's Agenda,' Debra J. Lewis not only suggests why pay equity is such a popular initiative with the state, but goes on to argue that the very reasons for its popularity undermine its potential for radical effect. She argues that pay equity is a procedural rather than a substantive reform, that it reinforces the male standard rather than questioning it, and that it divides rather than unites women workers. As a result, Lewis concludes, it is necessary for feminists to reseize the issue of wage discrimination in order to ensure that pay equity does not eclipse other strategies that could deliver greater gains for women workers.

By contrast, Sara M. Evans and Barbara J. Nelson, in examining the case of Minnesota, offer a more optimistic appraisal of the impact of pay equity on wages, the workplace, and social change generally. Minnesota was one of the first jurisdictions to enact pay equity legislation, and this legislation was used as a model for Canada's first pay equity statute. Evans and Nelson argue that two important lessons for an international perspective can be drawn from the Minnesota experience of implementing pay equity for public employees. The first concerns women's experiences in the workplace, which they summarize in the following terms: 'with vigilance and support from labour and feminist groups, pay equity can improve the wages of people working in female-dominated jobs. Without vigilance and support, job evaluation – the mechanism that determines whose wages will change and by how much – remains a technocratic tool justifying patriarchal, racial, and class assumptions about the value of workers and the kinds of jobs they typically hold.'

Their second, more complicated, finding concerns connecting work-place gains with changes in the operation of the market economy, the nature of the political system, and the organization of domestic life. Although the linkages in Minnesota between pay equity and these other arenas were indirect, the authors suggest that such need not be the case. While they find that the workplace value of pay equity depends on the context of its implementation, they also note that the market, political, and domestic effects of pay equity are even more contingent. They conclude that 'one of the most important lessons from analysing the pay equity movement in Minnesota ... is that social movement theories need to pay more attention to *translation processes*, the activities that transfer gains in one arena to gains in another. For reforms like pay equity, which are valuable to employees but difficult to control in the workplace, the possibility of social gains in other arenas is important in creating support for the policy.'

The last two essays in Part IV look at pay equity in the context of economic restructuring in order to evaluate both its potential and its limits. Joan Acker's essay looks beyond North American pay equity initiatives in order to consider why it is that pay equity is now on the political agenda for feminists in the Nordic countries. Prior to economic restructuring in the mid-1980s, the wage-solidarity collective-bargaining strategy in Sweden reduced the gender wage gap. She argues that the recent interest in comparable-worth pay equity policies is, in part, due to this restructuring, which has resulted in the weakening of coordinated bargaining and the virtual abandonment of the wage-solidarity policy. As solidarity arguments have weakened and market arguments have gained strength, the gender wage gap in the Nordic countries has increased. Acker argues that these conditions have encouraged Swedish and other Nordic women to think about new strategies, including pay equity. She concludes that, at the end of the twentieth century, pay equity has the potential to mobilize women workers in the same way that the campaign for a living wage mobilized men one hundred years ago.

In 'Pay Equity and Economic Restructuring: The Polarization of Policy,' Isabella Bakker examines the potential impact of several key economic trends, particularly the recent structural changes in employment, on pay equity in Ontario. She concludes that central elements in this restructuring may undermine the goals of current pay equity policies, or, at the very least, dramatically challenge their effectiveness. She cautions that feminists must begin to consider how pay equity policies will tie into new economic strategies aimed at addressing the restructuring of the economy.

How far can pay equity go in challenging the gendered hierarchy that permeates the labour market – the primary mechanism for distributing income in capitalist industrialized countries? The contributions to this volume help answer this question. The concluding essay pulls together the central themes woven throughout the collection and attempts to show how pay equity links up with other strategies aimed at challenging women's economic dependence on men and their exploitation by employers. Pay equity is both an ongoing political struggle that can be shaped by strategic decisions over legislation, implementation, and litigation and part of a larger process of the feminization of labour. What unites the following essays is a common belief that relations of gender and class are crucial to understanding how women's work is valued, and why women, generally, receive so little pay.

NOTE

1 Convention 100 requires ratifying countries to 'ensure the application to all workers of the principle of equal remuneration for men and women workers for work of equal value' ('Convention Concerning Equal Remuneration for Men and Women Workers for Work of Equal Value,' Art. 2, para. 1, 165, United Nations Treaty Series 303). As of 1986, the convention had been ratified by 104 countries, including such major industrialized countries as Canada, Japan, the United Kingdom, and West Germany. The United States has not ratified the convention. For a discussion of Canada's ratification of Convention 100, see Niemann (1984).

PART ONE

Setting the Stage

1 Pay Equity in Canada: Assessing the Commitment to Reducing the Wage Gap

Patricia McDermott

Since 1985, five Canadian provincial jurisdictions have introduced pay equity legislation. The statutes passed in Manitoba (1985), Ontario (1987), Nova Scotia (1988), Prince Edward Island (1988), and New Brunswick (1989) all claim to end discriminatory pay practices in the sectors they cover. Since feminists have been demanding a reduction in the persistent gender-based wage gap for decades, this new legislation deserves careful study. Indeed, only by close scrutiny of these statutes can such legislative initiatives be supported, amended, or discouraged in favour of better solutions for ending inequitable pay practices.

The first important factor that must be noted in an assessment of these five new pay equity acts is that they are all 'proactive.' This means that they have moved beyond 'complaint-based' *equal-pay-for-work-of-equal-value* provisions contained in the human rights legislation of Quebec, the Yukon Territories, and the federal jurisdiction since the late 1970s. These equal-pay-for-work-of-equal-value schemes require that complainants launch an action against their employers with the respective human rights commissions. Although equal-value provisions were clearly a significant improvement over the ineffective *equal-pay-for-equal-work* legislation in place in all other provinces since the 1950s, relatively few cases have been initiated under these statutes. The most revealing fact, however, is that the wage gaps in these three jurisdictions have not been significantly reduced, despite a handful of very successful cases. Indeed, the proactivity of all five of these recently introduced pay equity statutes clearly must be seen as a major improvement over complaint-based schemes. Under proactive legislation, employers are required to assess the extent to which they are engaged in discriminatory pay practices and must remedy the problem by implementing a wage-adjustment program. Although the proactive stance of this legislation is indeed a step in the right direction, a great deal more must be known about each of the five acts in order to determine whether a jurisdiction is truly committed to significantly decreasing the gendered wage gap.

Before we begin a more detailed discussion of the pay equity process, it would be useful to outline briefly how Canadian pay equity statutes operate. The five provincial acts have several characteristics in common. All are based on a system that involves a comparison between men's and women's jobs. Each requires that the jobs in an establishment be divided into 'classes' or 'groups' and designated, depending on the percentage of males and females in the group, as either a female or male 'job class.' Then, all the acts require that each job class is evaluated using a 'gender-neutral'[1] job-evaluation scheme. This 'gender-neutrality' requirement is a feature unique to Canadian pay equity legislation and was undoubtedly incorporated into Canadian schemes to avoid the kinds of problems that arose in the United States in which traditional job-evaluation exercises seriously underrepresented the true value of women's work (Steinberg and Haignere 1987, 157). Once the evaluations are complete, all of the statutes require that the compensation paid to the female classes be compared to that paid to comparable male classes. If this comparison reveals discriminatory pay practices, the legislation requires that employers adjust the wages paid for female jobs to equal those paid for the male jobs.

It must be stressed that this process may sound easier than it actually is. When it comes to implementing pay equity schemes, numerous technical difficulties usually emerge. Indeed, the very complexity of pay equity is itself an issue about which pay equity advocates should be concerned. An analysis of a complicated process unavoidably becomes, as we shall see, a complex discussion. However, only by having feminists delve into both the legal and the methodological intricacies of this legislative model will we be able to assess the limits of such an exercise and propose alternative, more equitable and accessible ways of closing the wage gap. Examining the technical issues will also clearly reveal that technical, legislative, and implementation decisions are clearly political decisions in that they directly affect the extent to which the undervaluation of women's work is measured and the consequent wage adjustments delivered by a pay equity scheme (Acker 1989).

The Coverage

The pay equity acts in Nova Scotia and Prince Edward Island cover both the narrow public service as well as most of the 'broader public sector,' which includes publicly funded health-care facilities, social-service agencies, educational institutions, and municipalities. Manitoba's act, however, contains a more restrictive definition of the broader public sector in that it excludes municipal employers, school-boards, and numerous other publicly funded organizations, such as nursing homes. New Brunswick's Pay Equity Act has the most limited coverage of all five statutes and includes only the non-managerial component of the provincial public service. It is interesting to note that both Newfoundland and British Columbia have decided to implement pay equity schemes that cover the narrow civil service without introducing legislation. Implementing pay equity without a statute can indeed be problematic unless a bargaining agent is involved to represent the interests of union members. Those in non-union positions, however, are likely to have no real input into, or protection from, the process without clearly articulated statutory rights to participation and appeal.

Ontario's Pay Equity Act is unique in that it covers the private as well as the entire public sector. The extension of the act to employers in the private sector has prompted one leading U.S. authority on pay equity to say in a front-page *New York Times* article that 'Ontario has gone the furthest in the world' (27 July 1989). When compared to other legislative initiatives, especially New Brunswick's, with its narrow coverage for only part of the public service, Ontario's act, by including the private sector, has undoubtedly taken the step most necessary in demonstrating a serious commitment to closing the wage gap. Simply introducing pay equity in the civil service and hoping that the private sector will 'follow the government's good example'[2] obviously represents a weak commitment to ending wage discrimination. Although the extent of coverage is indeed the most important measure of whether a government really wants to reduce significantly the differential between men's and women's wages in the province, a closer look at how an act actually operates is also critical to determining whether legislation will be effective in the sector that it is intended to cover.

As noted, all five provincial pay equity acts require that each establishment's workforce be divided into 'job classes'[3] in order to be able to undertake a pay equity exercise. These 'classes' are defined as a group of positions that have similar qualifications, duties, responsibilities, and pay schedules. Ontario's act permits a job class to contain only one person, while Manitoba's, Nova Scotia's, and New Brunswick's legislations require that there be ten people before a group of positions can be a job class, and thus qualify to be involved in the pay equity exercise.

Ontario's act does not permit a job class to consist of one person if the work this person does is unique in the establishment. It should also be noted, however, that Ontario's act covers only private-sector employers with ten or more employees. Although this restriction will mean that thousands of women working in small establishments in the private sector will not benefit from Ontario's legislation, this exclusion will not, in fact, limit coverage to as great an extent as would a ten-person job-class requirement because of Ontario's rather unusual and broad definition of 'employer.' In defining 'employer,' the act refers to 'all the employees of the employer' within a certain, potentially large, geographic area (such as the entire city of Toronto). Thus an employer with only one or two employees in multiple locations within one geographic area could meet the ten-person size requirement when the numbers of employees in all of the locations are added together. Also, these employees would not have to be in the same 'job class,' but could be in numerous classes, as long as the establishment size requirement is met.

It is unclear whether Prince Edward Island's act allows only one person to constitute a job class because the act is silent on this issue; however, like Ontario's act, it does not explicitly contain a ten-person requirement. Restrictions on the size of 'job class' can limit coverage to large numbers of people doing women's work. This issue must be studied more closely in order to mount a critique of current legislation and should likely be avoided in new legislation.

In terms of coverage it is obvious that a pay equity statute should cover both the public and the private sectors. Also, as noted, it is clear that restrictions placed on the size of a job class in Manitoba's, New Brunswick's, and Nova Scotia's acts serve to reduce the number of those doing women's work who can benefit from the legislation. Similarly, from a pay equity advocate's point of view, there is no justification for Ontario's decision to exclude those who work in private-sector establishments with fewer than ten employees. Feminist demands across Canada should be for pay equity laws that cover all those doing women's work, not just public-sector employees. The legislation should not exclude workers in the smallest (under ten employees) private-sector establishments since both the low wages and the low levels of unionization typical of such workplaces make these employees most in need of pay equity.

Gender Predominance

Once the job classes have been identified, all of the statutes impose a gender-predominance requirement. This requirement stipulates that, for a job class to qualify as either a 'female job class,' and potentially be entitled to a wage adjustment, or a 'male job class,' and provide a comparison in the pay equity scheme, a job class has to have a certain percentage of male or female employees. The first Canadian proactive pay equity act to establish a gender-predominance standard was Manitoba's, with its 70 per cent for both male and female job classes. Ontario's, the next statute to be passed, maintained the 70 per cent standard for male job classes but lowered that for female job classes to 60 per cent. Nova Scotia's and Prince Edward Island's legislation continued the trend and lowered both male and female predominance cut-offs to 60 per cent; however, New Brunswick's act, passed in 1989, reversed this downward trend and introduced the same standard used in Ontario's act – 70 per cent for male job classes and 60 per cent for female. Although it is unclear how gender predominance operates with regard to the size of *male* job classes, it is quite clear that the lower the *female* cut-off, the lower the number of women in any given establishment who will be covered. Thus any future legislation or proposed amendments to current legislation should have a predominance standard no higher than 60 per cent.

In terms of *male* predominance, it is not necessarily true that the lower the cut-off the better. Since male job classes enter the pay equity scheme as comparators for female job classes, it is probable that lowering the male predominance standard, and thus decreasing the number of jobs that are more clearly 'men's work,' would reduce the number of more highly paid jobs with which to compare, simply because the higher a proportion of men there are in a job, the greater the likelihood that it will be better paid. For example, a study done for the Ontario Public Service Employees Union demonstrated that, when wage data were analysed for the job classes in the unionized public service, each increase of 1 per cent in the number of women in a job corresponded with a decrease of $1.15 in weekly wages, producing an annual differential of $5,980 for a job class that was 100 per cent female (Lewis 1988, 120).

There has been very little study of how gender predominance functions in a pay equity exercise. It is possible, given a labour market so extensively segmented on the basis of gender, that the higher the gender-predominance standards, the higher the pay adjustments. For instance, it may be that the standard of 90 per cent that was used in some early U.S. pay equity exercises produced the most dramatic wage increases for those doing women's work. If this is so, perhaps it would be more equitable to match those with similar gender-predominance standards. For example, a female job class with 90 to 100 per cent women would be compared with male job classes (of equal or comparable value) that had 90 to 100 per cent men.

Feminists lobbying for initial pay equity legislation, or for amendments to an existing act, need to know more about how gender predominance operates in terms of both coverage provided by a statute and level of pay adjustments. The suggestion that the concept of gender predominance be abandoned must be approached with caution since it is a tool that helps reveal the impact of a highly segmented labour market on the wage differential between men and women.

Establishing Value

Once the male and female job classes have been identified, all five pay equity statutes require that each job class be assigned a value, determined by a job-evaluation system that uses the four standard factors: skill, effort, responsibility, and working conditions. It is true that Ontario's act is unique in that it requires the use of a 'job comparison' system, rather than a 'job evaluation' system. This distinction, however, has proved meaningless since Ontario pay equity exercises, like those in other provinces, have become synonymous with job evaluation. Indeed, section 6 of the Ontario act clearly suggests an evaluation must be done in order to find job classes of 'equal' or 'lower' value.

Job-evaluation systems have been widely used since the 1950s, primarily by large governmental and private-sector employers, to create and justify a classification and compensation structure. Unions have traditionally opposed the job-evaluation process and have generally accepted only the job-classification component of a full job-evaluation program. Typically most unions continued to bargain the wages that the jobs were to be paid according to the classification and also insisted on the use of seniority as the main criterion to establish who moved up to the better-paid jobs when an opening occurred. In other words, the unions did not agree that some jobs were actually 'more valuable' than others, they simply accepted the classification system as a framework within which to bargain.

In non-unionized settings, not only do employers construct the classification system, but they also decide what wage each level of the classification series should be paid. This decision is usually based on a 'job market survey' whereby a study of the wages paid for specific jobs in the regional labour market is used as a guide for the establishment's internal compensation structure.

A classification system and job evaluation are linked to the point where they are almost indistinguishable. Typically a classification involves a set of job descriptions that have escalating requirements of skill and responsibility associated with each level of a particular job (for example, computer technician, one through five). These escalating requirements can be established by some type of job-evaluation process, but they do not have to be. The employer, perhaps in the form of the human resources department, can simply decide that a clerk-typist *one* will perform these functions, while a clerk-typist *two* will carry out those functions, and so on. There are no set rules about the number of job titles that will be contained in a classification system: whether one job contains a set of functions is governed solely by the nature of the workplace and the decisions that the personnel department makes. Also, tradition enters the picture. Someone looking for a 'clerk-typist' position would expect the job to include typing and filing, along with a range of other possible tasks such as dealing with clients in person or by phone, photocopying, and taking and transcribing dictation. The duties are certainly firm-specific, as would be those assigned to each of the positions in a classification structure.

Once the job-classification system is in place, a job-evaluation exercise is typically conducted, creating a hierarchical structure within the organization. It is important to note that there are no standard rules about the compensation for various jobs – in one firm an accounts-receivable clerk could be paid more than a payroll clerk, whereas, in another, the reverse could be true. The evaluation process is supposed to establish, for a particular organization, what the job is worth to that organization.

One of the most common ways job evaluations are done is by having a 'rating team,' comprising a small number of employee representatives, look at a job description and rate each job on a series of 'subfactors.' For example, the factor 'working conditions' would be measured by ratings on a set of subfactors such as noise level, extreme temperatures, unpleasant fumes, night work. The average of the scores for all of the subfactors becomes the quantitative representative for the value of the job. As much research has demonstrated, such job-evaluation processes have been fraught with social as well as gender bias (Hartmann, Roos, and Trieman 1985, 3, 53). Since the raters are typically those who work in the establishment, there is a tendency to reproduce the hierarchical relationships that already exist within the organization. For instance, when the raters see a job description for 'clerk-typist,' they tend to think automatically about low-paid, traditional women's work, at the bottom of the establishment's structure and, consequently, again assess the job as one that *should* receive lower pay. Such an evaluation methodology, it could be argued, may have been acceptable in non-unionized settings where the purpose of the job evaluation was to establish a compensation structure that reflected the market, thus enabling employers to retain female clerical workers because they were paying them the 'going rate.'

Pay equity, however, challenges the use of the market as the sole determinant of women's wages and insists that employers evaluate and pay those doing women's work according to the same measures of value used in assessing their male employees. Perhaps the most crucial undervaluing has been in the area of skills and responsibilities. The classic example involves assigning value points for dexterity to someone who uses a screwdriver, while ignoring the fine motor skills employed in the typically female task of typing in clerical jobs or administering needles in nursing. Another excellent example is the assigning of more value points to a zoo keeper responsible for animals than to a child-care worker. Surely the most memorable example, however, is that of male jobs that receive job-evaluation points for working conditions involving what has been termed 'men's dirt' – axle grease and grime – while vomit and urine, for instance, which most of us consider even more unpleasant and which are encountered daily by health-care workers, go unacknowledged in job-evaluation schemes (Remick 1984a, 114).

All five pay equity statutes require that job-evaluation schemes be 'gender neutral,' yet not one attempts to define this important concept. Although it is impossible to analyse a job-evaluation system with a view to ensuring its gender neutrality, this kind of analysis is rarely carried out by the large management-consulting firms hired to undertake many pay equity exercises throughout North America. Two well-known American pay equity specialists have noted that 'most' pay equity exercises in the United States have employed 'the very management consulting firms that have been using biased job evaluation systems for decades' (Steinberg and Haignere 1987, 158). No doubt this same problem, indeed involving many of the same consulting firms, is again occurring in job-evaluation exercises in Canada. The results either justify the current compensation practices or produce wage adjustments that represent only a small fraction of the true undervaluation of women's work. The real danger, of course, is that women, because of these practices, will see their wages increase minimally, yet will be told that they now have 'pay equity' and will, therefore, have no recourse but to engage in undoubtedly lengthy and expensive litigation over the issue of gender neutrality.

In fact, just such cases over the plans of several large consulting firms have been launched at Ontario's Pay Equity Hearings Tribunal.

The Job Class

The issue of constructing appropriate job classes is closely related to those of gender predominance and evaluating work. As mentioned earlier, job classes are defined as a group of positions that have similar qualifications, duties, responsibilities, and pay schedules. The major concern is that appropriate job classes are structured. Typically a job class should include people who do *similar* work. Obviously it does not have to be the same work, but for a job-evaluation exercise to fairly assess a job class, those in it must be doing work that is both similar and of relatively the same value. If the value ranges vary greatly, and an average of all the values is used for the whole class, it is clear that those above the average would not get the full adjustment to which they were entitled. Indeed, if the values that result from a job-evaluation exercise vary to any significant degree within any one job class, it is very likely, given the logic of this exercise, that the job classes should be broken down further to reflect the clustering of value points.

For example, if a job class included an entire range of library workers and not just librarians, it is very likely that the librarians would not benefit from a pay equity exercise nearly as much as they would if they were evaluated alone. If, for instance, they were put in a job class with those doing work requiring less skill and training, the evaluation results from these jobs, when averaged in, would pull down the results for librarians. Consequently the job class would be matched with a lower-paid male comparator. Job class structures can also make lucrative potential male comparators disappear into 'gender-neutral' job classes. Similarly too narrow a definition of job class can function to reduce the number of female job classes entitled to wage adjustments as well as the number available for use as male comparators.

This job-class issue also raises some fundamental methodological problems about how job-content data are collected and analysed. Basic sound social-science research technique would require that a random, representative sample of positions be used to ensure that the data used to evaluate each job class accurately reflect the true value and are not skewed in any way. Thus social scientists would be concerned that both gender and social bias, discussed earlier, could enter the exercise when 'job-rating teams' are used to establish value. A clear preference would be for a methodology that would *not* involve the intervention of a rating team at all, but would move directly to the analysis of reliably collected data. Many of the major public-sector pay equity exercises in Canada have employed rating teams. It would be interesting to reassess the evaluation results using a closed-ended questionnaire methodology to see if the results in, for example, Manitoba's civil-service exercise differed significantly.

Method of Establishing Wage Increases

The key factor that reflects whether a jurisdiction is committed to closing the wage gap is how wage adjustments are calculated. In most pay equity initiatives in the United States, almost all employees in female job classes received some pay equity adjustment. American pay equity implementation typically employs an 'average pay line,' and if one's job rate fell below the pay line calculated for an establishment, the job class received a permanent wage increase.

Manitoba, the first jurisdiction in Canada to introduce pay equity legislation, allowed the use of an average-pay-line technique. It was, however, not a requirement, but simply an option presented, rather obliquely, in the statute. Ontario's act moved decidedly away from this approach and introduced the complex, *and much less costly,* 'job-to-job' comparison scheme. This job-to-job method of establishing wage increases made the achievement of an increase a very arbitrary exercise. To be entitled to a pay equity adjustment in Ontario, a female job class has to be lucky enough to be in an establishment with an 'appropriate male comparator,' which means a male job class with the same range of value points of the female job class seeking a wage adjustment (McDermott 1990). If there is more than one appropriate male comparator, the female job class, under Ontario's act, is entitled to a wage adjustment as that of the *lowest possible male comparator.* This is truly an amazingly low level of pay equity and clearly indicates the Ontario government's lack of a serious intention to close the wage gap.

Like so many details of a pay equity exercise, the designation of job classes, the manner in which gender-predominance standards are used, the method of establishing wage increases, and the techniques employed to evaluate jobs are, as we have argued earlier, political as well as technical decisions in that they can lead to a continued undervaluation of women's work and a consequent decreased cost for so-called pay equity. Indeed, in terms of the type of legislation that best closes the wage gap, the idea of job classes should be carefully assessed, and thought given to whether there may be a better approach. There is also a need for sociologists, trained in reliable questionnaire design, survey methodology, and data-analysis techniques, and not affiliated with commercial management-consulting firms, to become more involved in an assessment of current job-evaluation practices in pay equity exercises.

Conclusion

It is clear that a great deal of work must be done to ensure that the promise of pay equity does not slip through our fingers. When feminists assess the legislation offered by their governments, such assessments must be done carefully and demands for new legislation formulated clearly to ensure that the technical decisions made by the state are not the bare minimum that can be called 'pay equity.' It is obvious that many decisions about the shape of a pay equity process can be made to reduce the costs to employers. The impact of such decisions needs to be studied and the results used to create a political will to reform the legislation. Only continued monitoring of the resulting wage adjustments, along with the long-term effect on wage differentials, can demonstrate whether what has been offered as 'pay equity' can significantly, and permanently, close the wage gap. If it cannot, other solutions must quickly be sought.

   In jurisdictions in which no pay equity legislation has been introduced, advocates have to consider whether weak legislation is worth having, as opposed to no legislation at all. The fundamental weakness of Ontario's Pay Equity Act represents such a political compromise that it is unlikely to produce a significant decrease in the wage gap (McDermott 1990, 381). Amendments that make an already complex process even more complex run the risk of creating a bureaucratic quagmire that can stifle change. Once legislation is in place and employers have complied, and spent tens of thousands of dollars doing so, it is politically and practically difficult to encourage compliance with a new set of rules. Jurisdictions that have had a history of pay equity implementation must be carefully studied in order to avoid any pitfalls that they have en-countered, as well as to evaluate the success of one set of implementation decisions over another. Although it is tempting to ignore the details and deal at the level of rhetoric, the price could be ineffective legislation that does nothing to seriously reduce the wage gap.

NOTES

1 Manitoba's (section 9), New Brunswick's (Section 11), Ontario's (section 12), and Prince Edward Island's (section 14) acts all use the term 'gender-neutral,' while Nova Scotia's act refers to a system that 'does not discriminate on the basis of gender' (section 12).
2 'B.C. Pledges equity for women employees,' *Globe and Mail*, 12 September 1990, A-8
3 The acts in Ontario and New Brunswick use the term 'job class,' while Nova Scotia's act refers to 'classifications'; both Manitoba's and Prince Edward Island's acts simply refer to a 'class.'

2 The State of Pay Equity: Mediating Gender and Class through Political Parties in Ontario

Carl J. Cuneo

Between 1985 and 1987, two alliances representing opposing points of view on Ontario's proposed pay equity legislation vied for dominance. One, the labour-feminist alliance, whose most explicit organizational expression is the Ontario Equal Pay Coalition, was a joining together of labour organizations, such as the Ontario Federation of Labour; feminist organizations, such as the National Action Committee on the Status of Women; and women-of-colour groups, such as the Coalition of Visible Minority Women. The second alliance, which will be referred to in this essay as the 'male business alliance,' was an ideological, rather than an organized coalition, consisting of male business associations, such as the Canadian Manufacturers' Association and the Canadian Federation of Independent Business; neo-conservative organizations, such as the National Citizens' Coalition; and anti-feminist groups, such as REAL Women of Canada.

These two alliances effectively enunciated their respective positions in the publicly held debates around the *Green Paper on Pay Equity* and, through their lobbying of the province's three political parties, kept their viewpoints at the forefront during the policy-formulation stages of the debate on pay equity. Three stages were the amending processes on bills 105 and 154, conducted by the Standing Committee on the Administration of Justice for this legislation and, later, the amending process on Bill 154 in the Committee of the Whole House.

Neither of the two leading sides on this issue can be said to have wholly succeeded in its efforts. However, the Ontario Pay Equity Act, which represents the state's mediation of the conflicting interests of the two groups, is heavily weighted in favour of protecting the hegemonic interests of the white male business class at the expense of both white and visible-minority women, whose interests were either underrepresented or suppressed during the prelegislation phase of the debate on this issue. Consequently, the act, while mediating the interests of labour-feminist and male business alliances, incorporates class and gender relations, and inherent contradictions in those relations.

This essay examines the role of Ontario's three political parties in representing the two dominant points of view during the policy-formulation stages of this legislation. It begins by looking briefly at the background of the legislation and at the politicking that took place during the amending procedures on bills 105 and 154. The essay then takes a close look at nine of the central issues involved in the Ontario pay equity debate, with an examination, in each case, of the manoeuvres by the parties to achieve the aims they represented and to defeat those they opposed. While providing this issue-by-issue analysis, the essay also discusses the way the legislative process managed to overlook the interests of visible-minority working-class women.

Background

The political catalyst for pay equity in Ontario came from the collapse in 1985 of the long Tory rule and the election of a minority Liberal government. In order to maintain the confidence of the Legislative Assembly, the new government needed the support of either the NDP or the Conservatives. In an accord signed in May 1985, the NDP pledged to give the Liberals this support, provided the latter promised to introduce some pieces of legislation, one of which was equal pay for work of equal value in the public and private sectors. In the summer and early fall of 1985, the Liberal government consulted with women's, labour, and male business organizations. The options laid out in the resulting *Green Paper on Pay Equity*, tabled in the House on 19 November of that year, in turn helped to shape the issues addressed in the subsequent public debates by the labour-feminist and male business alliances.

Public lobbying on the legislation occurred in four state forums. First, in early 1986, the Liberal government formed two separate premier's business and labour advisory groups on pay equity in order to give it advice on the mechanics on how a pay equity act might be implemented in terms of job evaluations, pay equity plans, and timetables. Thus, business and labour were given a forum inside the state, and away from the public eye, in which to press their respective interests.

Second, between February and May 1986, the Public Consultation

Panel on Pay Equity received 236 written briefs and heard 149 oral presentations on the *Green Paper on Pay Equity* in Toronto, Windsor, Sudbury, Thunder Bay, and Ottawa (Ontario Legislative Assembly [OLA] 1986, 3370–1). It published *The Report of the Consultation Panel on Pay Equity* in August 1986 (Clark, Cook, and Dimma 1986). In it, the authors simply summarized the main points of the briefs, without making any recommendations. They also failed to recognize the presence of class and race/ethnic contradictions, although gender contradictions were acknowledged. In addition, they made a confidential oral report to Premier David Peterson and Ian Scott, the attorney general and minister responsible for women's issues.

Third, in late September and early October 1986, the Standing Committee on the Administration of Justice of the Ontario Legislature received 42 briefs and heard 28 oral presentations on Public Service Bill 105 from individuals, male business groups, women's organizations, feminist-union organizations, unions and employee associations, and community groups, as well as officials from the Ministry of Labour and the Workers' Compensation Board.[1]

In the fourth and final forum, held in early 1987, a reorganized Justice Committee heard 61 oral presentations and received 194 written briefs and letters from similar groups and individuals on the combined public- and private-sector Pay Equity Bill 154 of 1987 (Ontario Government 1987).[2]

The Green Paper and the public debates were bounded by Ontario administrative policy making on pay equity, embodied by a variety of state agencies, including the cabinet, board of management, the ministries of Labour and Justice, the Ontario Women's Directorate, the Legislative Assembly, and the premier's Business and Labour Advisory committees. While the Green Paper was in the public domain and its options were being debated through the Public Consultation Panel and the Standing Committee on the Administration of Justice, policies on pay equity were being shaped and reshaped in these other agencies of the Ontario state. Lobbying and state policy formulation affected each other: lobbying signalled to the state what different groups in society favoured and rejected, and this favouring and rejecting was being influenced by the state's own agenda, shaped by prior gender, race/ethnic, and class forces.

The Labour minister, William Wrye, introduced the Public Service Pay Equity Bill 105 into the provincial legislature for first reading on 11 February 1986 (OLA 1986, 3999–4000). After its public hearings, the

Standing Committee on the Administration of Justice partially completed a clause-by-clause amendment of the bill between 20 October and 18 November 1986. The NDP and Conservatives submitted a list of amendments that would expand the bill from the narrow public service, covering 29,000 women, to the broader public sector, covering 340,000 women. However, the Liberal government and the Conservative chair and the committee, Andy Brandt, argued that these amendments violated parliamentary tradition because the opposition parties were forcing on the government an additional expenditure of monies. (Only a minister from the governing party could move such amendments.) After the chair ruled the amendments out of order, the NDP and Conservative members of the committee outvoted the Liberal members to overturn the chair's ruling, and proceeded with their amendments.[3]

The Liberal party was now very much on the defensive as it watched the NDP and Tories 'gang up' on it by totally gutting its bill. The committee had approved eight amendments, all of them put forward by the NDP and supported by the Tories. These included expanding the bill to include the entire public sector; replacing 'pay equity' with 'equal pay'; rejecting the grouping of predominantly female and male job levels; accepting seniority as the only gender-neutral exclusion from pay equity; replacing the government's 60 per cent female job levels and 70 per cent male job levels by negotiations in unionized establishments and the employer's decision in non-unionized workplaces; rejecting comparisons of the job rate of female job levels with the lowest job rate of a male job level; banning employers' transferring of part of their general wage increases into pay equity (wage restraint); and having employers found guilty of wage restraint compensate their employees in the amount lost through the restraint.

In response, the Liberal members of the committee tried to stall the committee's deliberations as long as possible, and the Peterson government threatened to withdraw Bill 105. After widespread criticism of the bill, especially from the labour and women's movements, on 24 November 1986, Justice minister Ian Scott introduced into the legislature the combined public/private Pay Equity Bill 154 (Ontario Government 1987). Bill 105 was still in the Standing Committee on the Administration of Justice (OLA 1986, 3551–4), and the committee was thrown into considerable disarray over the relationship between the two bills and whether the committee should complete the amending of Bill 105.[4] The Liberals and Andy Brandt accused the NDP and Tory members of the committee of killing Bill 105 by overruling the chair and trying to expand the bill's scope, involving additional expenditures of government monies;[5] the opposition parties repeatedly accused the Liberal members on the committee of delaying tactics and slowing down the amending process.[6]

Bill 154, too, was sent to the Standing Committee on the Administration of Justice, which, after public hearings, put it through a clause-by-clause amendment. On 1 April 1987, Ian Scott, attorney general and minister responsible for the status of women, visited the committee to move eight government motions to incorporate Bill 105 into Bill 154.[7] The NDP – largely unsuccessfully – attempted to push for the incorporation into Bill 154 of some of its amendments approved in Bill 105.

The political dynamic among the three parties changed dramatically in the four months between the amending processes for the two bills. During the Justice Committee's consideration of Bill 105, Tory Phil Gillies had teamed with Evelyn Gigantes of the NDP to push through a number of progressive amendments. The other Tory members – O'Connor, Partington, and Villeneuve – and the only other NDP member – Charlton – were the supporting cast. At this point, the Tory party seems to have come under pressure from the construction industry to put the brakes on some of the more progressive amendments. This possibility, as well as the party's desire to regain strength after its defeat in the 1985 election, was likely what led to the Tories' replacing their more 'progressive' members on the committee considering Bill 105 with members who were much stronger advocates for business. Consequently, when the time came to consider Bill 154, Gillies was gone, and Baetz, Barlow, and Stevenson replaced O'Connor, Villeneuve, and Partington. The revamped committee included nine members – two NDP, the three Tories mentioned, and four Liberals – in addition to the two Tories in the chair, namely, Andy Brandt and Susan Fish as vice-chair.

In addition, responsibility for the new bill shifted to the Ministry of the Attorney General, under Ian Scott, from the Ministry of Labour, which had overseen Bill 105. In the amending process for Bill 154, the Liberals got most of the amendments they wanted, although they did accept some from the NDP. By now the Tories and NDP were no longer 'progressive' partners but had became enemies, allowing the Liberals to manipulate them easily. Thus, in the Justice Committee hearings on Bill 154, the Liberals lost none of their proposed amendments, the Tories lost 5 of their 6, and the NDP lost 42 out of its 53.[8]

By the time Bill 154 arrived in the Committee of the Whole House of the Legislative Assembly in June 1987, the Liberals were completely in charge. Twenty-five amendments were voted upon. None of the amendments proposed by either the NDP or the Tories passed, while all three of the Liberal amendments were passed by an all-party consensus, and the bill became law.

Central Issues

The central issues in the public debates were raised in the *Green Paper on Pay Equity* (Ontario Government 1985), and became the focus of intense debate between the labour-feminist and male business alliances, especially in the public hearings conducted by the Public Consultation Panel on Pay Equity in 1986 and in the Standing Committee on the Administration of Justice, which deliberated bills 105 and 154 in 1986 and 1987. Twelve of the most important are listed in Table 1, along with their respective legislative outcomes, in terms of wins, losses, and draws, for the two major alliances. Nine of these issues are discussed below, with a detailed analysis of the part played by Ontario's political parties in representing the two dominant points of view. To a lesser extent, this discussion includes comments on how this balancing process affected the interests of such underrepresented groups as visible-minority working-class women by incorporating gender and class into the Pay Equity Act.

Gender Predominance
Gender predominance concerns the percentage of women that must be in the female job class and the percentage of men that must be in the male job class before the female job class can be compared to the male job class (male comparator). In the public debates before the Consultation Panel and in the written and oral submissions to the Justice Committee on bills 105 and 154, the labour-feminist alliance opposed the 60 per cent minimum threshold for female job classes and the 70 per cent threshold for male job classes, and proposed setting the cut-off just above the portion of the labour force consisting of women (slightly above 44 per cent). The male business alliance, such as the Ontario Chamber of Commerce, desired a much higher threshold – around 80 to 90 per cent – although other male business groups, such as the Canadian Manufacturer's Association and Canada Mining Association, were willing to accept the Ontario government thresholds (Cuneo 1990, 29–33).

In the Justice Committee consideration of Bill 154, Evelyn Gigantes of the NDP argued for the removal of the 60 and 70 per cent gender-

TABLE 1
Wins, losses, and draws on centrally contested issues

Issue in dispute	Labour/ feminist alliance	Male business/ neo-conservative/ anti-feminist alliance
1 Gender predominance	Lost/Draw	Won/Draw
2 Model	Won	Lost
3 Sector	Won	Lost
4 Size of establishment	Lost	Won
5 Within-establishment comparisons	Draw/Lost	Draw/Won
6 Definition of establishment	Draw/Won	Draw/Lost
7 Annual pay equity adjustments	Lost	Won
8 Phasing in of pay equity adjustments	Lost	Won
9 Pay equity adjustments vs. expected wage increases	Lost	Won
10 Within-bargaining-unit comparisons	Draw	Draw
11 Separate pay equity bureau or commission	Won	Lost
12 Exclusions	Lost	Won

predominant thresholds because they would prevent women below the 60 per cent level from qualifying for pay equity adjustments, even though they suffer discriminatory wages, and she moved to eliminate the definition of female and male job classes and to substitute 'the current and historical ratio of women and men in the job, and prevailing and historical sex stereotyping of the job.'[9] The Liberals continued to argue in favour of their thresholds; they defended the 10 per cent differential between female and male job classes on the grounds that the full-time Ontario labour force consists of 10 per cent more men (about 55 per cent) than women (about 45 per cent).

Liberals Chris Ward and Eleanor Caplan suggested that the abandonment of any thresholds would convert female and male job classes into battlegrounds over subjective considerations of historical incumbency and sex stereotyping; it would leave women defenceless, and force them into the complaints procedures simply to establish their job classes. The NDP responded that the government's thresholds would leave the many unorganized private-sector women below 60 per cent without union guidance on the use of historical incumbency, forcing them to rely on a complaints procedure. In the end, the Tories teamed up with the Liberals to defeat the NDP proposals.[10] When Bill 154 was later under consideration in the Committee of the Whole House, Gigantes attempted to change the definition of the female job class, and again the Tories joined the Liberals in defeating the NDP amendments (OLA 9 June 1987, 1209–33, 1227).

Since the 1987 Ontario Pay Equity Act specifies a 60 per cent threshold for female job classes and a 70 per cent threshold for male job classes, the male business class alliance won this dispute and the labour-feminist alliance lost. Although some provision was made for negotiating lower figures in the case of historical incumbency and sex stereotyping, these were not mandated by the legislation (Ontario Government 1988, s. 1[5]).

Race/ethnic criteria were ignored in the state's definition of gender predominance. There was no consideration of race/ethnic predominance, which ensured that gender predominance would be defined along dominant white/English-Canadian lines. Although gender predominance is used in reducing gendered pay inequities based in systemic discrimination, it also has the following potentially negative consequences for gender differences: it may divide and create tensions among women by qualifying some for pay equity adjustments (those in female job classes with at least 60 per cent women who can find one or more male comparators), while disqualifying those who fail this test; it can set up a male standard (male job points and male wages) by which women are to judge their own job worth and wages, rather than establishing a more independent standard based on women's needs, interests, and experiences (for example, the double day of labour). Since male job points and wages are heavily weighted in terms of different labour markets on those factors valuable to the employer, and since labour markets are structured along male-dominated lines, gender predominance, in effect, imports the external male market standards into the establishment to set the job points and wages of female job classes. In terms of class effects, although gender predominance in unorganized workplaces may lead to greater discussion among workers about pay inequities, and hence to a push for unionization, it may also divide workers as tensions about changes in one's place along the finely tuned job-hierarchy increase.

Model: Proactivity vs. Complaints
Three pay equity models are generally recognized: complaints, proactive or employer-initiated, and integrated. Under the complaints model (such as the Canadian Human Rights Act), it is entirely up to a woman or her

agent – in most cases, her union – to launch a complaint about unequal pay for work of equal value. In contrast, under the proactive model, legislation mandates the negotiation of job-evaluation schemes and pay equity plans, with specific compensation adjustments to be paid out according to a set time schedule in unionized workplaces. Where no union exists, the employer has the responsibility to initiate this process, and employees typically do not have much input. Under the integrated model, there is a combination of both proactivity and full rights under complaints procedures.

The labour-feminist alliance opposed the complaints model as ineffective and too burdensome for individual women; in the past the complaints model produced few gains. The alliance supported either the proactive model alone or its combination with complaints procedures in an integrated model; either would provide unions with the legislative teeth needed to back up their bargaining demands around pay equity. The male business alliance opposed both the proactive and the integrated plans, preferring the much weaker complaints model.

In the Justice Committee and the Committee of the Whole House, the NDP represented the proactive model pushed by the women's and labour movements. It criticized Bill 154 for being only partly proactive: women in workplaces with 10 to 99 employees had only the complaints model to use since their employers did not have the obligation to develop plans. The Progressive Conservative party raised little criticism of the proactive or integrated model, and offered no amendments that would replace them with a complaints model. The Liberal party could be said to have mediated the demands of the male business community and the labour-feminist alliance by devising Bill 154 along the lines of a partly complaints and partly proactive model.

Depending on one's interpretation, the 1987 Ontario Pay Equity Act is either a proactive model (where a bargaining agent is present) and employer-initiated (where a bargaining agent is absent), or an integrated model, with a complaints procedure set up under a hearings tribunal to adjudicate disputes over implementation of the act. As such, it was considered by many to be one of the most important victories for the labour-feminist alliance.

The principle of proactivity has two potentially contradictory consequences for gender: on the one hand, it places a powerful instrument in the hands of the union for bringing together female and male members and for showing leadership and initiative on issues of gender discrimination; on the other hand, where there is an entrenched male leadership in the union local, proactivity may inadvertently exacerbate tensions between women rank-and-filers, with little direct access to pay equity technical expertise, and a male staff and executive who enjoy such access and expertise. Similarly, proactivity has potentially contradictory consequences for class relations: while it places a powerful instrument in the hands of the union bargaining agents in negotiating pay equity adjustments, thereby strengthening one working-class organization (trade unions), it also institutionalizes (or reproduces) the industrial-relations divisions between organized and unorganized workers by leaving unorganized workers without much effective input into the formulation of pay equity plans, other than through complaining to the Pay Equity Commission and Hearings Tribunal (Ontario Government 1988, s. 22).

Sector

In Ontario, discussions occurred over the application of pay equity to three sectors – the narrow public service (mainly the civil service), the broader public sector (education, health, social and community organizations, municipalities, etc.), and the private sector. Most existing proactive legislation applies only to the public sector; for example, that of Manitoba, Prince Edward Island, Nova Scotia, Minnesota, and Oregon. The labour-feminist position was that there had to be a single, all-inclusive pay equity law encompassing both the public and the private sectors. The male business alliance, however, opposed the extension of pay equity to the private sector, especially if it was to be proactive.

The sector question was much less an issue once Bill 154 was introduced because Ian Scott put forward amendments to fold Bill 105 into Bill 154, thereby expanding Bill 154 to include the narrow public services. There was an all-party consensus on this move. With regard to its desire for one piece of legislation, it could be concluded that the labour-feminist alliance was represented by all three parties, while the male business alliance lost its parliamentary representative. At no point in either the Justice Committee or the Committee of the Whole House did the Tories introduce any amendments that would remove the private sector, or the broader public sector, from Bill 154. The 1987 Ontario Pay Equity Act therefore represents a victory for the labour-feminist alliance in that it is a single, all-inclusive legislative enactment applicable to the civil service, the broader public sector, and the private sector.

The all-inclusiveness of the act has positive consequences for gender by bringing together women in both the public and the private sectors under the same legislation. Fear had been expressed that women would be pitted against one another if women in the private sector, who suffer relatively larger wage gaps, were either excluded from the act or treated separately in a different statute from public-sector women, who suffer smaller wage gaps. The coverage of both public and private sectors in the same act potentially strengthens, or at least does not harm, working-class solidarity.

Size of Establishment

Related to the sector question is that of size of establishment; that is, should pay equity apply to all firms, regardless of size, or should it be applied only to the largest firms because of their greater resources and ability to pay? In the public debates before the Consultation Panel on Pay Equity and in the Standing Committee on the Administration of Justice, the male business class, especially small-business associations, argued that small firms (those with fewer than ten employees) should be exempted from pay equity legislation, while the labour-feminist alliance argued that all firms, regardless of size, should be covered by the legislation (Cuneo 1990, 41–3).

In section 3 of Bill 154, the Liberal government excluded private-sector employers with fewer than ten employees (Ontario Government 1988). In the Justice Committee's deliberations on this bill, Evelyn Gigantes of the NDP strongly opposed this exclusion with the argument that it would eliminate thousands of women from the proposed pay equity law and moved to strike the 'fewer than ten' exclusion from section 3 of the bill. She ran into strong opposition from the Tories, especially Baetz and Barlow, who made arguments on behalf of small business. The Tories joined the Liberals in voting down Gigantes's amendment, and the original Liberal section 3 carried.[11]

When Bill 154 went through the amendment process in the Committee of the Whole House, Gigantes again moved to amend section 3 by eliminating the 'fewer than ten' exclusion. She argued that this exclusion would particular affect immigrant and visible-minority women, many of whom are concentrated in such small firms. The Liberals and Tories voted down the NDP amendment by a 65-to-18 margin, and the 'fewer than ten' exclusion became law (OLA 9 June 1987, 1217–18, 1227).

The second issue concerning size of establishment had to do with the obligation of employers with 10 to 99 employees to develop pay equity plans. Under subsection 11(1) and section 19 of Bill 154, the Liberal government stipulated that employers with 10 to 99 employees were not obligated to develop pay equity plans, although they could do so if they wished. In the Justice Committee's deliberations on this bill, the NDP strongly objected because, as with the federal Canadian and Quebec legislation, it meant that women in such firms would be forced into a complaints procedure to obtain pay equity; in other words, proactivity would not apply to them. The result would be that 84 per cent of Ontario firms, covering 570,000, or one-quarter of all women, would not be obligated to post plans.

Gigantes moved to amend section 11 by requiring *all* employers to develop pay equity plans. The Tories, on the grounds that small firms do not have the resources to develop plans and that the NDP amendment would make the bill even 'more interventionist,' joined the Liberals in defeating the NDP amendment.[12] The NDP did not introduce a similar amendment in the Committee of the Whole House, but they had pointed out earlier in the House that many visible-minority women would be forced into a complaints procedure because they are concentrated in firms with 10 to 99 employees (OLA 17 December 1986, 4299).

A third issue related to the size of establishment concerns the relation between the presence or absence of a union and the obligation to develop pay equity plans. In the Justice Committee's study of Bill 154, the NDP moved to add a subsection to section 11 requiring that all firms with 10 to 99 employees, and having a bargaining agent (fully or partly *unionized*), develop pay equity plans. The employer in similar-sized non-unionized firms would have no such obligation. The NDP rationale, according to Gigantes, was that 'where there has been a history of labour-management negotiations in an establishment, it would be quite a natural phenomenon for these labour-management negotiations to be continued around the issue of an equal pay plan.'[13] The Tories and Liberals defeated this amendment. Gigantes made one more try later in the Committee of the Whole House by moving two amendments, to require the development of pay equity plans in firms with between 10 and 99 employees, where a bargaining agent is present. She pointedly argued:

we are talking here about firms where the employer has, over a period of time, negotiated with unions about pay scales and has negotiated with union representatives of women employed in that firm about job classifications, hours of work and benefits. Why is it that, when we get to the question of pay equity, women do not have the right to be represented by their union on this question in relationship to the employer? ... Why shut them out? Why, in fact, disrupt? This is disruptive. Why disrupt a pattern that is in place in a particular work place by saying, 'On this one subject we are not going to have the union representing those female workers involved in something that is an essential change in the work place under this legislation?' (OLA, 10 June 1987, 1261)

The Liberals objected to the NDP amendment on the grounds that unions in such workplaces still had the right under the existing sections to negotiate pay equity plans. The Tories joined the Liberals to defeat both amendments by a 56-to-17 margin (OLA, 10 June 1987, 1261–2, 1272, 1275).

On the three size-of-establishment issues, the 1987 Ontario Pay Equity Act represents a victory by the male business alliance over the labour-feminist alliance. The Tories and Liberals successfully represented the male business alliance against attempts by the NDP to eliminate small-workplace exclusions and restrictions. The 'fewer than ten' exclusion is divisive for working-class women in two ways. It creates a division between low-income women in workplaces with fewer than ten workers (whom it completely disqualifies from pay equity adjustments) and higher-income women in workplaces with ten or more employees (whom it qualifies for pay equity adjustments). The exclusion also creates divisions among working-class women on the basis of race and ethnicity, since low-income immigrant women and women of colour are more likely than are white women to be found in workplaces with fewer than ten employees (especially in the garment industry). Further divisions among women are created by giving the strong proactive model to mostly white unionized women in workplaces with more than 100 employees, while saddling women in workplaces with 10 to 99 employees, more of whom are non-white and immigrant, with the weaker complaints model. In addition, union rights are undermined by the lack of a clear requirement of employers with 10 to 99 employees to negotiate pay equity with bargaining agents in their establishments.

Within-Establishment Comparisons
In the *Green Paper on Pay Equity* (Ontario Government 1985, 4, 16, 39), the Ontario government assumed that comparisons between female-predominant and male-predominant jobs could be done only within establishments, not between establishments. On the whole, this premise was accepted by the male business and labour-feminist alliances, although the latter wanted provisions for related-establishment comparisons when male comparators could not be found in female-predominant establishments, such as child-care centres.

In the Justice Committee's amendments to Bill 154, the NDP attempted to move a related-establishment provision and the granting to the Pay Equity Commission of the right to determine the mechanisms for job comparisons in all-female establishments that did not have the appropriate male comparators. The Tories and Liberals opposed both amendments. Because the 1987 Pay Equity Act is restricted to comparisons within establishments only, and in view of the fact that neither alliance took a strong position supporting between-establishment comparisons, neither can be said to have won on this issue.

Although there is a sense in which within-establishment comparisons can be said to bring workers together to discuss their conditions of labour and hence contribute to their intracorporate solidarity, the exclusion of interestablishment comparisons also serves to reinforce gender contradictions within the working class, since part of the gendered wage gap is located at these junctures. To take an extreme example: women working in day-care centres earn far less than do male workers in the steel industry. It would be interesting to compare the job-worth points of women day-care workers and male steelworkers *across* establishments. Male business representatives and governments have usually ruled out this type of comparison on the grounds that wage differences across establishments are caused by 'objective' market forces rather than by systemic discrimination. But numerous gender-related factors – such as the exclusion of women from heavy steel–making through managerial and co-worker action and inaction on sexual harassment – are embedded in 'objective' market forces (see Field 1983).

Definition of Establishment
The *Green Paper on Pay Equity* (Ontario Government 1985, 16–17) outlined three possible definitions of establishment. First, in the *functional* definition, 'establishment' is marked by the boundaries of a compensation plan or personnel policy *within* a company. Thus, one company may constitute two or more establishments, and comparisons could be made only within, not between, such functional units. Second, the *geographic* definition marks physical boundaries of a territorial area, such as a municipality. Comparisons could be made between an establishment's divisions located in the same municipality, not between divisions of the establishment located in different municipalities. Third, the *corporate* definition sets the widest possible boundaries of an establishment as all organizations included under a corporate entity.

The labour-feminist alliance favoured the corporate definition, while the male business alliance supported either narrow geographic bound-aries within municipalities or the functional definition set within geo-graphic boundaries; in other words, comparisons would be allowed only within a compensation plan and at a specific physical location.

Before the Justice Committee began amending Bill 154, several Ontario construction associations sent a packet of letters to Tory Andy Brandt, pleading that, in the new pay equity act, job comparisons not be allowed within the same establishment between on-site male skilled tradesper-sons (such as bricklayers) on construction projects and off-site female office workers.[14] In the committee's amendments to Bill 154, the Tories declared their opposition to subsection 6(5) because it would allow com-parisons between female and male job classes throughout an establish-ment defined on a geographic basis. Evelyn Gigantes pointed out that the construction industry's concerns were unwarranted: 'any construc-tion employer who has a brain in his head and a lawyer at his disposal is going to make sure that the unorganized women staff in his office will be compared to a male, comparable, unorganized, job class in the office. That is what [sub]sections 4 and 5 do for the employer, so relax. If you are looking after the employer, relax, it is all there in the Bill.'[15]

Rueben Baetz of the Progressive Conservatives moved to include the functional definition in a new clause in section 1 that would treat as two separate establishments both on-site trades and off-site office em-ployees in a construction establishment in a single geographic area. When Baetz encountered opposition from the other two parties to his amendment, he became incensed, declaring: 'this is a pretty sad com-mentary on this committee. We have heard from the construction in-dustry time and time again ... They are the people who know what is going on in the industry ... and they have made what we think is a very sensible logical request ... I just want to make it clear that our party has listened to the construction industry on this one.'[16]

In the Justice Committee, the NDP moved to strike the Liberal geo-graphic definition of establishment in Bill 154 and replace it with a corporate definition in which ' "establishment" means all of the em-ployees in Ontario of an employer.'[17] Gigantes reasoned thus: 'We be-lieve the geographic division of the establishment ... is one which employers on different sides of a boundary line, which might be a street, will be able [to use] to avoid comparing the comparable work done by employees who might work across the road from each other. It is a very artificial division.'[18] She added that, since minimum wages were set across the province, with no variation between geographic regions, job

classes should also be compared across the province within an establishment, with no artificial geographic boundaries. The Tories and the
Liberals joined forces to defeat this amendment.[19]

In an effort to rescue some semblance of the corporate definition, the
NDP moved a new section 2 that would allow 'two or more employers
and the bargaining agent or agents for their employees,' where they
negotiate a 'central agreement,' to treat their separate establishments as
a single establishment; this may also be done for 'municipalities in the
same geographic division,' even where they are not unionized.[20] Gigantes argued that the purpose of this amendment was to cover the
centralized negotiations in the Ontario Hospital Association and other
such groups. Surprisingly, the Liberals did not oppose this amendment,
perhaps because it was primarily 'permissive in nature'; the amendment
thus carried and became one of the few NDP additions to the 1987
Ontario Pay Equity Act.[21]

A weaker, but not insignificant, supplement to the corporate definition
would be a ban on contracting-out to avoid pay equity. In the Justice
Committee, the NDP moved that the following clause be added to the
definition of 'employee' in section 1 of Bill 154: ' "employee" means a
person who performs any work or supplies any services for compensation and includes employees of contractors and subcontractors performing work or supplying services."[22] Gigantes argued that 'what the
employer can do in order to get around the aegis of this act is to contract
out ... If a hospital has cleaners on staff and the hospital will have to
make wage adjustments under this legislation, the hospital may seek to
avoid making wage adjustments by contracting out ... This is an item
which has been raised to us as a committee time and again by women's
groups.'[23]

The Liberals and Tories joined forces in defeating the NDP amendment.
Undaunted, the NDP reintroduced its amendment later in the Committee
of the Whole House. Gigantes repeatedly argued that, not only would
the legislation as currently written not prevent contracting-out to avoid
pay equity, but it would accelerate contracting-out for the same reason.
By a vote of 65 to 18, the Tories and Liberals again defeated the NDP
amendment (OLA 9 June 1987, 1227).

The failure of the NDP attempt to ban contracting-out as a means of
avoiding pay equity may have severe consequences for immigrant and
visible-minority women who are concentrated in cleaning services that
are often contracted-out at lower wages. On the third reading debate of
Bill 154 in the House, Tory MPP Shymko gave an example of this oc-

curring right under the noses of his colleagues in the Ontario provincial government:

If you look at the system of contracting out jobs, you will have an immigrant Portuguese woman cleaning my office in the Whitney Block paid some $4 an hour less that the lady [sic] cleaning my colleague's office in the Legislative Building doing the same work. One is a public servant of the government of Ontario, a civil servant paid according to the unionized rate. The other lady [sic] doing the same work is being paid $4 an hour less because she is contracted out. This bill does not resolve the issue. (OLA 15 June 1987, 1369)

The 1987 Ontario Pay Equity Act enshrines the geographic definition of establishment, but on a broad basis as the boundaries of a 'county, territorial district or regional municipality' (Ontario Government 1988, s. 1[1]). Because neither the corporate definition favoured by the labour-feminist alliance nor the functional definition set within the geographic definition supported by the male business alliance was inserted in the act, the two alliances can be said to have duelled to a draw on this particular issue. However, the legislation tilted somewhat in the direction of the labour-feminist alliance because of the acceptance of the NDP provision for expanding the boundaries of an establishment by combining two or more establishments within or between geographic divisions through negotiations in unionized workplaces between one or more bargaining agents and employers, and in non-unionized workplaces between employees and employers.

The geographic definition of establishment has positive gender and class consequences in that women workers can identify with other women workers, and be compared with male job classes, on a basis broader than that which would have been allowed under a functional definition. Municipal boundaries of 'establishment' can potentially lead to the creation of working-class solidarity on a community basis, which has been the unit of analysis in many historical working-class studies (see Palmer 1979; Kealey 1980). However, the geographic definition can also have negative effects on gender and class. Within many corporate establishments, it splinters the workforce along gender lines, impeding the intermunicipal identification of women workers and comparisons of their job classes with male job classes. Within the same corporate establishment male warehouse workers usually have higher wages than female retail workers, but where, for example, the warehouse and retail outlets are physically located in different municipalities, comparisons between their job classes cannot be conducted under the geographic definition, unless agreed to by both the employer and bargaining agents (or the non-unionized employees).

Annual Pay Equity Adjustments

In Ontario, as in other jurisdictions throughout North America, male business associations have argued that pay equity would cost them billions of dollars and could lead to bankruptcies and a downturn in the economy (Cuneo 1990, 116–26). Business associations therefore demanded that pay equity costs not exceed 1 per cent of the previous year's payroll, with a possible cap on the number of years (around four) during which they might be expected to make pay equity adjustments. The labour-feminist alliance objected to the use of 1 per cent as a maximum; instead it argued that it should be a *minimum*, with an upper limit of 3 per cent.

In the Justice Committee's study of Bill 105, the NDP proposed amendments obliging employers to use at least 3 per cent of annual payroll to pay equity adjustments. In addition, the NDP wanted a 3 per cent lump sum given to the lowest-paid women in the first year of adjustments. The Conservatives had difficulty with the size of these pay-outs, favouring a minimum of 1 per cent per year.

By the time the Justice Committee considered Bill 154, the Tories sided more with the Liberals. As a result, the NDP no longer demanded that at least 3 per cent be paid annually in pay equity adjustments. Instead, it fell back to the position that pay equity adjustments should be at least 1 per cent per year and also moved that the lowest-paid women should achieve equal pay before anyone else. The Liberals opposed this proposal because of the requirement that all positions in a job class receive the same dollar increases in pay equity adjustments. Instead, the Liberals pushed their 'cascading' clause, in which the lowest-paid women would receive an extra amount in pay equity adjustments until they caught up with the next-lowest paid, and so on up the ladder of inequalities. By the time Bill 154 arrived at the Committee of the Whole House, the NDP had dropped all of its cost demands, with the exception of the amendment banning wage restraint as a means of achieving pay equity (see below).

The 1987 Pay Equity Act most closely reflects the male business alliance demand of 1 per cent per year: employers are required to pay out annually at least 1 per cent of the previous year's payroll, but not any more (although they may if they so choose). It seems clear that the labour-feminist alliance lost, and the male business alliance won, on this issue.

Phasing In of Pay Equity Adjustments
In the *Green Paper on Pay Equity*, the Ontario government considered the following method of phasing in the legislation: 'the phase-in could be divided into two parts: a period during which the plan is to be formulated and implementation is to begin; and a second stage during which the implementation is to be accomplished ... Under the employer-initiated model or integrated approach, the phase-in could be related to the size of the employer, based on the number of employees in the establishment' (Ontario Government 1985, 35).

If pay equity was to be imposed on employers, this method would have been consistent with their interests. In contrast, the labour-feminist alliance opposed a drawn-out implementation process, with no final date for implementation – especially because those women who suffer the greatest wage gaps (not necessarily the lowest-paid) would have to wait the longest for the full adjustments to which they would be entitled under the legislation.

On the issue of phase-in, the NDP closely represented the views of the labour-feminist alliance, and the Liberals and Tories the views of the male business alliance. The Liberals inserted a series of clauses into Bill 154 that effectively gave smaller establishments a longer time period to post their plans and to make their first adjustments. The NDP introduced a number of amendments that essentially moved these adjustment dates up. These were voted down by the Tories and Liberals. The NDP also moved to have all employers required to complete full pay equity within five years of the first adjustment date, with 20 per cent of the total pay equity adjustment allotted to each year. This proposal was also voted down by the other two parties. However, perhaps surprisingly, when the NDP moved that full pay equity be achieved in the public sector within five years of the first adjustment date, the Tories supported it, and it passed against the opposition from the Liberals. This section was not removed in the Committee of the Whole House, and today is part of the Pay Equity Act.

Regarding the mandatory posting dates, in the Justice Committee, the Liberals moved a number of amendments that effectively stipulated that such dates coincide with the date of the first adjustment. Despite opposition from the NDP, these amendments passed because of support from the Tories. However, after arguments against it were made by the

NDP, the Liberals reconsidered and moved to reinsert the earlier mandatory posting dates.

. On the issue of phase-in, the 1987 Pay Equity Act bears a remarkable similarity to the passage from the Liberal government's Green Paper quoted above. The dates for mandatory posting of pay equity plans, first pay equity adjustments dates, and final adjustment dates, by sector and size of organization, are shown in Table 2 (see also Pay Equity Commission 1988a, 3). Three principles seem evident from this table. First, the smaller the organization the more lenient are the dates for mandatory posting and first adjustments. This stipulation is based on the government's assumption that the administration of pay equity would be more costly per employee for small employers, especially those without personnel departments. Second, private-sector organizations, which mounted a vociferous opposition to pay equity, are treated more leniently than are public-sector state organizations in two ways: the public sector must begin its adjustments in 1990, the same year it must post its plans, whereas the private sector is given an extra year to begin adjustments; and public-sector organizations must complete all adjustments by 1 January 1995, whereas private-sector organizations are given an indefinite amount of time, subject to the 1 per cent per year requirement (Pay Equity Commission 1988c, 4). Third, since average compensation decreases with the size of the organization, the lowest-paid women in the smallest organizations – who are perhaps in greatest need of adjustments – would have to wait the longest. It is clear that the male business class won on this issue.

The stages-implementation schedule potentially pits women against one another by giving earlier pay equity adjustments to those in larger firms, which, as previously noted, generally have higher job rates, than to those in smaller firms, which generally have lower job rates. In this respect, the law treats higher-paid women, and perhaps new middle-class women, better.

Pay Equity Adjustments vs. Expected Wage Increases
The labour feminist alliance was concerned that employers would simply use pay equity as a bargaining chip to play off against other collective-bargaining demands from unions. Concern was expressed that employers could achieve their pay equity obligations by lowering general wage and benefit increases and diverting these expected increases into pay equity settlements. The male business alliance preferred the total freedom to play pay equity off against other demands in regular collective

TABLE 2
The stage implementation by sector and size of organization

No. of employees and sector	Mandatory posting	First adjustments	Final adjustments
Public Sector	1 January 1990	1 January 1990	1 January 1995
Private Sector			
500 or more employees	1 January 1990	1 January 1991	No mandatory deadline; at least 1 per cent of the previous year's payroll must be used for pay equity adjustments each year, until pay equity is achieved.
100–499 employees	1 January 1991	1 January 1992	
50–99 employees; plans posted	1 January 1992	1 January 1993	
10–49 employees; plans posted	1 January 1993	1 January 1994	
50–99 employees; no posted plans	inapplicable	1 January 1993	1 January 1993
10–49 employees; no posted plans	inapplicable	1 January 1994	1 January 1994
0–9 employees; excluded	inapplicable	inapplicable	inapplicable

Source: Adapted from Pay Equity Commission (1988a, 2; 1988b, 3)

bargaining; in fact, some business associations warned that, if a proactive pay equity law were enacted, they would simply divert funds from general wage increases negotiated in regular collective bargaining into pay equity negotiations and adjustments (Cuneo 1990, 51).

These public debates among lobby groups were reflected in the political amending process. In Bill 105, the Liberals inserted a ban against wage reduction in section 9, which read: 'An employer shall not reduce the compensation payable to any employee or reduce the rate of compensation for any position in order to achieve pay equity' (Ontario Government 1986). In the Justice Committee, Gigantes moved to strike and replace this section with the following ban against wage reduction *and* restraint: 'An employer shall not reduce *or restrain* the compensation payable to any employee or reduce *or restrain* the rate of compensation for any position in order to achieve equal pay for work of equal value.'[24] Gigantes worried that, in its public service bill, the provincial government could restrain the wages of its male employees by holding back part of their general increases in order to pay for women's pay equity adjustments. Brian Charlton of the NDP questioned whether 'reduce' covered 'restraint,' which 'has been part of a major debate in the labour community for a decade now. What is "reduce"? Is "reduce" a dollar reduction in wages or is "reduce" when one loses real buying power, real dollars.'[25] The Liberals opposed the NDP amendment with the argument that it would result in unions and unorganized workers flooding the Pay Equity Commission with complaints that their wages had been unfairly restrained because of pay equity. The Tories sided with the NDP to narrowly defeat the Liberals in a 5-to-4 vote, and the amendment passed.[26]

In Bill 154, the Liberals inserted a subsection (9 [1]) identical to that which appeared in Bill 105, and the NDP responded in the Justice Committee with the same amendment. In the debate, Gigantes objected to three categories of workers having to pay for pay equity by taking a smaller wage increase: men, women who do not qualify for pay equity adjustments, and women who do qualify. In the last case, women, by having their wages restrained, would be paying for their own pay equity adjustments. As Gigantes argued: 'As a female employee, I have the employer taking money out of one of my pockets and putting it into my other pocket and somehow I am supposed to feel happier. To me, that is not only unfair but deceptive ... We do not think that employees, either male or female, should be punished because there has been discrimination in the past. They should not be punished in the future in terms of having lower general annual wage increases. It is not their fault. These decisions are management decisions in the end.'[27]

Under her amendment, she again wanted employees to have the right to complain to the commission that their wages had been unduly restrained because of pay equity. Barlow, a Tory, complained that the NDP would allow the government to set wages by dragging employers before the commission to prove that they had not decreased wages to fund pay equity. Chris Ward of the Liberals opposed the NDP amendment by coming close by asking women to pay for their own pay equity adjustments: 'The argument that is being made here [by Gigantes] strikes me as being similar to many of the arguments we have heard from [business] groups and organizations that say they should be exempted from any impact of this legislation. The fact is that nobody wants to bear the cost in some way or other and the fact is that everybody has a role to play in bearing some of the cost.'[28] Ian Scott, Liberal attorney general and minister responsible for women's issues, was more direct when, on 18 November 1986, he told a group of employers: 'We are going to try and help you in this way by saying that, of the amount that you allocate annually to wage increases, a certain proportion should be devoted to dealing with this [pay equity] adjustment ... Inflation is at four percent. If you are increasing wages two percent, a certain proportion of that two percent should be directed to solving this [unequal pay] discrepancy over a period of time.'[29] The Tories sided with the Liberals and defeated the NDP amendment. In the Committee of the Whole House, the NDP again introduced its wage-restraint amendment. The same debate took place, and the Tories and Liberals joined forces to defeat the amendment by a 56-to-17 margin (OLA 9 June 1987, 1224–6; 10 June, 1275).

On this issue, the male business alliance won and the labour-feminist alliance lost. The Liberals and the Tories were the representatives of male business-class interests, and the NDP of working-class women's interests. Because of this defeat, there is no clear prohibition in the 1987 Ontario Pay Equity Act against employers diverting part of general wage increase to pay equity adjustments, although this may be a matter that the Pay Equity Hearings Tribunal will have to decide. This situation perhaps goes a long way to explain why business, after so vociferously opposing proactive pay equity legislation, has now, on the whole, gone along with it.

This issue is fraught with negative class and gender implications. In a number of workplaces, resentment by male workers against women workers has already arisen over the belief that their general wage increases will be lower, so that employers can make their pay equity adjustments. As Gigantes expressed it, the intent of her amendment would have been 'to make sure that women do not pay for their own equal pay payouts and that their male colleagues do not have to sit around feeling, for a period of up to 17 years, that the reason they did not get the increases they might have expected is those blankety-blank women are getting equal pay.'[30] This situation potentially harms working-class solidarity around pay equity, unless unions set up education workshops to work through such resentments. On the positive side, such workshops may be successful in educating male workers against the traditional family wage and lead them to favour paying women a fair wage for the worth of their jobs, independent of any household connection to a man. In the long run, such a change in view has considerable potential for integrating women into internal trade-union politics and in general support for, and activity in, the union.

Conclusions

Despite its initial vociferous opposition to the legislation, business has been willing to go along with it because, compared to the labour and women's movements, it did not appear to lose as much. By design or otherwise, devices were set up in the legislation whereby pay equity would not cost employers any more in terms of labour expenditures than they would otherwise have to bear in the absence of pay equity. The defeat of the NDP wage-restraint amendments meant that business could simply shift some of its labour costs from general wage increases to pay equity adjustments without suffering much of an overall increase in costs. In addition, the non-coverage of establishments of fewer than ten employees, the lack of obligation to develop pay equity plans for employers with 10 to 99 employees, and the gender predominance thresholds weaken the legislation from the point of view of women and unions.

The state's agenda was only partly a product of the period of public consultation that began in early 1986. In a sense, the public consultation was partly a sham and partly an effective device for getting opposing points of view embodied in the legislation. That Bill 105 was written and presented in public (11 February 1986) *before* the lobby groups delivered their oral and written briefs to the Public Consultation Panel on Pay Equity (February to April 1986) and *before* the public hearings by the Standing Committee on the Administration of Justice on Bill 105 (September to October 1986) and later on Bill 154 (February to March 1987) makes the state's public-consultation process fairly dubious. Worth questioning, too, is the remarkable similarity of Bill 105 and Bill 154 on the following issues: 60 per cent predominantly female job classes or levels; 70 per cent predominantly male job classes or levels; a separate pay equity commission; pay equity adjustments at 1 per cent of annual payroll; lack of any ban on wage restraint; job comparisons only within establishments; comparisons throughout the establishment; the *principle* of grouping of job classes or levels; proactivity; casual part-time work exclusion; temporary-training exclusion; temporary-skills exclusion; and comparisons with the lowest male comparator. In these respects, it could be argued that pay equity resulted from a combination of internal state decision making, pre-1986 lobbying within and outside Ontario, and the influence of state practices in other jurisdictions. Certainly, lobbying in Ontario during the three periods of public consultation had no effect on these features of the legislation.

There is the contrary argument, however, that lobbying during the three periods of public consultation had important effects on the legislation. Suggestive of this is the fact that Bill 154 had some features that were not in Bill 105, such as: coverage of the private sector and the broader public sector; the exclusion of establishments with fewer than ten employees; phased implementation of pay equity adjustments by size of establishment; the lack of any requirement for employers with 10 to 99 employees to develop pay equity plans; the geographic definition of establishment; the explicit division of functions between a pay equity office and a hearings tribunal; and the exclusions of red-circling, seniority, merit, and relative bargaining strength. But these latter provisions were a result of the complex interplay among state administrative decision makers *after* 1985; lobbying efforts during the three public consultation periods by the labour-feminist and male business alliances; and the discussions and debates among the Liberals, Tories, and NDP during the amending process. For all the reasons and facts cited in this paragraph, the wins, losses, and draws by the male business and labour-feminist alliances discussed in this essay cannot be interpreted simply as the effects of lobby-group pressure on the final outcome of the legislation.

However, the representations of the contradictions of gender, class, and race/ethnicity are also apparent in the legislation. While the interests of the business class are well represented in the legislation, especially through the efforts of the Liberal and Progressive Conservative parties, some concessions are made to the working class, represented by the NDP. In addition, the interests of men were represented in the legislative process by all three parties (for example, the exclusion of domestic-labour issues), with several concessions to women.

The interests of the white and dominant Anglo-Saxon collectives were well represented in the legislation by all three parties through the suppression of minority race/ethnic criteria. But class, gender, and race/ethnicity never occur separately in society. It is their interaction in concrete reality that received representation in the legislation. The most extreme poles are the dominant hegemonic representation of the white male business-class interests in the legislation by the Progressive Conservative party for much of the time and the Liberal party for some of the time, and the suppression of visible-minority female working-class interests, which had no party representative. Between these poles are combinations of representations: white business women fared better than visible-minority working-class women, white business women fared better than white working-class men, and so on. All of this was a product of the fine-tuning of the legislation in the amending stages.

Despite being in a minority situation, the Liberal government of David Peterson was quite in control of the agenda on pay equity. It managed to defeat directly through votes, or indirectly through stalling tactics, attempts by the opposition parties to change the spirit of the legislation as written through amendments the Liberals did not support. The Tories did an about-face from appearing to come close to representing the labour-feminist alliance during the amendments to Bill 105, to its more traditional representation of the male business alliance in the amendments to Bill 154 in both the Justice Committee and the Committee of the Whole House. In fact, it could be argued that the Tories were minor players, taking a back seat that consisted of voting with the government to forestall a more progressive piece of legislation envisaged by the NDP and Evelyn Gigantes, who took a leading creative role, despite the failure of most of their efforts to amend the legislation.

NOTES

1 Public Archives of Ontario (hereafter PAO). Standing Committee on the Administration of Justice (hereafter SCAJ), RG 18 F, Acc. 20499, Box 4, Exhibits (Bill 105); Box 6, Transcripts J-17 to J-29, 23 Sept. to 8 Oct. 1986. Unless otherwise noted, all references to 'Transcripts' in this essay will be to Box 6 in the files of the Justice Committee held at the PAO, with the above call number.
2 PAO, SCAJ, RG 18 F, Acc. 20499, Boxes 4 and 5, Exhibits (Bill 154); Box 6, Transcripts J-51 (23 Feb. 1987) to J-69 (11 Mar. 1987)
3 Transcript J-32, 27 Oct. 1986
4 Transcript J-38, 2 Dec. 1986, 2–5
5 Transcript J-78, 7 Apr. 1987, 15
6 See, for example, Transcript J-35, 4 Nov. 1986, 10–12. Evelyn Gigantes of the NDP exclaimed: 'What we have seen is the government refusing to allow this bill [105] to proceed through the amendment state.' Transcript J-37, 18 Nov. 1986, 20
7 Transcript J-74, 1 Apr. 1987, 16

8 This numerical summary of the Justice Committee oversimplifies the complexity of the amending process. Not included in this summary are amendments submitted but never discussed as well as amendments that were discussed but withdrawn without a formal vote or decision being taken. In addition, because of discussion and debate, several of the approved amendments were different from those initially submitted by the parties to the committee.
9 Transcript J-73, 31 Mar. 1987, 4
10 Transcript J-73, 31 Mar. 1987, 3–20
11 Transcript J-76, 6 Apr. 1987, 2–8
12 Transcript J-70, 30 Mar. 1987, 7; Transcript J-72, 31 Mar. 1987, 1–2, 5–7; Transcript J-74, 1 Apr. 1987, 25–9
13 Transcript J-77, 6 Apr. 1987, 39–40
14 For example, the Council of Ontario Construction Association, Sewer and Watermain Contractors Association, Ontario General Contractors Association, Niagara Construction Association, and the ECAO Electrical Contractors Association of Ontario. See PAO, SCAJ, Box 5, Folder on Exhibits for Bill 154, Vol. IV, Exhibit No. 152, Mar. 1987. See oral presentations by the Council of Ontario Construction Association, Box 6, Transcript J-65, 5 Mar. 1987, 30–45; Transcript J-69, 11 Mar. 1987, 1–15.
15 Transcript J-77, 6 Apr. 1987, 21
16 Transcript J-81, 8 Apr. 1987, 49
17 Transcript J-82, 9 Apr. 1987, 6
18 Transcript J-82, 9 Apr. 1987, 6
19 Transcript J-82, 9 Apr. 1987, 6–8
20 Transcript J-81, 8 Apr. 1987, 54–5
21 Transcript J-82, 9 Apr. 1987, 19–20
22 Transcript J-82, 9 Apr. 1987, 5
23 Transcript J-82, 9 Apr. 1987, 5–6
24 Transcript J-36, 17 Nov. 1986, 11; emphasis added
25 Transcript J-36, 17 Nov. 1986, 39
26 Transcript J-37, 18 Nov. 1986, 2
27 Transcript J-74, 1 Apr. 1987, 4
28 Transcript J-74, 1 Apr. 1987, 8
29 OLA, 20 November 1986, 3498. This is a tape transcript of Scott's statement read in the Legislature by Evelyn Gigantes. Scott denied making such a statement. Gigantes paraphrased from this statement in the Justice Committee's clause-by-clause amendment of Bill 154. See Transcript J74, 1 Apr. 1987, 3.
30 Transcript J-74, 1 Apr. 1987, 7

3 Litigating Our Way to Gender Neutrality: Mission Impossible?

Judy Fudge

Pay equity embodies the simple idea that people should not be paid less because they work at jobs that have become identified as women's work. But the problem is that this simple idea has become obscured by a complex maze of statistics and procedures generated by economists and lawyers. According to Willborn, 'if there is one universal truth, it is that the complexity of an issue increases in direct proportion to the number of lawyers and economists dealing with it' (1989, 157).

This essay focuses on the Pay Equity Hearing Tribunal's approach to the issue of gender neutrality under the Ontario Pay Equity Act in order to illustrate how the implementation process in Ontario has the potential to become a litigation nightmare. Unlike most other proactive pay equity initiatives, Ontario's Pay Equity Act establishes an independent tribunal in order to resolve disputes that arise during the implementation process. Such recourse is particularly important with respect to the legal requirement in Ontario that the job-comparison system used to evaluate female and male jobs be gender neutral because it gives feminists and trade unions an opportunity to challenge the sex biases that are alleged to infect traditional job-evaluation systems. However, the preliminary decisions issued by the tribunal concerning the gender neutrality of job-comparison systems suggest that its approach reinforces the Pay Equity Act's shift in focus from systemic discrimination to individual group equity (McDermott 1990, 407). In this essay the implication of this approach will be identified and examined, and an alternative method for resolving the issue of gender-neutral job-comparison systems will be briefly sketched in the conclusion.

Job Evaluation and Gender Neutrality

The Canadian pay equity initiatives go beyond the vast majority of their American counterparts in at least one crucial respect: each of the Canadian statutes requires that the mechanism used to evaluate the worth or value of jobs to employers be gender neutral (McDermott, 28). Typically, other jurisdictions have relied on traditional job-evaluation systems that have not been modified to eliminate possible gender biases in their methodology. Because the Canadian pay equity statutes specifically require job-evaluation, or, in the case of Ontario, job-comparison, systems to be gender neutral, the elimination of gender bias in the evaluation technique should, in theory, result in higher wage adjustments for women workers. For this reason the gender neutrality of traditional job-evaluation systems is an extremely contentious issue in Ontario.

A gender-neutral job-comparison system must be used to compare the relative value of work performed in Ontario. The Pay Equity Act simply requires that the value, defined as a composite of skill, responsibility, effort, and working conditions, of female and male job classes be compared using a job-comparison system (s. 5); it does not define a job-comparison system. The Pay Equity Commission[1] has issued guidelines that address the issue of a gender-neutral job-comparison system[2] in order to guide the parties through the self-managed process. However, the Pay Equity Hearings Tribunal, which is charged with deciding complaints under the act, does not treat the guidelines issued by the commission as binding.[3] Consequently, it is inevitable that the tribunal will be faced with the task of developing criteria for gender neutrality under the Pay Equity Act. How it goes about doing this is crucial.

Both the commission and the tribunal have been careful to distinguish job-comparison from job-evaluation systems.[4] Regardless, many employers and unions have used, and are continuing to use, job evaluation as the basis for job comparisons under the act.[5] Thus, it is likely that, in most cases, unless the Hearings Tribunal decides otherwise, job-evaluation plans will be the basis of gender-neutral job-comparison systems.

'Job evaluation' is a generic term that refers to a formal procedure for hierarchically ranking a set of jobs with respect to their value or worth to a particular employer. Such procedures have a long history in Canada, and they have become quite common in both the public and private sectors, particularly in larger organizations (Kaufman 1986, 3). Although there are many different job-evaluation methodologies for ranking the value of jobs, some elements are common to most job-evaluation systems. According to Acker, 'job evaluation is a process of assessing the worth of particular job categories on a number of dimensions or compensable factors usually including knowledge and skill, effort, responsibility, and working conditions. A numerical score is assigned for each factor and a total score for the job is computed. Jobs are then ranked according to their scores and the wages of jobs with similar scores are compared to determine the presence or absence of pay inequity' (1987, 183).

The appropriateness of using existing job-evaluation plans for measuring the value of work had received a great deal of attention (Acker 1987; Schwab 1985; Burton 1987; Remick 1984c; Steinberg and Haignere 1987; McArthur 1985). According to the authors of a study of the pay equity implementation process in Minnesota, the 'pre-existing methods of evaluation used by most jurisdictions implementing comparable worth merely applies to women's jobs the same values and criteria that have been designed to rate traditional men's jobs' (Evans and Nelson 1989a, 170). Moreover, the conclusion that most existing job evaluations are biased in favour of jobs traditionally occupied by men is widely accepted in much of the pay equity and comparable-worth literature (Acker 1987; Schwab 1985; Burton 1987; Remick 1984c; Steinberg and Haignere 1987; McArthur 1985). But despite these criticisms, researchers have concluded that job evaluation is a useful tool for identifying and correcting wage discrimination if job-evaluation plans are closely scrutinized and carefully modified to minimize implicit gender bias (Hartmann, Roos, and Treiman 1985, 5). To this end, a growing body of literature has emerged that has developed methodological standards or criteria for minimizing gender bias in job-evaluation systems.[6]

However, it is important to recognize that, 'while research can determine the conditions that minimize sex biases, it can never prove that such biases will be absent from comparable worth analyses. This is because most jobs are sex-segregated' (McArthur 1985, 67). The existence of a highly segregated labour market allows for the possibility of different standards being applied in the evaluation of jobs predominantly held by men and those predominantly held by women. Moreover, with a sex-segregated labour market 'the possibility arises not only for different standards to be applied, but for a systematic undervaluing or, indeed, non-recognition, of the importance of some characteristics of women's jobs' (Burton 1987, 130). Such is the case because the characteristics found in jobs typically held by women are not necessarily found in the jobs typically held by men.

The Ontario Pay Equity Commission, in recognition of much of this research, has stated that the search for gender bias is an exploratory process with no hard and fast rules for ensuring the identification of all gender bias (Ontario Pay Equity Commission *Newsletter*, 1[9]). Despite this caveat from the commission, it has issued guidelines on how to minimize gender bias in job-comparison systems. However, it is the tribunal that is charged with developing a legal standard for neutral job comparisons in order to resolve challenges brought before it to particular job-comparisons schemes.

The Ontario Pay Equity Act and Gender Neutrality

The requirement of gender-neutral evaluation and comparison systems in Canadian pay equity legislation is an important step forward towards 'true' pay equity: 'a wage setting system in which wages are pegged to unbiased sex-neutral evaluated points, with some flexibility to respond to market forces, but with controls to keep inequities from creeping back over time' (Acker 1989, 43). However, gender neutrality is more of an aspiration than an established standard (McArthur 1985). So far, none of the Canadian statutes provides any indication of what is to count as a gender-neutral job-evaluation or -comparison system (McDermott 28). In Manitoba, for example, where there is a legislative requirement that a gender-neutral job-evaluation system be used to compare female- and male-dominated jobs, the civil service used a ready-made system – a system that has been impugned as gender biased elsewhere (Acker 1989). The important point of this example is not whether the job-evaluation system was, in fact, gender neutral, but that the Manitoba legislation provided neither criteria nor a mechanism for resolving disputes over the gender neutrality of the evaluation mechanism. This absence of legislative or regulatory standards over what constitutes a gender-neutral method of evaluating and comparing female and male job classes gives rise to a host of problems; different methods will result in different evaluations of the same job and, thus, different pay equity adjustments. The choice of a particular method for evaluating and comparing job classes will have different financial implications for employers and employees. Moreover, the problem of determining a gender-neutral job-evaluation or -comparison system is further exacerbated by the fact that many of the job-evaluation systems historically used for the purpose of compensation have been impugned as gender biased. If such challenges are successful, they will erode entrenched managerial prerogatives and potentially disrupt managerial power. The choice of a job-evaluation methodology, which is the corner-stone of the current pay equity initiatives, is, therefore, likely to raise a number of problems for employers and unions, as well as for different groups of employees.

Under most of the Canadian pay equity statutes, the issue of gender neutrality will be resolved in negotiations that reflect the relative bargaining strengths of the parties. But, unlike the other Canadian pay equity statutes, the Ontario Pay Equity Act provides a mechanism for resolving disputes that does not, in theory, depend on entrenched managerial prerogatives, the advice of management consultants, or the relative bargaining strengths of the parties. In Ontario, when an employer and a union cannot agree on an aspect in the pay equity implementation process, either party may request the Pay Equity Commission to appoint a review officer, whose job it is to attempt to settle the dispute. If the parties are unable to reach a settlement, the review officer may issue an order binding on both unless they seek a hearing on the matter before the Pay Equity Hearings Tribunal. The review officer's order is not a precedent for any other parties, and copies of the order are available only to the parties to the dispute. In the event that either of the parties is unhappy with the review officer's order or the officer was not able to settle the dispute, a complaint may be brought to the Pay Equity Commission. Ultimately, such disputes may be referred to the Pay Equity Tribunal, a quasi-judicial body, for final resolution.[7]

But simply providing a means of adjudicating disputes arising over the issue of gender neutrality does not solve the problem that the parties, whether they be employers, unions, or groups of employees, have different interests at stake in the selection of a mechanism for comparing the value of job classes. What the Ontario Pay Equity Act does is provide a traditional adjudication process and litigation model for resolving potential conflicts that appears to depoliticize some of the most contentious aspects of the implementation process. However, the problem with this mechanism for resolving what is essentially a political controversy over the nature and meaning of pay equity is that the legislation does not define some of its most crucial concepts. By failing to define such central terms as 'employer' and 'gender neutrality' and delegating the task to the Hearings Tribunal, the legislature achieved a political compromise between business organizations and women's groups and trade unions. Consequently, the Hearings Tribunal must resolve what are essentially political problems and, in doing so, will determine the magnitude of pay equity adjustments paid to workers in women-dominated jobs in Ontario. The site of the struggle over the meaning of pay equity, therefore, has shifted from the explicitly political and economic realms of the legislature and the bargaining table to the legal terrain of an administrative tribunal – a terrain that is characterized by its own peculiar procedures, styles of address, standards of proof, and forms of argument.

The Choice of a Litigation Strategy: The Ontario Nurses' Association

Although the government emphasized the self-managed process as the primary means for implementing pay equity, it is clear that in many crucial instances this process has broken down. By far the most frequently occurring issue in dispute has been the selection of a gender-neutral job-comparison system.[8] The commission has already been swamped with complaints on this issue (Gorrie 1990).

So far, the majority of disputes that review officers have been called upon to resolve have arisen in the health sector (Ontario Pay Equity Commission *Newsletter*, 2[12]), and most of them have involved the Ontario Nurses' Association (ONA), the union that represents 55,000 nurses employed in hospitals, nursing homes, and public-health units across the province. The ONA has adopted a strategy of litigating crucial issues in the pay equity process in order to get the highest possible adjustments for its members. It has estimated that it will spend $1.5 million litigating pay equity issues in 1990 (Pigg 1990).

It is not possible, however, to understand the ONA's litigation strategy outside of the general labour-relations climate for nurses. Across Canada, nurses have become increasingly more militant. In the past few years, nurses in Alberta and Quebec have engaged in protracted illegal strikes, which received a great deal of public attention, and in Manitoba nurses recently went on a legal strike to back their contract demands. While some of the militancy of Canadian nurses is attributable to changes in the organization of their work (Menzies 1990, 210–12), much of it results from the fact that nurses believe that they are seriously underpaid for the work they do.

The vast majority of ONA members can engage in collective bargaining, but they do not have the right to strike.[9] Rather than directly challenging the legal restrictions on the collective power of its members, the ONA has opted for a strategy of using the Pay Equity Act to increase nurses' wages. This strategy is available and attractive to the association for several reasons. The first is financial. The ONA does not need a large strike fund, since most of its members are not permitted to strike; it, therefore, can devote a large portion of its resources to an extremely expensive and lengthy litigation battle. This capability puts it in a somewhat unique position among unions representing mostly women workers that simply do not have the financial resources needed to litigate pay equity. The composition of the membership and leadership of the ONA is the second reason that a pay equity strategy is attractive to it. Nearly all of the ONA's members are women, as are its leaders. Consequently, the union's decision to devote a great deal of its resources to litigating pay equity is not likely to create division among its members. Unions that represent men and women workers would likely have to face a backlash from their male members if union resources were devoted to a cause that would benefit only those members performing work in female-dominated job classes. Moreover, it is also possible that an aggressive stance in favour of pay equity would have a negative impact on the wages of members employed in male-dominated job classes (Warskett 1990). Therefore, unions with a heterogeneous membership are likely to face high political costs in terms of internal division if they choose to litigate pay equity. The ONA does not have this problem. Third, because of the nature of nurses' work, a gender-neutral job comparison is likely to result in a favourable evaluation for the purpose of pay equity. That nurses are highly trained, have a great deal of responsibility, and often work in very stressful conditions, all suggest that, if traditional job-evaluation methodologies were modified to identify and value much of nurses' work, pay equity should lead to fairly high wage increases for them. In fact, in much of its educational literature, the commission uses pictures of nurses to draw attention to the object of the pay equity legislation. And, finally, because nurses are employed in the broader public sector, the government could increase nurses' wages without unduly disturbing private-sector wage relativities or market compensation rates.

There are two major thrusts to the ONA's litigation strategy: establishing an expansive definition of employer and challenging conventional job-evaluation systems on the grounds that they are not gender neutral. The ultimate object of the first thrust is to argue that nurses are not employees of specific hospitals for the purpose of pay equity, but rather are employed by the Ontario government because the government funds the health-care system (Pigg 1990). Were such to be established, it would not only provide a wide range of highly paid potential comparators (the police, for example), but also result in a larger pool of money being set aside for pay equity adjustments because the government's payroll is so much larger than a hospital's.[10]

The objective of the second thrust of the ONA's litigation strategy, that of challenging the job-comparison systems proposed by several hospitals on the grounds that they are not gender neutral, is to have these complaints consolidated and thereby force a decision on the gender neutrality of the job-comparison system that could be treated as a precedent, binding throughout the health-care sector. If the ONA succeeds in this, it is likely that many of the pay equity plans already posted would be found not to be gender neutral. Moreover, if the ONA is successful in arguing that the methodology of conventional job-evaluation techniques is biased against positively registering the value of women's work, job evaluations that were gender neutral would likely result in more money for women workers.

Litigating Gender Neutrality: The Early Case Law

The ONA has brought several cases to the tribunal that involve challenges to job-comparison systems that are based on traditional evaluation methodologies on grounds that the systems did not meet the requirement of gender neutrality imposed under the Pay Equity Act. A number of preliminary matters, including the qualification of expert witnesses and whether the consulting firms that developed and marketed the impugned pay equity job-comparison systems can participate as intervenors in the hearing, have been raised in these cases. These issues must be decided before the tribunal can resolve the central one of whether the job-comparison system in question is gender neutral.

As part of its litigation strategy of challenging the gender neutrality of job-evaluation systems, the ONA brought an application to the tribunal, stating that the Regional Municipality of Haldimand-Norfolk, which had earlier been found by the tribunal to be the employer of the public-health nurses,[11] had failed to bargain in good faith in its choice of a gender-neutral job-comparison system. During the course of the hearing, William M. Mercer, the management-consulting firm that had developed the job-comparison system purchased by the municipality, made an application for intervenor status, which, if successful, would enable it to call witnesses, to cross-examine the ONA witnesses on the issue of gender bias in its plan, and to make submissions. The ONA characterized Mercer's job-evaluation methodology as 'off the shelf' or 'a priori,' and the consulting firm, of course, feared that, if the tribunal decided that the plan was gender biased, the decision would have a long-term adverse effect on its business. The municipality supported Mercer's application for intervention, and the ONA opposed it. On 26 June 1989, the tribunal issued a unanimous oral ruling denying Mercer intervenor status, emphasizing 1 / that evidence relating to the gender neutrality of the Mercer plan or any other plan is relevant only insofar as it relates to the gender-neutral comparison system and pay equity plan that the parties are required to negotiate; 2 / that the employer intends to lead evidence with respect to the Mercer plan as it has been tabled and negotiated in the case; and 3 / that Mercer has only a commercial and incidental interest in the proceedings.[12]

This decision did not, however, end the preliminary issues that the tribunal was required to deal with before it could get to the main issue in the dispute between the ONA and the Municipality of Haldimand-Norfolk – whether the Mercer plan used by the municipality violated the statutory requirement of gender neutrality. The ONA sought to introduce expert opinion on a range of issues pertaining to women's work and gender bias. However, the municipality and the ONA disagreed over the relevance and qualification of the expert witness (Dr Pat Armstrong), with the result that two days of hearings were consumed on this issue by the process of examination, cross-examination, and submission. Noting that the case was 'a first look at the issue of the gender neutrality of a proposed pay equity plan,' the tribunal stated that, although it was ultimately responsible for deciding the legal standard for gender neutrality, it could be assisted by expert opinions.[13] But rather than unconditionally accepting expert evidence, the tribunal balanced the need for a fair, accessible, and expeditious hearing against the countervailing need to understand the technical issues involved, while at the same time avoiding prolonging the proceedings or clouding the issues by calling upon too many experts or soliciting too much expert evidence. Acknowledging that the scope and admissibility of expert evidence may vary in any given case, the tribunal qualified Dr Armstrong as an expert witness, but limited her testimony to the nature of women's work in the health-care sector, specifically, her view that nursing skills are general, complex, overlapping, invisible, and unrecognized, insofar as it forms a basis of the critique of the municipality's proposed methodology (O.N.A. v. Haldimand-Norfolk [No. 4], 53). However, it refused to allow Dr Armstrong to comment generally on the Mercer comparison system. Relying on its previous oral ruling that denied Mercer's application for intervenor status, the tribunal stated that the issue of the Mercer comparison system in general was not before the tribunal, but rather that the gender neutrality of the proposals tabled by the municipality was.

The preliminary decisions in the *Haldimand-Norfolk* case suggest that the tribunal is not prepared to establish general methodological standards for gender-neutral job-comparison systems. This is somewhat surprising, given the fact that much of the criticism of job-evaluation systems as gender biased is directed to their general methodology and not to their application to a particular workplace. However, in written reasons issued at the request of Mercer for clarification on the issue of intervenor status under the Pay Equity Act, the tribunal emphasized that the issue of gender neutrality must be decided on a case-by-case basis, even when the same job-comparison system is under attack.[14] Moreover, the tribunal suggested that it did not have the jurisdiction to hear and adjudicate a job-evaluation methodology outside a specific workplace because the act did not impose any obligations on companies that developed and marketed job-evaluation methodologies.

This emphasis on the particular workplace as the focus of the inquiry into the gender neutrality of a job-comparison system was reinforced and extended by a different panel of the tribunal in *O.N.A. v. Women's College Hospital (No. 1)*.[15] The ONA alleged that the comparison system adopted and proposed by Women's College Hospital was gender biased and unlawful in the circumstances of the case. Once again, the management-consulting firm that developed the job-comparison system that was in dispute – Stevenson, Kellogg, Ernst, and Whinney (SKEW) – applied to intervene in the case. However, unlike *Haldimand-Norfolk*, where there was some question of whether or not the Mercer plan was an a priori system, the Aiken plan developed by SKEW was a generic plan and had been recommended by the Ontario Hospital Association for use by its 223 member hospitals.[16] Thus, in seeking intervenor status, SKEW not only emphasized its commercial interest in the outcome of the case, but also argued that it could ensure that the issues arising out of the Aiken plan would be dealt with and that further complaints by the ONA against other hospitals could be avoided with respect to the issue of gender neutrality (*O.N.A. v. Women's College Hospital [No. 1]*, 64). Women's College Hospital supported SKEW's application on the ground that, as the marketer of the Aiken plan, SKEW had a vital interest in the outcome of the hearing. By contrast, the ONA argued that its complaint related to the comparison system proposed by the hospital and whether it was gender neutral when applied to the particular workplace and was not an inquiry into the nature of comparison systems or the Aiken plan generally.

The tribunal concluded that SKEW should not be granted intervenor status. In doing so, it emphasized the private nature of, rather than the public interest in, the proceedings. Moreover, it made much of the fact that the Ontario Pay Equity Act did not employ the term 'job evaluation plan' but rather obligated the employer and the bargaining agent to negotiate a 'gender neutral comparison system (s. 14[2]).' The tribunal stated that the issue in the case 'is the gender neutrality of the proposals put forward by the Hospital regarding the comparison system to be used to evaluate the jobs in that particular workplace. The issue is not the gender neutrality of the Aiken plan.'[17] Characterizing SKEW's interest as commercial and incidental to the main issue, it turned to consider whether SKEW's participation at the hearing would ensure that further complaints by the ONA against other hospitals would be avoided. By employing circular reasoning, the tribunal concluded that 'one cannot simply employ the reasons and decisions of this panel relating to Women's College Hospital and apply it to another hospital without ensuring that those reasons are applicable to that hospital' (*O.N.A.* v. *Women's College Hospital [No. 1]*, 75). Moreover, it found that adding SKEW as a party would not only delay the proceedings, but also subject the ONA to a double defence because SKEW would, as well as having to disprove the ONA's allegations, also be assisting the hospital.

None of the reasons offered by the tribunal is particularly compelling. The tribunal adopted a very narrow interpretation of the jurisprudence, which establishes the rights of parties to participate in hearings. Moreover, it is difficult to understand why it adopted such a narrow and individualized approach to the issue of gender neutrality of the Aiken plan when more than one hundred hospitals adopted it as the basis of their job-comparison systems. The issue of whether the legal standard of gender neutrality is essential to the Pay Equity Act is capable of being used to achieve true pay equity and is not simply a private matter between two parties. Moreover, the tribunal's distinction between job-evaluation plans and gender-neutral comparison systems seems artificial, especially in light of its statement that 'the reality appears to be that job evaluation plans may be utilized as the basis of bargaining proposals under [section 14]' (*O.N.A.* v. *Women's College Hospital [No. 1]*). The tribunal's concern that SKEW's intervention would have unduly prolonged the hearing in the *Women's College Hospital* case is also not very persuasive. If it had permitted SKEW to intervene on the grounds that, in effect, it was the methodology of the Aiken plan that was being challenged by the ONA, then a decision in the Women's College Hospital case would have put an end to any gender-neutrality litigation involving the Aiken plan in Ontario hospitals.

Despite the fact that the ONA was attempting to limit the tribunal's inquiry into gender neutrality to the application of a job-comparison system to a particular workplace, the association proceeded to file identical complaints against hospitals that had proposed the same job-comparison system used by Women's College Hospital. In fact, the ONA successfully applied to the tribunal to have complaints concerning the gender neutrality of the job-comparison systems at two hospitals heard together with the complaint against Women's College Hospital. Consequently, Peat, Marwick, Stevenson, and Kellogg (Peat Marwick, formerly SKEW) requested that the tribunal reconsider its decision in *Women's College Hospital (No. 1)* on the ground that the applications filed by the ONA against the various hospitals focused on the Aiken plan itself and not on the job-comparison systems proposed by each hospital. It argued that, since the tribunal's decision to deny it intervenor status was so clearly predicated on the fact that the ONA's complaint involved the proposals made by Women's College Hospital, there was reason to believe that the decision was wrong.

The tribunal split over the request for reconsideration, with a majority denying the request. Although the majority admitted that 'there may be a perception that ONA is attacking the Aiken Plan in general rather than focusing on individual workplaces and the comparison system applied to them,' it held that the decision of the ONA to bring additional applications against other hospitals does not change the issue in the *Women's College Hospital* case.[18] Moreover, the majority went on to emphasize that its 'decision on the merits in this case will focus on the particular workplace and any remedy given to any party will be restricted to the particular circumstances found at Women's College Hospital' (*O.N.A.* v. *Women's College Hospital [No. 2]*, 183).

By contrast, the employer's representative on the tribunal would have allowed the reconsideration. In her view, the basis for the tribunal's decision to deny Peat Marwick's application to intervene at first instance was the fact that the issue before it was confined to the particular workplace in question. However, the subsequent behaviour of the ONA in challenging any use of the Aiken plan suggested to this member of the tribunal that 'we are no longer dealing simply with one employer's proposal for one workplace, but a proposal which is common to three hospitals before us, and directly applicable to the vast majority in Ontario' (*O.N.A.* v. *Women's College Hospital [No. 2]*, 187). According to her, the majority disregarded 'the practical exigencies and consequences of its decision' (188).

Implications of the Tribunal's Approach to Gender Neutrality

As the cases dealing with the intervenor status of management-consulting firms that market job-evaluation methodologies proceeded, the tribunal narrowed the impact that any decision concerning the gender neutrality or bias of a job-comparison system could have. According to the majority of the tribunal in *Women's College Hospital (No. 2)*, a decision regarding the gender neutrality of a job-comparison system is limited to its application in the particular workplace, despite the fact that the tribunal acknowledged that a job-comparison system that is used in a particular workplace typically is based upon a job-evaluation methodology that is widely marketed. If the tribunal allowed companies that develop and market job-evaluation plans to intervene in cases where the issue is gender neutrality, it could have crafted decisions that established broad guidelines for gender-neutral job-comparison systems. The result would have had a wide-ranging impact for unions and employees who do not have the resources to litigate gender neutrality on a plan-by-plan basis.

There are likely several reasons why the tribunal adopted a narrow case-by-case approach to the issue of gender neutrality. It was advocated by the Ontario Nurses' Association, which is at the forefront of litigation under the Pay Equity Act. But it is not obvious why the ONA would urge the tribunal to adopt a narrow approach to the issue of gender neutrality, given its long-term object of knocking out the Aiken plan in Ontario hospitals. The answer to this probably lies in the gap between political realities and legal formalities. Although the cases establish that any finding of gender bias would be legally limited to the particular workplace, a decision that a comparison system based on Aiken was gender biased would have the practical effect of getting rid of the Aiken plan in hospitals across Ontario.[19] The downside of the decision is, however, that it will not have any effect on the range of job-evaluation systems that are currently being marketed for pay equity purposes. It is possible that a finding of gender bias in the *Women's College Hospital* case might not affect the use of the Aiken plan outside of the health-care sector.

This analysis of the ONA's strategy does not explain why the tribunal adopted a narrow approach to gender neutrality. This question is particularly pressing, given that the purpose of the Pay Equity Act is to redress systemic wage discrimination. By failing to provide general legal standards for gender neutrality that address the methodology of job-comparison systems, the tribunal is, in effect, requiring women workers and their representatives to bring individual legal challenges to specific plans. The problem with this requirement is that few unions are as well placed as the ONA to adopt a litigation strategy.

The reason the tribunal adopted a narrow approach to gender neutrality likely has to do with the nature of an adjudicative process governed by principles of judicial review and the structure of the Pay Equity Act. The Pay Equity Act is an extremely contentious piece of legislation, and both employers and unions have demonstrated a willingness to turn to the tribunal to resolve disputes. Because of its path-breaking nature, it is likely that the tribunal is taking a cautious and incremental approach in order to avoid the possibility of successful legal challenges to its decisions in the superior courts. By clearly limiting its decisions on gender neutrality to the facts of each case, the tribunal may be trying to preserve its jurisdiction to decide crucial interpretive issues. However, by doing so it has reinforced the act's individualized approach to what is identified as a systemic problem.

Moreover, the tribunal's decision to limit the inquiry of gender neutrality to a particular workplace reflects the structure of the Pay Equity Act. The Ontario Pay Equity Act embodies a central paradox: although it is designed 'to redress systemic gender discrimination in compensation for work performed by employees in female job classes,' it does so on the basis of gender-neutral job comparisons in an individual employer's establishment. Consequently, while the problem of gender wage discrimination is identified as systemic, the remedy replicates the individualized and atomized ordering of the private market system for determining compensation. Sex-based wage discrimination must be neutralized, but not, it seems, at the expense of the autonomy of individual employers to establish compensation schemes that reflect their own priorities. That is why the government did not impose standards for gender-neutral job-comparison systems, but rather put in place an adjudicative mechanism for resolving disputes. By limiting its inquiry into gender neutrality to job-comparison systems as they are applied to individual workplaces, the tribunal is simply reflecting the narrow approach to equity embodied in the act.

Unless the tribunal reverses the approach that it has taken in its preliminary decisions, gender bias will be fought establishment by establishment rather than in terms of the general methodology of job-evaluation plans. Not only will the impact of decisions be limited to the particular workplaces, but the emphasis on individual litigation will simply invite the use of a range of delaying tactics. To date, litigating gender neutrality has been an extremely long and expensive process. The hearings on the gender neutrality of the job-comparison system in *Haldimand-Norfolk* ended in December 1990, over two years after the initial application, while hearings in the *Women's College Hospital* case are scheduled into April 1991. The delay in getting a decision on the substantive issue, the legal standard of gender neutrality, creates problems for the self-managed process. How are parties to agree on gender-neutral job-comparison systems until the tribunal offers some guidance regarding the legal standard it will impose?

Even if the tribunal were to change its approach and offer general legal standards for gender neutrality that were binding beyond a particular workplace, it would not help those employees in establishments where pay equity plans, based on what are subsequently found to be gender-biased job-comparison systems, have already been posted. Under the Pay Equity Act, an employee in an unorganized workplace has ninety days from the posting of the plan to review it, and a further thirty days to object to it, after which it is deemed to be approved (s. 15[8]). Many plans in large private-sector establishments have already been posted, and the time limits for complaints have long since expired. Because of the length of time it has taken the tribunal to issue its first decisions on the legal standard of gender neutrality, they will have little practical effect for the many women who work in establishments where pay equity plans have already been posted.[20] And because the Pay Equity Act does not impose a requirement on employers to file pay equity plans with the commission, there is simply no means of determining whether gender-biased job-evaluation systems have been used in any establishments.

Conclusion: Developing Minimum Standards for Gender Neutrality

The problem with an approach that requires us to litigate our way to gender neutrality is that litigation favours a few at the expense of the many. Only large, well-financed, women-dominated unions can afford, both politically and economically, to litigate. Moreover, the fact that the tribunal has indicated that it will not be issuing minimum standards for what constitutes a gender-neutral job-comparison system limits the effect that litigation will have on the majority of women workers who are not able to engage in such an expensive business. Although it is possible that the substantive decisions in particular cases will be used by unions in the negotiation process, unless the union has the resources to litigate, it is not likely to have much effect. And the situation for unorganized workers is even worse, for they have even fewer collective resources.

One way of solving the problems created by an individualized approach to gender neutrality is for the Ontario government to amend the Pay Equity Act so that it provides general standards for gender-neutral job-comparison systems. Minimum standards can be developed by drawing upon the existing research on the use of job evaluations to implement pay equity (Weiner and Gunderson 1990; Pay Equity Commission, Ontario 1989). Moreover, there are simple statistical tests of correlation that could be used in large establishments to determine whether a particular system is gender biased (Haignere, 163). In order to ensure that employers meet the minimum statutory standards for gender neutrality, it is necessary to amend the Pay Equity Act to impose an obligation upon employers to file their pay equity plans with the Pay Equity Commission. The commission would then be charged with performing an audit to ensure that the plan is not based on a gender-biased methodology. The time, effort, and expense that are now consumed by the commission in appointing review officers to investigate and settle complaints involving gender neutrality could be better spent in auditing pay equity plans. Litigation could continue to play a limited role if necessary; but its role should be supplementary rather than primary. It could be used both to fine-tune standards and to deal with unforeseen circumstances. By itself, litigation is too indirect and too costly a method for implementing pay equity (Willborn 1989, 155). An approach that emphasizes the self-interest of individual litigants as the primary means of resolving disputes that arise over crucial elements in the Pay Equity Act is unlikely to result in a solution that addresses the systemic nature of wage discrimination.

NOTES

1 The Pay Equity Commission is an independent commission charged with the responsibility of administering the Pay Equity Act, 1987, S.O. 1987, c. 34. It reports to the Minister of Labour.

2 Pay Equity Commission Implementation Series, no. 9; Pay Equity Commission *Newsletter*, vols. 1(7), 1(9), 2(11); Pay Equity Commission, *How to Do Pay Equity Job Comparisons*

3 It is clearly stated in the Pay Equity Commission's guidelines that the guidelines will not restrict the Pay Equity Hearings Tribunal in its review of the cases.

4 Pay Equity Commission, *How to Do Pay Equity Job Comparisons*, 19; *O.N.A.* v. *Women's College Hospital (No. 1)* 1 P.E.R., 53 at 67

5 In addition, both the Manitoba Pay Equity Act and the equal-pay-for-work-of-equal-value guidelines issued under the Canada Human Rights Act explicitly contemplate the use of modified job-evaluation plans or systems as the basis for determining the value of, and making comparisons between, female and male jobs. See Manitoba Pay Equity Act, C.C.S.M., c. P.13, enacted by S.M. 1985–86, c. 21, s. 9(1)(a), which refers throughout to a 'single gender-neutral job evaluation system' as the method of achieving pay equity in the Manitoba civil service, and Canada Human Rights Act, R.S.C. 1985, c. H-6, Equal Pay Guidelines, 1986, SOR/86-1082, s. 9, gazetted 10 Dec. 1986, effective 18 Nov. 1986.

6 For some sociological literature on this topic, refer to Steinberg and Haignere (1987), Haignere (1990), Weiner and Gunderson (1990), McArthur (1985), Remick (1984c). Moreover, both the Ontario Pay Equity Commission and the Pay Equity Bureau of the Manitoba Department of Labour have published guidelines on how to minimize gender bias in job-comparison and -evaluation systems. Ontario Pay Equity Commission, *How to Do Gender Neutral Job Comparison Systems*, and Manitoba Labour, Pay Equity Bureau, *Job Evaluation* and *Job Analysis*.

7 Of course, it is always possible for one of the parties to apply to the courts for review of the tribunal's decision on the grounds that the tribunal has made an 'error of jurisdiction' in applying its enabling legislation. The area of law known as administrative law deals with the legal rules that regulate the relationship between the ordinary courts and specialized tribunals. The availability of judicial review slows down the entire pay equity procedure and complicates it considerably. So far, the courts appear to be adopting a deferential stance to the tribunal. See *Haldimand-Norfolk and the Ontario Nurses' Association* (1989), 1 P.E.R. 188 (Ont. Div. Ct.); affirmed by the Ontario Court of Appeal, September 27, 1990.

8 The Pay Equity Commission *Newsletter* 2(12), June 1990, 5

9 The majority of nurses in the province of Ontario are covered by the Hospital Labour Disputes Arbitration Act, R.S.O. 1980, c. 205, which prohibits employees falling under it from striking.

10 According to s. 13(4) of the Pay Equity Act, the employer must put aside at least 1 per cent of its payroll during the twelve-month period preceding the first adjustments for pay equity purposes.

11 *O.N.A.* v. *Haldimand-Norfolk (No. 3)* (1989), 1 P.E.R. 17 (P.E.H.T.); *Re Haldimand-Norfolk and O.N.A.* (1989), 1 P.E.R. 188 (Ont. H.C.); Ontario Court of Appeal 27 September 1990, affirming the tribunal's decision.

12 For the text of the tribunal's ruling, see *ONA* v. *Haldimand-Norfolk (No. 4)* (1989), 1 P.E.R., 49 at 51.

13 *O.N.A.* v. *Haldimand-Norfolk (No. 4)* (1989), 1 P.E.R., 49 at 50

14 *O.N.A.* v. *Haldimand-Norfolk (No. 5)* (1989), 1 P.E.R., 77 at 85

15 (1989) 1 P.E.R. 53

16 See the discussion of how the Ontario Hospital Association went about selecting a job-comparison system to recommend to its member hospitals in Shakes (1990). See also *O.N.A.* v. *Women's College Hospital (No. 2)* 1990, 1 P.E.R., 178 at 184.

17 *O.N.A.* v. *Women's College Hospital (No. 1)* (1989), 1 P.E.R., 53 at 67

18 *O.N.A.* v. *Women's College Hospital (No. 2)* (1990), 1 P.E.R., 179 at 183

19 Although the tribunal's decisions in the *Women's College Hospital* cases would appear to limit a finding of gender bias in the application of a job-comparison system to a particular workplace, it would be unlikely for any Ontario hospital to continue to use the Aiken plan. To do so would be to invite a legal challenge – a challenge that the ONA would likely win. This analysis is supported by the fact that several other cases brought by the ONA challenging the use of the Aiken plan in different hospitals have been adjourned until the tribunal issues its decision in *Women's College Hospital* regarding the gender neutrality of the Aiken plan.

20 It might be possible to complain that a posted plan that has been deemed to be approved under s. 15(8) violates s. 7(1) of the Pay Equity Act, which requires employers to maintain compensation practices that provide for pay equity.

PART TWO

The Ontario Compromise

4 Making Sense of Pay Equity: Issues for a Feminist Political Practice[1]

Sue Findlay

The introduction of Ontario's Pay Equity Act (1987) was heralded by many feminist advocates of equal pay for work of equal value in other parts of Canada and the United States as an impressive precedent in the development of pay equity legislation. The act extends coverage typically limited in most other legislations to women in the public service to women in all workplaces in the broader public sector and those employed by firms with ten or more employees in the private sector. Although pay equity advocates in Ontario recognized the limits of pay equity legislation that relies on job-evaluation methods to determine wage adjustments (Lewis 1988; Evans and Nelson 1989a; Acker 1989), most of them considered the extension of the legislation to these sectors a step forward in addressing the wage issues facing some of the poorest-paid women in the labour force in Ontario.

There is a major flaw in the Ontario legislation, however. Almost 50 per cent of the women in workplaces covered by the act are unable to claim pay equity adjustments under it.[2] These include women who are located in what is referred to as 'the predominantly female sector' – that is, in workplaces that lack appropriate male comparators, such as libraries, child-care centres, community and social services, and small health-care services in the broader public sector, and garment factories in the private sector. Many of these workplaces are exclusively female.

In this essay, I use my experience as a consultant to the Pay Equity Commission to explore how 'femocrats'[3] and community-based feminist pay equity advocates, including members of the Equal Pay Coalition[4] and feminists in trade unions, have participated in developing the government's response to this problem and some of the factors that have limited our capacity to define policies that work for the predominantly female sector. My intent is to examine the way in which the state engages feminists in limiting reforms, and thus to help us identify our opportunities to challenge these limits in our ongoing struggles for state reforms.

The difficulty of applying pay equity legislation to women in the predominantly female sector is not unexpected. Indeed, it was recognized in the negotiations for and drafting of the legislation in Ontario. The legislation was introduced with the proviso in section 33 of the act that the Pay Equity Office of the Pay Equity Commission 'shall conduct a study with respect to systemic gender discrimination in compensation for work performed, in sectors of the economy where employment has traditionally been predominantly female, by female job classes in establishments that have no appropriate male job classes for the purpose of comparison under section 5 and, within one year of the effective date, shall make reports and recommendations to the Minister in relation to redressing such discrimination.'[5]

The Pay Equity Office conducted its study in two stages. In the first, the scope of the problem was outlined in nine sector studies, and five options were recommended to the minister of labour as ways for women in the predominantly female sector to achieve pay equity adjustments.[6] In the second stage, these five options were tested, and four of them were recommended to the minister as ways to achieve pay equity for women in the predominantly female sector.[7] In its second report to the minister, the commission recommended the proxy comparison approach – a method of comparing female job classes in the 'seeker' establishment to male job classes in an establishment external to it – as the solution best suited for exclusively female establishments in the broader public sector.[8]

However, after careful consideration of the report, the government rejected the proxy comparison approach on the grounds that it was inconsistent with a basic principle underlying the act: 'that work traditionally performed by women be paid the same as work traditionally performed by men that is of *comparable value to the employer in the employer's establishments.*'[9] The minister acknowledged that his proposal would make it impossible for child-care workers and visiting homemakers to achieve pay equity adjustments (*Globe and Mail*, 19 April 1990). Approximately 105,000 women workers in establishments covered by the act would be unable to claim pay equity adjustments. Confirming the position taken by the government in the *Green Paper on Pay Equity* in 1985, he argued that other policies, such as increases in the minimum wage or employment equity legislation, should be used to address the issue of low wages of women in workplaces where no male comparators can be identified. His report made it apparent that the Pay Equity Act was never intended to apply to all of the women workers in Ontario as promised, as suspected by the Equal Pay Coalition despite the inclusion of section 33 in the legislation.

The minister's rejection of the proxy comparison approach certainly reflects the limits of the government's willingness to intervene in the wage-setting practices of employers in the broader public sector and the private sector. However, what became obvious to me in my work as a consultant to the Pay Equity Office in both stages of the study of the predominantly female sector was that the proxy comparison approach itself, as recommended by the feminist oriented Pay Equity Commission, also had distinct limits. Not only would the approach be difficult and expensive (in time and money) for the small non-unionized low-budget workplaces that characterize the broader public sector to negotiate and/ or administer, but the pay equity adjustments required would undercut programs and/or put an unreasonable burden on their clients. As yet, the government had not responded to persistent requests by feminists and trade unionists for a pay equity fund to support pay equity adjustments in the broader public sector. For many of these workplaces, then, a victory for the commission's proxy comparison approach would have introduced another round of relatively futile exercises in which overextended workers expend much energy and expense to define pay equity adjustments that would, in most cases, force employers to cut services or increase clients' fees.

The limits of the recommendations of the Pay Equity Commission cannot be simply attributed to a lack of commitment on the part of the commission staff. Many of the staff and management of the commission are feminists; some have a trade-union background. They would argue that they are as committed to finding ways to achieve pay equity adjustments for women in predominantly female establishments as feminist advocates working outside the state. But, regardless of their commitments, their work is circumscribed by their location in a state bureaucracy that Mahon (1977) has described as an 'unequal structure of representation.' While the interests of all the players may be seen to be represented in the making and implementation of policies (for example, through endless and varied consultations), they are represented in a way that gives priority (and resources) to the economic interests that dominate society rather than the interests of women, the working class, and racial minorities. Pay equity legislation, then, is not a simple response to feminist demands, but a more complex and 'unstable equilibrium of compromise' (Poulantzas 1978) in which demands for equal pay for work of equal value are negotiated within the 'unequal structure of representation' to protect employers' 'rights' to set wages and, in doing so, to maintain systemic wage discrimination.

The concept of 'the unequal structure of representation' is useful in describing the hierarchy of interests reflected in the policy-making process of the state bureaucracy and some of the limits faced by femocrats inside the state, but it does not account for how this structure was produced or adapted to incorporate new public issues, such as those related to gender and race. To the extent that the structure is defined as one in which the struggle among the classes/interests of society is simply reflected within the state (that is, in struggles among state bureaucrats), it can be a deterrent for the exploration of how our practices as femocrats and community-based feminist activists, such as those in the Equal Pay Coalition, shape the development and implementation of the policies of the Ontario government in relation to employment initiatives for women workers. Structures are quite correctly seen as determining the roles that we are given to play in the policy-making process, and the concept of the 'unequal structure of representation' is important in providing us with an understanding of how these roles are limited and how a representative bureaucracy is organized to displace the direct representation of issues by the public to the political level. But such a formulation by itself does not account for our everyday experiences as agents (subjects) in the process of change rather than as simple objects. From the articulation of our issues at the community level to our ever-increasing participation in various stages and aspects of the production and delivery of state policies, many of us are engaged in the making of policy.

Dorothy Smith's institutional ethnography offers a way to move beyond the structuralist paradigm. Shifting from a reliance on theories that define political power in terms of structures organized by the state to maintain the interests of capital, Smith uses the more textured and dynamic term 'relations of ruling' to convey her understanding of power as being more 'pervasively structured than can be expressed in traditional concepts provided by discourses of power' and, most important for my work, to bring 'into view the intersection of the institutions organizing and regulating society with their gender subtext and their basis in a gender division of labour.' Power is maintained, then, not by force or by dominance of particular interests in the state but by a practice of ruling that involves a 'continual transcription of the local and particular actualities of our lives into abstracted and generalized forms ... that enter them into the relations of ruling' (Smith 1987, 3). It is this process that must be revealed and understood then if we are to fully account for the limits of our political reforms. As such Smith proposes 'an organization of inquiry that begins with where women actually are and addresses the problem of how our everyday worlds are put together in relations that are not wholly discoverable within the everyday world' (1987, 47). Not only does her method of inquiry provide us with a way of seeing the disjunction between our realities and the policies designed to address our realities, but it tells us how our practices are essential to the maintenance of the relations of ruling. With this perspective, we have not only the basis for a critique of state policies, but a standpoint for the development of alternative practices that can be used to challenge the relations of ruling in our everyday lives.

To unravel the specific 'truth' about the limits of the pay equity legislation and the particular role that we as feminists play in producing these limits, then, I begin with my experience as a consultant to the Pay Equity Commission and the knowledge I gained of how our everyday practices as feminist activists and femocrats in the policy-making processes shaped these limits. In my analysis of this experience, it becomes clear that our political practices can be understood only in the context of how the state regulates the representation of our interests in the policy-making process.

The Story: The Policy-making Process at Work

My task was quite specific. I was to conduct consultations with 'stakeholders'[10] in the broader public sector about the acceptability and feasibility of the proxy comparison approach as a method of identifying male comparators for female job classes in exclusively female workplaces that included libraries, child-care centres, community and social-service agencies, and health-care units. Those consulted included employees, their union representatives and/or provincial associations, and employers. Members of the Equal Pay Coalition were not consulted in process; however, it was understood that they would review the recommendations before they were submitted to the minister of labour.

I was excited about working for the Pay Equity Office on what seemed to be a method that would make it possible for workers in exclusively female workplaces to win pay equity adjustments. As the January 1989 report issued by the commission had noted, 'it is likely that those groups advocating the interests of women in these sectors would be pleased with the approach taken' (Pay Equity Commission 1989b, 86).

But I soon began to wonder whether consultations with representatives of the broader public sector would have any effect on the development of an option that already seemed to be quite firmly in place. Much of the work of defining the approach had been set out previously in the first report to the minister of labour and in subsequent discussions within the commission and with the commission's advisory committee. Questions that we raised at this time about the proxy comparison approach itself – about the validity of adjustments based on comparisons using different job-evaluation systems, the potential abuse of wage line comparisons used to support employers' red-circling of male jobs, the potential conflict of interest between the Pay Equity Office and the Pay Equity Hearings Tribunal should the former attempt to identify appropriate proxy organizations, the use of a single option for such a diversified sector – were defined as technical issues that could be accommodated within the proposed model. My task was not to question the proxy comparison approach as a policy option but to determine how it could best be implemented. The consultations, then, were structured around a draft proposal developed by the Policy and Research Branch that focused attention on the technical details of implementing the proxy comparison approach and presented little or no room for debate about the approach itself.[11]

Consulting the 'Stakeholders'

I asked those identified as stakeholders for their views on the acceptability and feasibility of the implementation of the proxy comparison approach as put forward in the draft proposal prepared by the Pay Equity Office, as well as their views on potential proxy organizations, such as the Ontario Public Service, municipalities, and school-boards.

Of those consulted, only union representatives had the technical knowledge and experience in implementing the act to comment critically on the Pay Equity Office's draft proposal. They argued strenuously for a definition of the proxy comparison approach that would recognize their rights to bargain in the selection of the proxy organization and the method of comparing the job classes in the proxy and seeking organizations. They did not approve of the role proposed for the Pay Equity Office, and were particularly opposed to any suggestion that the Ontario Public Service serve as *the* proxy organization for all seeking organizations.[12] However, most of their concerns focused on how the proposal would affect the organized workers they represented, rather than the majority of workplaces in the broader public sector, which were, in fact, not unionized.

Employees and employers, however, expressed minimal interest in the proxy comparison approach. Some found the proposal too complicated to assess in any comprehensive way; others were engaged in new initiatives that had displaced the proxy comparison approach.

For example, many library workers and their union representatives were arguing that it was better to identify male comparators by expanding the definition of 'establishment' and 'employer' rather than using proxy organizations. Most of the library workers in small municipalities had been readily absorbed into the pay equity plans of their municipal governments. And the Administrators of Medium Sized Libraries in Ontario was urging its members to adopt a similar strategy, although the costs prompted a resistance from municipalities that the smaller libraries had not encountered. Workers in larger libraries, who argued the need for autonomy to protect them from any possibility of political control by the municipal government, favoured the proxy comparison approach as long as it did not 'put them in the pocket of the municipality.'

In the smaller non-unionized 'transfer payment agencies'[13] in the community and social-service and health sectors, those consulted lacked the experience and expertise to assess the workability of the option, nor did they have any alternatives. Employers and employees in predominantly female workplaces had for the most part lost interest in the Pay Equity Act, 1987, as a way to increase their wages because the act was clearly restricted to job class–to–job class comparisons within the same workplace.[14]

The exception to this was child-care centres represented by the politically oriented Ontario Coalition for Better Child Care. Encouraged by the success of the child-care centres in the region of Ottawa-Carleton in negotiating parity with their counterparts who worked for the regional government, the coalition was debating the relative merits of adjustments based on the average adjustment received by child-care workers in community colleges, or those based on adjustments received by workers in either the municipality or the Ontario Public Service. A minority in the coalition had begun to consider the implications of defining the provincial government as the employer.

What was most striking in the consultations in these two sectors, however, was the preoccupation of both workers and employers with the issue of funding for salaries in general, and for the pay equity adjustments in particular. I seemed to be asking the wrong questions. The lack of an appropriate male comparator was clearly secondary to the fact that most of these agencies could not afford pay equity adjustments. Most of those consulted argued that the proxy comparison approach must be accompanied by a commitment from the government to establish a pay equity fund if the option was to work in the broader public sector.

If the perceptions of representatives of these agencies were accurate, the proxy comparison approach would be an exercise in futility for most establishments in the sector, requiring them to go through a complex and expensive process of evaluating work, only to find themselves unable to afford the adjustment without seriously damaging other aspects of their service. However, the commission considered funding was a political issue and the business of the Ministry of Labour rather than an issue that could be addressed in the context of the proxy comparison approach. My arguments about the centrality of funding were marginalized by commission staff as advocacy rather than objective analysis.

Redefining the Problem
After the consultations with the stakeholders I found it impossible to ignore the limits of the proxy comparison approach as defined by the commission. At the same time, the success of the library workers in defining the municipal government as employer,[15] and the decision of the Pay Equity Hearings Tribunal to uphold the Ontario Nurses' Association's claim that the Regional Municipality of Haldimand-Norfolk should be identified as the employer of those in the Police Commission for purposes of the Pay Equity Act gave me an alternative to propose. It was becoming clear that the proxy comparison approach was not necessarily the only or the best way to find male comparators for predominantly female workplaces.

Information that I had gathered in consultations with representatives from transfer-payment agencies convinced me that the tribunal's rationale in defining the regional municipality as the employer of the Police Commission could be applied to the relationship between the transfer-payment agencies and the provincial government as well. Representatives from these agencies had described their negotiations with the regional officers of the Ministry of Community and Social Services in a way that demonstrated a relationship between them that went beyond the funding of services to one that regulated the wages of workers in these agencies. In spite of the differences among the programs and funding formulas that determine provincial contributions to transfer-payment agencies, regional officers are integrally involved in the development of agency budgets. Funding criteria of the ministry to a large extent determines/stipulates the percentage of funds that can be allocated for administrative costs within the approved budget criteria that clearly favours the development of services rather than increases in wages. The standards stipulated in the legislation under which these services operate reinforce this pattern. Although the provincial government – and many of the agencies themselves – like to maintain the notion that these agencies are relatively autonomous, governments at both the provincial and the federal levels have established a set of practices that regulate how their services are delivered and what their workers are paid.

The provincial government is prepared to step in when the quality of services is threatened, as it is by the difficulties agencies are encountering in hiring and maintaining qualified staff at the wage level they can offer, but individual employers (social-service-agency boards) are still considered to be responsible for the wages – and pay equity adjustments – of their workers. Government responses to wage issues in the broader public sector have been limited to 'emergency measures,' to responses to the 'squeaky wheel,' rather than any comprehensive plan commensurate with the way in which that sector actually regulates wages. The Ministry of Community and Social Services is willing to provide special grants when the provision of services is threatened (for example, low-wage grants to increase the salaries of child-care workers; increases in visiting homemaker's wages following the threat of the main provider – the Canadian Red Cross – to dismantle its programs throughout Ontario), but it is made quite clear that these grants are not considered to be part of or in lieu of pay equity adjustments. A strategy that focused on the responsibility of the government as employer would expose these practices, whereas requests for a pay equity fund or increases in their individual grants obscures them. It would be a strategy that not only produced male job-class comparators, but challenged the wage gap between public-service workers and those in the broader public sector.

While I began my work on the proxy comparison approach with a concern about how it could accommodate the differences among establishments within the broader public sector and went on to the more serious issues of how it could address the funding of pay equity adjustments, I was now convinced that the lack of male comparators was secondary to the issue of who sets the wages in the broader public sector and who should be defined as the employer. The assumption, implicit in both the act itself and the proxy comparison approach, that wage-setting practices in the public service, private sector, and broader public sector were identical had to be challenged if women in the broader public sector were to achieve pay equity adjustments.

Advising the Commission

I was now faced with a dilemma. My task had specific limits – I was to consult stakeholders on the feasibility and acceptability of the proxy comparison approach. Yet, the consultations had convinced me that the primary issue for these workers was the definition of employer, that is, identifying who actually regulates the wages of women workers in the broader public sector. The evidence that I had gathered from all parts of the sector showed that the wages of women workers in most exclusively female establishments were largely regulated by either the provincial or the municipal governments.

While I was in the final stages of 'making sense' of the consultations, the Pay Equity Commission was being pressured by the Ministry of Labour to complete its second report to the minister. Time deadlines ended my debates with the commission, and my work (*The Proxy Comparison Approach: Can It Work in the Broader Public Sector?*) was summarized in the commission's report in four double-spaced pages that failed to reflect the major concerns about funding pay equity adjustments and alternatives to the proxy comparison approach that had emerged in the consultations. My report was put 'on the shelf' in the commission's library – as was the proxy comparison approach itself after its rejection by the minister of labour.

To summarize, then, the proxy comparison approach appealed to very few of those consulted in the broader public sector – mainly to union representatives who had become experts in job-evaluation procedures. In the more affluent parts of the sector (for example, library workers, nurses), challenges to the definition of establishment/employer implicit in the Pay Equity Act, 1987, made through applications to the Pay Equity Hearing Tribunal (by the ONA) or the bargaining process (CUPE-organized library workers), were favoured over the proxy comparison approach. Neither of these strategies had been considered by the unorganized parts of the broader public sector. However, it was these challenges that prompted me to examine the role of the provincial government in the wage-setting practices of transfer-payment agencies in the health and social-service sector. My analysis, in turn, led me to recommend that, for purposes of the Pay Equity Act only, provincial and municipal governments be defined as employers of establishments in which workers' wages are shaped by the funding policies and legislation of these governments.

On the basis of my work for the Pay Equity Commission, I came to three conclusions. First, the reason pay equity legislation does not work for women in the predominantly female sector is because the Pay Equity Act fails to address the specificity of the wage-setting practices in either the broader public sector, where the practices of the provincial and municipal governments are more central to the regulation of wages than individual boards, or the private sector, where multi-branch corporations determine the wages of local workers. Modelled on legislation developed for women in the public service, where the definition of employer was not an issue, Ontario's Pay Equity Act was extended to the broader public sector and the private sector without understanding how the differences in the wage-setting practices among them could challenge this definition.

Second, the failure to resolve this issue for women in the predominantly female sector reflects the way in which feminist pay advocates are largely rooted in what 'makes sense' for organized workers, as much as it reflects the limits of political will expressed in the minister's rejection of the proxy comparison approach. Women in the predominantly female sector are largely unorganized. Regardless of how committed pay equity activists are to finding ways to achieve pay equity adjustments for these women, their perspectives are rooted in institutional practices that have been developed for their work with the organized sector. Even where these practices conflict with the realities of unorganized workplaces, there is little time for those feminists to develop alternatives and gain support for them from their unions. With the introduction of the act, their time is monopolized by negotiating on behalf of their constituents, that is, organized women. Their understanding of what 'makes sense,' then, is shaped by what 'makes sense' for organized workers. Regardless of the success that unionized workers (some nurses and librarians) had in identifying male comparators by extending the definition of employer, and the obvious difficulty that non-unionized workers would experience in negotiating the proxy comparison approach, it was this understanding that persisted. Feminist trade unionists resisted the development of any general strategy that would name the provincial government as either *the* proxy organization or the employer of the many transfer-payment agencies that lacked male comparators.

Third, the limits reflect the dangers of representative bureaucracies where in-house experts are substituted for any meaningful consultation with either organized groups or those who are truly 'stakeholders' in the policies that are being developed. Although consultation with stakeholders may be regarded as a necessary part of the policy-making process, the way in which it is defined and implemented is critical to those most affected by and/or opposed to the proposed policy option.

At issue then are our political practices as feminists working inside and outside the state – how they are shaped in our ongoing relationship with the state and the institutions in which we are located, and how they limit our own capacity to represent the interests of women workers in the policy-making processes – rather than any real lack of alternatives that could be developed within the legislative framework.

Making Sense of Our Practices

Any account of the limits our political practices as feminists pose to pay equity reform must be grounded in an understanding of how the state has organized the representation of women's interests in the policy-making processes of the state bureaucracy in the past two decades, and how this has influenced our political practices. The struggle for reform in liberal democracies is embedded in a complex structure of representation that characterizes the policy-making process at all levels of the political system, from constituency organizations of political parties to the federal legislature. Since the Second World War, this structure has been extended to include departments and programs in state bureaucracies.

In the 1960s, militant radicals challenged the inequities of the state decision-making processes and the policies proposed by them, and charged the state with supporting the interests of capital at the expense of the people. They wanted to participate more directly in the representation of their interests in the policy-making processes of the state. In response to these challenges, state policies in the late 1960s and early

1970s in Canada were marked by commitments to participatory democracy through to programs and policies that would increase the opportunities of community-based groups to participate in decisions that affected their lives, and to equal-opportunity policies that were intended to promote a more representative state bureaucracy. At the same time, however, it was clear that limits had to be placed on both the state's commitment to participatory democracy and our integration into the decision-making process of the state – limits as to who could participate, and how and when – that would regulate our demands in relation to the interests of capital.

Among the challenges facing governments in liberal democracies in the 1960s were those posed by a revitalized feminist movement that demanded reforms to resolve the contradictions between women's economic rights and opportunities and their ability to exercise them. These challenges gave some urgency to the status-of-women issue in Canada as it did in other liberal-democratic countries in the Western world, but the governments of these countries were not equipped at that time to mediate the clash between feminist demands for equality and the interests of the dominant groups in society in maintaining a sexual-hierarchical division of labour. The state had neither the expertise on women's issues to respond to their demands nor a relationship with feminist organizations that could, in practical terms, provide the basis for containing/regulating their demands in relation to the interests of the dominant groups. Before the state could respond to specific issues, particularly those that were rooted in capitalist wage relations or the relations between women and men, it was necessary to establish ways to regulate feminist demands for reforms and to organize the representation of women's interests in the policy-making process of the state bureaucracy.

In Canada, the federal state has played the central role in organizing this representation of women's interests. In a series of royal commissions, task forces, advisory committees, and internal interdepartmental committees beginning with the Royal Commission on the Status of Women in 1967, the state has defined not only its own responsibilities, but also those of the provincial governments, thereby providing the model for how women's interests would be integrated into the policy-making processes at all levels of government. During the 1970s, a network of advisers was established within bureaucracies, first, at the federal and, then, at the provincial level. However, the capacity of femocrats to represent women's interests or, indeed, the demands of feminist organizations was limited by the imposition of the rules and regulations of the bureaucracy on our everyday work. Our impact on the policy-making process was, in turn, limited by the location of the status-of-women issue in Mahon's 'unequal structure of representation.'

Although there were no explicit rules specifying the limits of our participation in the policy-making processes, the status-of-women issue was gradually absorbed by the state in ways that shaped the definition of our issues, our community-based organizations, and the way in which we related to the state policy-making processes.[16] By the 1980s, technical issues increasingly vied with our political concerns in our negotiations for reforms by the state. We learned to be 'reasonable' in our presentations to elected and appointed officials,[17] to work within the legislative timetables of the state, to comply with demands for representative organizations in spite of the fact that they may conservatize the definition of our issues, and to tailor our administrative practices to conform to the funding criteria of the state.[18]

It was only when these practices were in place that the federal government initiated the process of defining its response to women's employment issues in the private sector, and of adopting a more proactive policy to increase the representation of women in the public service. In 1983, the federal government appointed the Royal Commission on Equality and Employment (the Abella Commission). Although the main focus of the commission was employment equity, it also set the framework for the development of pay equity legislation in Canada in the 1980s – recommending proactive legislative strategies to implement both affirmative action and equal pay for work of equal value, and shifting the definition of both issues to an equity framework that called for policies that would recognize what was fair to employers as well as the rights of women and other disadvantaged groups.[19]

Within this framework, feminists found a way to influence the development of Ontario's Pay Equity Act, 1987, both as feminist advocates and femocrats committed to equal pay for work of equal value for all women workers in Ontario and employers. It was the Equal Pay Coalition that led the feminist struggle for pay equity reforms – defining and coordinating the response to government proposals and articulating compromises that were acceptable to the majority of feminists. It was femocrats in the Ontario Women's Directorate who organized the development of legislative proposals for pay equity within the state as well as the public consultations on them.

In the face of strong employer resistance to pay equity feminists were forced to make many compromises in the process of negotiating their interests, including the agreement to defer the resolution of the issue of how women in predominantly female establishments would achieve pay equity in exchange for concessions on other demands. The acceptance of section 33 – the government's commitment to have the Pay Equity Commission identify ways to apply the Pay Equity Act to all of the women in Ontario regardless of whether they could identify male comparators within their establishments – was an example of these compromises.

As my account shows however, feminists had little success in either defining a solution that reflected the situation facing women in this sector or pressuring the government to honour its commitment. The proxy comparison approach offered by the Pay Equity Commission did not 'make sense' to most of those consulted in predominantly female workplaces in the broader public sector, nor did trade unionists offer a real alternative to it during the consultations I conducted. In both these cases, the limits of their proposals (or the absence of proposals) can be explained by the way in which their work as union representatives and as administrators and implementors of the Pay Equity Act, 1987, absorb them in a set of practices that limit both the effectiveness of their proposals and their influence in the policy-making process. How do these practices work in the Pay Equity Commission and the organizations we work in at the community level?

The Pay Equity Commission
The ability of the commission to produce workable policy options to apply the Pay Equity Act to women workers in the predominantly female sectors (section 33) was limited from the beginning of the project: limited by the mandate of the commission as specified in the Pay Equity Act, by its lack of independence from the government and its particular relationship to the Ministry of Labour, and by the Ministry of Labour's location in the unequal structure of representation that characterizes the policy-making process of the provincial government. All of the factors contributed to what emerges as a serious contradiction between the political commitment to pay equity articulated in the preamble to the act and the rather narrow implementation of this commitment.

The Pay Equity Commission was established to implement the Pay Equity Act. The act is very specific about who is eligible or obliged to negotiate pay equity adjustments and how it shall be done. The work of the commission – the work of implementing the act – was defined therefore in essentially administrative, technical, and legal terms, including research to specify the technicalities of the act, public-education programs, and procedures to respond to complaints from employers and employees related to the enforcement of the act. In spite of the fact that the Pay Equity Office of the commission includes a research and policy branch, policy development in the commission – and those hired to make policy – is oriented to the technical questions of implementing the act.

The issue of pay equity adjustments for women in predominantly female workplaces had been narrowly defined in section 33 of the legislation as one of the lack of male comparators. Because of this narrow definition of the problem, the options were quite limited. By the time I was hired to conduct the consultation, the commission was quite firmly committed to the proxy comparison approach and was focused on the question of how it could be implemented.

The commission's administrative mandate and the technical orientation that arose from it were clearly at odds with the highly political task of resolving the issue of pay equity for women in the predominantly female sector. The minister of labour is considered to be responsible for 'political' issues related to pay equity. As a fundamentally administrative body, the commission had neither the mandate nor the expertise (research and policy staff are hired for their technical expertise in areas such as job-evaluation methods) to confront the challenges that pay equity for the predominantly female sector posed to the principles underlying the act – or to respond to the essentially political questions about the limits of the legislation raised by employees and employers during the consultations I organized.

However, the realities of the issue that became apparent during the study organized by the Policy and Research Branch of the Pay Equity Office, as well as the decisions emerging from the Pay Equity Hearings Tribunal, undoubtedly challenged the commission to go beyond its mandate and question its technical approach. And while the policy-making process is infinitely messy and must not be simplified, it is important to note two ways in which potential for the development of more radical options was likely contained.

The most obvious one is the dominance of the technical approach – a dominance that not only defined the work of the commission's staff as noted above, but effectively insulated them from the issues raised in our consultation with employees and employers. Their issues were labelled 'political,' and my presentation of those issues to the commission was labelled 'advocacy' as opposed to analysis. Within this framework, consultations with 'stakeholders' had a very specific and narrow purpose. The perspectives of union representatives engaged in applying the act were of some use to the Policy and Research Branch, but there was really no place for the views of the majority of representatives from non-unionized transfer-payment agencies concerned with the funding of pay equity adjustments. And, given the limited role of consultants, I was unable to either represent their views effectively or find a place for my own argument that the commission should make a recommendation to the minister that would define the provincial government as employer for workplaces in the broader public sector.

Similarly, the views of the Equal Pay Coalition had little direct impact on the development of the recommendations to the minister of labour. As a voluntary organization, the coalition lacked the resources to do the kind of research they considered necessary to define workable options. But they also wanted to pressure the commission to get on with its work rather than rely on the unpaid labour of coalition members to produce the kind of studies that would in fact be useful for the coalition. The coalition's refusal to present a brief to the commission on options to achieve pay equity in predominantly female workplaces[20] was both practical and strategic. The coalition did present the commission with an excellent review of its sector studies in December 1988,[21] but had no formal input into the development of policy options for the final report to the minister. Consultation with the coalition was reduced to a rather perfunctory review of the commission's final recommendations to the minister of labour on policy options for the predominantly female sector.

It could be argued that the need for consultation with the coalition was displaced by the appointment of the Commissioner's Advisory Committee in 1989 (a committee that included one of the key spokespersons for the coalition). But I would think that closer to the truth is the fact that the technical orientation of the commission's policy-making process and the time pressures from the political level made it difficult for either the coalition or the advisory committee to make inputs that made sense to the commission's staff.

The structure of the Pay Equity Commission also plays a role in limiting the commission's response to political issues. In particular, the clear distinction between the work of the Pay Equity Office and the work of the Pay Equity Hearings Tribunal established in the Pay Equity Act[22] has contradictory consequences for the implementation of the act. This distinction may be necessary to build support among the business community for the implementation of the act – to convince suspicious employers that the tribunal is sufficiently neutral to be able to represent their interests in disputes about enforcement. But it has the unfortunate consequence of justifying the isolation of the issues raised in the work of the tribunal from the research and policy work of the Pay Equity Office, and reducing tribunal decisions that could be treated as precedents for changes to the Pay Equity Act to individual case decisions. The success of legislative strategies rests not on the passage of the legislation, but on both the implementation and the interpretation of this legislation – how it works in particular cases. As Evans and Nelson (1989a) argue, pay equity legislation must be seen and treated as a procedural reform – to be reviewed and revised on the basis of the problems that are exposed as it is implemented. This perspective is particularly useful for us to advance in Ontario where the government is attempting to apply a very specific and narrow definition of pay equity modelled on U.S. legislation for women in the public service, not only to the Ontario Public Service, but to the broader public sector and the private sector. As we are discovering, differences in the wage-setting practices among these sectors is one of the factors that makes it difficult to apply the legislation in a consistent manner.

But the ability of the Pay Equity Commission to take on political issues suffers from more than the dominance of the technical approach or the separation of tribunal decisions from the policy-making process of the Pay Equity Office. The effectiveness of the commission as a policy-making body is also limited by its relationship to government. The Pay Equity Commission reports to the minister of labour, who represents the issue of pay equity in Cabinet and the Legislature. Its influence on government policy depends on its ability to influence the minister and Cabinet.

Commissions and advisory councils are regarded by many social activists as a necessary part of our strategies for state reform. They are regarded as visible indicators of government support for their issues, as mechanisms to represent their interests effectively in the policy-making process or, in the case of the Pay Equity Commission, to implement political commitments. In addition, they are seen to provide spaces for activists to struggle within the state. Those established as responses to feminist issues are often staffed by or engage community-based feminists whom we respect in their processes. In varying ways we trust them to represent our interests in the appropriate way.

In fact, the power and influence of these mechanisms are often quite limited in ways that are not always apparent to the outsider. For example, their staff may have considerable expertise, but they have little authority in relation to the minister to whom they report and are often effectively marginalized in the development of government policy. It is the time-tables and the priorities of the government that shape their work rather than the issues that they may be seen to represent by those who argue for their existence. Appointed and funded by governments that may in fact have limited commitment to the issue they represent, they are caught between accountability to the inside and the outside.

If government policy offered us a definitive solution and commitment to our problems, perhaps these mechanisms would be more useful. But government policies are imperfect at best – particularly those that tackle systemic issues such as wage discrimination and those that emerge from battles among opposing interests as only 'a good first step.' What we need if reforms are going to work are organizations that have the flex-ibility to participate in procedural reform and the authority to influence the policy-making process rather than mechanisms that appear to be designed to limit reform. Our use of commissions and advisory councils as policy instruments often serves only to legitimate political commit-ments that are then contained by another arm of the state.

The subordination of the policy work of the Pay Equity Commission to government priorities is, of course, rarely made explicit – particularly at the political level. In many cases, the heads of commissions and advisory councils rarely see their respective ministers. Who they do see is their counterparts in the ministers' administrations. It is the Ministry of Labour that organizes the commission's relationship with the minister and determines in very practical and often mundane ways the work of the commission and the influence it can wield.

These relationships between government administrations and quasi-independent bodies such as the Pay Equity Commission are often quite problematic – not because of 'personality differences,' but because of structural issues such as overlapping or competing mandates, compe-tition over resources, and issues of secrecy and control that characterize the way in which administrations go about their work. In most cases, these administrations effectively control and limit the work of the quasi-independent bodies. In the first place, the ministry provides the infra-structure that regulates the work of the Pay Equity Office (rules and regulations regarding staffing, financial administration, processing of documents, and so on). It is the Ministry of Labour – through the Policy

Branch – that 'polices' the work of the commission in relation to government's timetables. It is no secret that relationships between the commission and the Policy Branch of the Ministry of Labour are strained – and for good reasons, considering the control function that the branch must play.

Second, although the mandates of the commission and the ministry are different in theory, they, in fact, both act as advisers to the minister of labour. The overlap between the commission and the Ministry of Labour was quite clearly displayed in the process of developing options for the predominantly female sector. The Policy Branch of the ministry actually repeated much of the work of the commission in preparing the minister's discussion paper on policy options, including consultation with the same 'stakeholders' contacted for the commission's study. The duplication of efforts between the ministry and the commission is particularly confusing and annoying to the employees and employers who feel they are asked to spend too much time consulting and have minimal impact.

Third, the Policy Branch has the potential to influence the minister more directly than does the commission. Ministry staff see her or him more frequently – they know her questions, they know more about the 'policy environment' that will influence Cabinet discussions and decisions, they have access to financial-planning information that will affect the responses of her Cabinet colleagues to her proposals. They not only have access to this information, however; they can control access to this information, thus putting the commission at a real disadvantage. When faced with differences of opinion between her advisers in the Ministry of Labour and those in the commission, it is likely that the minister would side with ministry officials – after all, they are more directly accountable to her than the staff of the relatively autonomous commission.

Finally, the location of the Ministry of Labour itself within the unequal structure of representation of the provincial policy-making process regulates/determines the status of the pay equity issue in relation to the hierarchy of government's priorities and the distribution of its resources. The Ministry of Labour is relatively powerless as an advocate for wage reforms in a government where policies are shaped by a commitment to business interests. Historically, such ministries have been noted for their capacity to limit workers' demands, to establish relationships with organized labour to control workers' demands for wages in exchange for other benefits (Mahon 1977). The accord between the Liberals and the NDP shifted this balance of power to some degree – permitting the passage of the Pay Equity Act. But by the time the commission was embarked on the process of implementation in 1989, the Liberals had won a majority and feminists were generally under attack for being too militant.[23] In this climate of opinion, it undoubtedly 'made sense' to the commission to appear to be as 'reasonable' as possible, in the hope that the minister would be persuaded to recommend the proxy comparison approach to Cabinet. Representation of the concerns of those consulted about funding would have led to what the minister might have regarded as an untimely discussion of the complicated and very expensive issue of the government's responsibility for pay equity adjustments for the broader public sector. But regardless of what kind of commitment the minister herself might have had, there was no political incentive or pressure to apply the Pay Equity Act to workers in the predominantly female sector, particularly to those in exclusively female workplaces.

Feminist Pay Equity Advocates

Feminist pay equity advocates in Ontario are not overjoyed with the Pay Equity Act. It is 'a good first step,' but it has all of the flaws of a reform that has been produced from years of negotiating on the issue of equal pay for work of equal value with opposing interests. It is a compromise – and to a large extent, an inevitable compromise engineered in the policy-making processes of the state.

But the compromises that we have made on equal pay for work of equal value have not all emerged from our relationship with the state. We have, over the years, also found ourselves working in organizations whose structures and practices narrow the reforms we wanted. Like femocrats in the Pay Equity Commission, the influence of pay equity advocates is limited by the structures in which they work and the respective relationships of these structures to the state. Like the feminists working inside the state, their political agenda as advocates of equal pay has, to the extent that they are drawn into this process, been compromised by the way in which they have been absorbed as individuals into the technical tasks of bargaining pay equity plans as representatives of particular unions, litigating cases at the Pay Equity Hearings Tribunal, appearing as expert witnesses before the tribunal, or acting as advisers or consultants to the Pay Equity Commission. While these tasks present feminist advocates with the opportunity to engage in the implementation of the Pay Equity Act, 1987, they engage us in a set of institutionalized practices that focus our attention on organized workers and divert us from the political task of representing the interests of most of the women in the broader public sector who are neither unionized nor financially able to support the litigation process. It is these practices that dominate the work of pay equity advocates in spite of attempts by the Equal Pay Coalition to establish pay equity clinics to support unorganized workers or to have the government legislate the application of settlements from the unionized to the unorganized sector.

Feminists working from a trade-union base potentially have more freedom to interpret and challenge the act than do feminists employed by the Pay Equity Office of the commission, although perhaps not as much as those working for the Pay Equity Hearings Tribunal. But this potential is limited by the way in which unions have integrated the pay equity issue. Their responsiveness seems to depend on a combination of factors, including the gender balance of the union, the clients they serve, and the resources available. Public-sector unions such as CUPE and OPSEU have taken an active role on pay equity by appointing pay equity advisers/coordinators and educating their membership about their rights through pay equity manuals and workshops, and the Ontario Federation of Labour continues to speak out for the needs of women in the predominantly female sector. Male-dominated unions working primarily in the private sector, however, have not been as responsive. To date it has been the female-dominated unions, such as the Ontario Nurses' Association and the Women Teachers' Federation, that have led the challenges on the interpretation of the definition of 'employer.'

However, the fact is that the perspectives of feminist trade unionists on solutions for the predominantly female sector are rooted in their work with organized women workers who still represent only a minority of women in the Ontario labour force. Unorganized women have little or no voice in relation to pay equity and most of them are overwhelmed by their everyday work and lack the resources to pursue the issue at the political level. Even relatively well-organized provincial associations such as the Ontario Association for Interval and Transition Houses find themselves caught up in myriad negotiations with the government about funding that leave them little time for pay equity.[24]

The Equal Pay Coalition, as an organization standing slightly outside the relations of ruling in which femocrats and feminist trade unionists are variable enmeshed, could play an important role in mobilizing support for amendments to the legislation that would speak directly to the needs of the unorganized. But, in fact, the membership of the coalition has historically been dominated by trade unionists and lawyers who had the knowledge and expertise to define a feminist position on equal value, and thus the work of the coalition inevitably (and unintentionally) reflects the same bias in favour of organized workers as does the work of trade unionists and those working in the Pay Equity Commission. The coalition has found it difficult to come up with creative responses to the opportunities for amendments presented by section 33 of the act, or to the proposals that have been rather too hastily generated by the new New Democratic government since September 1990. Much-needed discussions of political strategies to advance the interests of the unorganized are often displaced by the incredible array of practical and technical details that feminists address as they implement the legislation.

There are at present few alternatives to the Equal Pay Coalition as a vehicle for feminist work on equal value. The growing complexity of our issues in the last two decades led us to organize ourselves into single-issue coalitions, and by now the coalition has virtual ownership of the pay equity issue in Ontario. It is difficult if not impossible for pay equity to be taken up by any other feminist organization.[25] Assessment of pay equity legislation is far too complex for any but the fully initiated expert to undertake. Time, if we have it, may give us a chance to address some of the limits that have emerged in the process of our struggles to define and implement pay equity legislation. Coalition members, exhausted by the long, hard struggle to negotiate the legislation and their responsibilities to implement it, may be inspired by the new 'opportunities' presented by the apparent willingness of the NDP government to pursue solutions for women workers in the predominantly female sector to direct their energy to the needs of the unorganized.

The fate of the unorganized women workers in relation to pay equity depends very heavily on the extent to which both the membership of the coalition and organized labour can move beyond the focus on strategies rooted in the specifics of the organized sector to develop strategies that speak to the specificities of the unorganized sector.

Conclusion

There is no simple formula that we can draw on to define a relationship with the state that would guarantee the reforms we want. But, in the struggle to define ways for women in predominantly female establishments to achieve pay equity adjustments, it was clear that our reforms were shaped in three major ways: one, by the balance of power at the political level where public issues are translated into political commitments; two, by the presentation of our interests in the policy-making processes of the state bureaucracy where the implementation of these commitments is organized; and three, by the institutionalization of our own political practices as we participated in these processes.

There is no doubt that the relative power of the New Democratic Party during the years of the accord with the minority Liberal government accounts for the passage of such a progressive piece of legislation. Pay equity legislation may have been on the Liberal agenda, but it is unlikely that the legislation would have been extended to the broader public sector or the private sector without pressure from a social democratic party that was willing to challenge what has historically been considered to be the right of employers to control their wage-setting practices, including those that have denied women's rights to equal pay for work of equal value. Part of the problem we have had in defining ways for women in predominantly female establishments to achieve pay equity adjustments can be explained in terms of the Liberal retreat from this commitment to intervene in these practices when it won a majority in the 1987 election.

What is often obscured by our focus on winning political commitments, however, is how the policy-making process within the state bureaucracy limits the way in which these commitments are implemented and our capacity as feminist activists outside the state to challenge these limits, and how our enmeshment as trade unionists and feminist activists in institutionalized practices that subordinate our issues to the 'main business' of both the state and the unions weakens our power to challenge these practices. Our struggles are often limited by the contradictions between the institutionalized practices that shape our work and the specificities of women's exploitation and oppression.

Feminists engaged in the pay equity struggle may be breathing a sigh of relief as the first social-democratic government in the history of Ontario comes to power. The New Democratic government has the power to make its commitments to pay equity a reality. It has the power to withdraw the previous government's decision to intervene in the judicial review of the Pay Equity Hearings Tribunal decision in the *Haldimand–Norfolk* case. Challenges to the act from the organized sector as well as tribunal decisions provide the new government with the appropriate guidelines for ways to make the act work for *all* of the workers in Ontario. It also has the power to address these challenges and declare the provincial government to be the employer of establishments in the broader public sector regulated by its funding policies and legislation for purposes of the Pay Equity Act.

However, it is unlikely that the New Democratic government's commitment to pay equity for women workers in the predominantly female struggle represents the last word on this issue. Commitments to manage financial deficits are clearly in competition with this commitment, and the new policy makers appear to be lapsing into the same 'squeaky wheel' strategies that marked the policies of previous governments. But a more serious question is whether the New Democratic government will address the limits of the legislation borne, as it were, out of compromises struck when business interests dominated the development of government policy. The advent of a social-democratic government presents us with the opportunity to do this and, given two years of experience implementing this legislation, many practitioners are in an excellent position to recommend ways to make it work in ways that more closely represent what feminists intended.

The challenge then is to design a process that will capture this intent and our experience on pay equity issues both inside and outside the state. It will have to be a new and more open process – one in which the voices of unorganized as well as organized workers will be heard, one that will rely on dialogue between workers and the state rather than on those that represent our interests within the state, and one that will break the division of labour among political, technical, and financial issues and address them in language that is accessible to all. Central to this challenge then is a rethinking of many of the liberal democratic structures and practices that we have taken for granted – or invoked – in our struggles for reform, and a redefinition of politics that is rooted in the particulars of our issues and in practices that facilitate our action on and control over these issues. Reflecting on our experience of the limits of pay equity could be a 'good first step' in the process.

NOTES

1 This essay is dedicated to the memory of Carole Geller, long-time friend and feminist activist and the first executive director of the Manitoba Pay Equity Bureau, with whom I spent endless hours debating the 'nature of the state' and how it would take up our demands for equal pay for work of equal value.

Many people have participated in the production of this work. In particular, I would like to thank Joan Acker, Pat Bird, Ann-Marie Delorey, Irene Harris, Rianne Mahon, Brigid O'Reilly, and Judi Stevenson for their comments. I would also like to thank Chris Gabriel who worked with me on the report.

2 In a joint campaign to pressure the provincial government to extend the coverage of the Pay Equity Act in the summer and fall of 1989, the Ontario Federation of Labour and the Equal Pay Coalition claimed that more than one million women are excluded from coverage. These include women in predominantly female workplaces, those in workplaces of fewer than ten and part-time workers.

3 'Femocrats' is a term that originated in Australia to describe feminists who work within the state bureaucracy. It is intended to distinguish these feminists from community-based feminists, and as such it has an analytic function. It is not intended to project any judgment about those who have chosen the state as a terrain of struggle, although by labelling them it does invite an examination of their practices. For further discussion of this term, see Watson (1990, ix).

4 The Equal Pay Coalition was organized in 1970s to pressure the provincial government to establish legislation to promote equal pay for work of equal value. In the 1980s, following the strategy adopted by American feminists, the coalition lobbied for pay equity legislation. The membership of the coalition has been drawn from the ranks of feminists who have entered the trade-union movement since the middle of the 1970s, as well feminist lawyers specializing in labour law.

5 Section 33(2)(e), the Pay Equity Act, 1987

6 *Report to the Minister of Labour by the Ontario Pay Equity Commission on Sectors of the Economy Which Are Predominantly Female, as Required under the Pay Equity Act, section 33(2)(e)* (January 1989). In this report, the Pay Equity Commission estimated that out of the 1.7 million women working in establishments covered by the act, 875,000 would be unable to identify appropriate male comparators. In its 1989 campaign to pressure the government for action to meet this issue, the Ontario Federation of Labour argued that this figure was really closer to one million.

7 *Report to the Minister of Labour by the Ontario Pay Equity Commission on Options relating to the Achievement of Pay Equity in Sectors of the Economy Which Are Predominantly Female* (October 1989)

8 The commission's argument suggested that private-sector establishments driven by competition might abuse the option by seeking male compara-

tors that would lower the wages of their workers (p. 85 of the commission's report on the predominantly female sector).

9 'Policy Directions: Amending the Pay Equity Act,' Ministry of Labour (February 1990), p. 4. Proportional-value comparison with male job classes with different values within predominantly female workplaces.

10 This is a contentious and imprecise term used in government discourse that sidesteps the political issue about the disjunction between who is selected by the government as a 'stakeholder' and who really has a 'stake in the policies being formed.' For the most part, I have elected to refer to the specific groups consulted.

11 'Determining Pay Equity Adjustments using the Proxy Comparison Approach,' Pay Equity Commission (August 1989), internal document prepared by the Pay Equity Office. In brief, the method of applying the proxy comparison approach relied on a cooperative proxy organization supplying information on its female and male job classes to the Pay Equity Office, which would, in turn, convert this information to wage lines against which the seeking organization would evaluate its female job classes.

12 Union representatives consulted were also opposed to the use of wage lines, arguing that they could be abused by employers interested in lowering or red-circling male wages.

13 Transfer-payment agencies are those agencies that are funded by transfers of funds in a variety of ways from the provincial government. They include agencies in the community and social-service sector and the health sector.

14 The Pay Equity Commission inadvertently encouraged this perspective in its distribution of the model of the Mariposa Agency as a guide for filing pay equity plans for predominantly female workplaces. The model made it quite clear that there was no way that these agencies could calculate pay equity adjustments.

15 It also gave pay equity practitioners the basis for new challenges in applying the act.

16 Feminist practices have been regulated by the state in a number of ways, including funding support that encouraged the development of 'representative' national and regional groups that were considered to be appropriate participants in the policy-making process, the separation of our issues from their economic and social roots and a generalizing of their definition in terms of equality with men, the definition of reforms in terms of further research, legislative change, and human resource

training that encouraged the professionalization of feminists and their organizations that represented an orientation compatible with that of the state, formalizing of access to the policy-making process by the appointments of feminists to the federal Advisory Council on the Status of Women (established in 1973), state-organized consultations on government policy during International Women's Year, ongoing consultations on the policies of the state organized by the Women's Program in the Department of the Secretary of State and Status of Women Canada, and the ongoing liaison functions of the Women's Program. See Roxanna Ng's *The Politics of Community Services* (1988), for a description of how the state penetrates feminist services. Gillian Walker (1988) describes this process in relation to the issue of wife battering as one of absorption and articulation.

17 In 1989, the minister responsible for the status of women and the Conservative cabinet refused to meet with the National Action Committee on the Status of Women because they did not like what they had to say or how they said it.

18 For an elaboration of how these practices work, see Working Group on Sexual Violence, 'Feminist Manifesto' (Vancouver 1985). Attempts in the 1990s to 'repoliticize' such groups as the National Committee on the Status of Women undoubtedly reflect a positive step towards reclaiming our capacity to maintain our feminist perspectives in representing women's interests in the development of state policies.

19 *Equity in Employment: A Royal Commission Report* (October 1984; Minister of Supply and Services Canada)

20 The Pay Equity Commission ran several advertisements requesting submissions about ways to identify male comparators for predominantly female establishments. They received relatively few replies.

21 Equal Pay Coalition, 'Bringing Pay Equity to Those Presently Excluded from Ontario's Pay Equity Act,' 13 December 1988

22 This distinction is concretized in the staffing of the Pay Equity Commission. The staff of the Pay Equity Office is appointed under the Public Service Act, while members of the tribunal are appointed by the lieutenant-governor.

23 Barbara McDougall, then federal minister responsible for the status of women, was praised by many of her party colleagues for her refusal to meet with the National Action Committee on the Status of Women in May 1989. NAC was and is considered to be far too demanding and critical of government policies for a broader public-sector group. See also

the Feminist Manifesto published by the Working Group on Sexual Violence (Vancouver, April 1985)

24 Excepted from this fate are the child-care workers whose pay equity interests are represented by the very well-organized Ontario Coalition for Better Child Care. One of the actions that the coalition has taken in relation to pay equity is to speak in support of the complaint that the Pat Schulz Child Care Centre in Toronto has lodged with the Pay Equity Commission that identifies the provincial government as its employer for purposes of the Pay Equity Act.

25 As I discovered at the Women and the State conference in 1987, feminists who try are either hopelessly confused by the complexity of the legislation or are looked upon with great hostility by both pay equity activists who are sensitive to criticism and other feminist activists who feel they have sacrificed their right to pose alternatives by not participating in the coalition. For further details, see Findlay (1987a) and McDermott (1987).

5 Limited Possibilities and Possible Limits for Pay Equity: Within and Beyond the Ontario Legislation

Pat Armstrong and Hugh Armstrong

A great deal of time, effort, and ink have gone into critiquing the Ontario Pay Equity legislation and the women who were party to its development (see, for example, Armstrong and Armstrong 1990; Lewis 1988; Warskett 1990). Such critiques are necessary if others are to avoid the problems inherent in the legislation and if we are to maintain our vigilance. They help combat the assumptions that nothing else can be done and that everything possible has been done. However, it is also necessary to focus on how to get the most out of the legislation that is in place, both to ensure that as many women as possible get some money and to ensure that efforts around pay equity are part of a larger struggle to gain better conditions of work for all women. The legislation does not inevitably lead in one direction. It has contradictory implications. In order to reap the long-term as well as the short-term benefits of pay equity, we need to understand and build on these contradictions.

This essay considers four contradictory implications of the Ontario Pay Equity Act. It argues that the legislation could serve to support the contention that the market is, for the most part, an objective means of allocating rewards. In this scenario, the legislation would offer few grounds for further demands designed to improve women's conditions of work. Or it could provide a basis for fundamentally challenging a reliance on market forces. Similarly, the job-evaluation schemes used to implement pay equity could either reinforce existing hierarchical work structures that perpetuate major inequities or be employed to restructure work along more egalitarian lines. Furthermore, the legislation could result in a greater unity among women, leading to additional collective strategies for change. But it could just as easily increase divisions among women, rewarding some and leaving the rest doing women's work at women's wages. And, finally, the Pay Equity Act could be applied in ways that restrict the impact to a few employers but in doing so may increase differences among employers that would encourage demands from them for a more uniform and simple policy. In order to simplify the analysis, the contradictions are presented here as alternatives but they should be understood as existing simultaneously. Both kinds of outcome are possible at the same time.

Legitimating and Delegitimating the Market

Pay equity implies that the market can and should determine relative values derived from 'the productivity-based job content characteristics of the jobs' (Remick 1984d, 289). Indeed, it is primarily based on the assumption that the market currently does determine this for men and that the solution is to apply the same criteria to women. Like human capital theory, it assumes that what men, at least, are paid reflects the requirements of the job and the capacities of the workers. The purpose is to apply the same market rules to women, to fix this particular glitch in an otherwise fair system (Brenner 1987; Steinberg 1987). Once the rules have been 'neutralized,' 'cleansed' of gender-bias, women will have no one to blame but themselves or their jobs for their pay.

Pay equity thus may leave unquestioned the major wage differentials among workers and leave unanalysed the power relations that are central to wage determination while serving to legitimate the dominance of the market. It may also serve to reinforce the notion that wages are determined exclusively in the market, and thus in isolation from households, volunteer work, and the underground economy. With the emphasis on the discriminatory values that create pay inequities and on a one-time pay equity plan to correct the situation,[1] this approach may shift the focus away from the structural conditions that help keep women doing women's work at women's wages. Moreover, it may end up helping to justify the major pay inequities that remain.

But this need not be the case. Equally integral to the notion of pay equity is a challenge to the market. When Ontario's pay equity legislation began with a recognition of 'systemic discrimination' (Pay Equity Act, S.O. 1987, c. 32, s. 4), it was in effect saying that the market does not work in an objective manner. By requiring both public- and private-sector employers to develop pay equity plans, the legislation was also implying that employers would resist paying women comparably to men. It suggested that free-market rules were not the only ones that applied and that employers had a vested interest in the current situation. In the process, the legislation increased the opportunities for exposing the profit to be made from 'discrimination,' from the non-application of free-market forces. And the negotiation of the plans, along with uneven application of the legislation, can provide yet another indication of the importance of power in wage determination.

Pay equity legislation thus can offer the opportunity to expose the myth of objective market forces. It can be used to demonstrate how women's low pay is embedded not simply in the ideology but also in the structure of work in and out of the market. It can be used to press for strategies that move beyond a focus on market wages to address the complexity of women's conditions.

Job Evaluation: Reinforcing and Undermining the Hierarchy

Pay equity also implies job evaluation. Although unions have frequently supported job evaluation on the grounds that it at least establishes the rules in an explicit way, job evaluation was developed as a management tool. Job-evaluation schemes were explicitly designed to establish and reinforce hierarchy, wage differences, and management's place (Haignere 1990; Remick 1984a; Treiman and Hartmann 1981). They regularized and bureaucratized the power relations involved in determining what constitutes a job and how the job is evaluated, in the process suggesting that objectively determined job characteristics, rather than power, determined position in the hierarchy and pay for the job. Introduced when only a minority of women were in the labour force and when services for people did not account for much of commodified production, most schemes were initially intended to measure jobs in the male-dominated workplaces of the primary and secondary sectors. Most still reflect these origins.

Consequently, job-evaluation schemes are much more likely to value what men do, particularly in the goods-producing sectors or at the top of the hierarchy, rather than what women do, especially in human-service work. Moreover, given their purpose and history, they are more likely to reinforce and justify, rather than challenge, women's position and pay. Fit into a predetermined male-dominated hierarchy, few women are likely to do more than establish comparisons with some men near the bottom (see Armstrong 1988b).[2]

Many of the job-evaluation schemes involve workers directly in the process. Employees often fill in the questionnaires that provide the basic data on job content and are sometimes involved in attaching grades to various job characteristics. But it is usually male managers and their experts who determine what information is collected, who instruct employees on what counts in terms of relative worth, and who establish the value attached to various job characteristics. In addition, the complex, technical nature of the process can mean that most workers are excluded from significant involvement. Few have the specific skills necessary to evaluate the evaluations. Those who do develop the skills may be overwhelmed by the time involved and the complexity of the task. And they may get so involved in the technical details that it becomes difficult for them to envisage the long-term implications of the evaluation scheme for women. Moreover, the male workers – and even the female workers – may retain many traditional ideas about the value of women's work (Acker 1989, 91–8).

Thus, in spite of some employee involvement, these schemes may serve to transform a political process into a technical one (Acker 1989). The establishment of both content and worth may be handed over to experts who predetermine what is counted, how it is counted, and what values are attached to what is recorded as being worthy of recognition. The technical nature of the evaluations and the reliance on management experts may mean that women have few tools with which to develop a critique and have no meaningful involvement in the evaluation process. Instead, they may be presented with results that denigrate their contribution but that suggest these are objectively determined measures of worth.

But again, this need not be the case. The Pay Equity Act broke new ground in calling for job-evaluation schemes that are free from gender bias, and in requiring employers to 'describe the gender-neutral comparison system used' (s. 13[2][a]). Because such schemes are part of the pay equity plan, they are also subject to appeal before the independent hearing tribunal. The act thus provides an invitation for women to expose the values inherent in these schemes. Women can use this requirement in the act to expose the complex nature of women's work, to challenge the old criteria, and to get more money for women.

These goals require much more than a tinkering with existing job-evaluation schemes. They require much more than adding examples that are relevant to women's work, much more than adding a few extra points for the kinds of working conditions women face, much more than arguing that women's experience as volunteers is relevant or that women looking after patients are really doing supervisory work, just like the men. Redefining women's skill, effort, responsibility, and working conditions to fit into the pre-established categories that reflect male hierarchies does not address the gender bias integral to most job-evaluation schemes.

Using job-evaluation schemes for women means we must begin by recognizing that most women do work that is different from that of most men. Women's work requires different kinds of skill, effort, responsibility, and working conditions within different kinds of organizational structures (Acker 1989; Armstrong and Armstrong 1983a, 1983b). Unlike most male jobs, much of women's work involves a variety of skills employed simultaneously. It frequently involves switching from one level of task to another level and from person to person, often in ways that involve different methods of communication. It usually involves the provision of comfort, emotional support, and care. It frequently involves coordination and cooperation with others, under conditions where women have little formal authority. In many cases, precisely because it is women who do the work, the actual responsibility is very different from what is formally defined. Women's work, much more so than that of men, means providing services for people, and such work creates its own special kinds of stress, its own special odours, its own special kinds of sound, its own special kinds of effort. Moreover, it is often the combination of these conditions, and the problem of dealing with people under these conditions, that constitute the main effort involved in women's work. Existing schemes do not, and most cannot, capture these aspects of women's work.

What is involved in women's work has, to a large extent, been unrecognized. The skill, effort, responsibility, and working conditions remain largely invisible not only to the job-evaluation experts but also to many of the women who do the work. They remain invisible in part precisely because so many women do such work, resulting in an assumption that they are simply doing what comes naturally. This invisibility is further reinforced by standards derived from male jobs, where discrete tasks, skills explicitly taught, and visible products or results at the end of the line are much more the norm. These assumptions mean that it is very difficult to record the complexity of women's work, even when women themselves are describing their work.

The very structure of job-evaluation schemes makes it difficult to document these different aspects of women's work. Few schemes begin with the understanding that women's work is different, or with the purpose of making the invisible visible. Moreover, the structure of questionnaires often provides limited space for descriptions of the work, often requires women to fit into predetermined categories derived from men's work, and often asks for estimates of time allocated to each task. The overlapping, multi-level character of women's work disappears in the process. The questions not asked are often as important as those that are. The requirement that supervisors check responses may serve to ensure that women present only the formal requirements of the job, excluding much of their actual responsibility, skill, and effort in their attempt to fit into the specified hierarchy. Furthermore, instructions to evaluators and the rules for fitting job descriptions usually make it clear that the purpose is to reproduce the relative positions of employees, making it difficult to break out of traditional evaluations of women's work.

The final stage of such schemes is to attach values to the aspects of the work that have been recorded. (Of course, what has not been captured cannot be evaluated, and many aspects of women's work remain invisible in most evaluation methods.) Many schemes have predetermined weights for various factors, weights that favour the work that men do and that reflect management's values (Haignere 1990). Most schemes place high values on independence, responsibility for supervision of others, formal education, or other factors that characterize jobs done by men at the top, and many of these factors may be double or even triple counted. At the same time, factors such as teamwork or the kinds of skills required to deal with clients or patients are usually not valued at all.

That job-evaluation schemes are biased in terms of what is captured, of how that work is captured, and of how what is captured is evaluated offers the opportunity to question traditional assumptions about women's work. Indeed, the Pay Equity Act encourages us to challenge job-evaluation schemes at all these levels. In order to capture and evaluate women's work, we need job-evaluation methods that are fundamentally different from those currently in place. These new approaches must be based on different assumptions about organizations and worth, and on the recognition that the jobs of women and men often require significantly different kinds of skill, effort, responsibility, and working conditions. Such approaches would recognize and value such aspects of women's work as cooperation; the importance of doing a multiple of tasks simultaneously or of switching from one level of task to another;

the difficulty involved in achieving cooperation when workers do not have access to formal authority; the stress involved in dealing with the young, the old, and the victimized.

The challenges to old schemes and the development of new ones can be made in ways that expose for both women and men the complexity of the very different skills that women employ, the different kinds of responsibility they share, the effort they expend, and the conditions they face. But this can work only if we avoid trying to squeeze women into traditional male hierarchies and male skill, effort, responsibility, and working-condition categories. We cannot, for example, simply demand that schemes call what nurses do the supervision of patients and in this way fit women into the male categories. Instead, we have to establish that women's particular work is valuable both in itself and in comparison with that of men.

To do this, we need to develop our own experts and own expertise. But this task, too, must be accomplished in a different way if we want to do more than simply get more money for some women today. We need experts who are thoroughly versed in the specific nature of women's work and who understand the problem of making the invisible visible (see, for example, Armstrong and Armstrong 1983b; Stratham, Miller, and Mauksch 1988). And we need to develop this expertise in ways that involve as many women as possible, not only in the process of developing critiques but also in exposing the complex nature of women's work. We need strategies that make job evaluation a source of continuing strength for women, based on a recognition of women's shared capacities at work.

Division or Unity

Pay equity may also imply divisions among women and between women and men. Because the Ontario act is based on comparing female job classes with male job classes, it may well be that, although reductions in pay to achieve pay equity are explicitly prohibited, the act will primarily serve to freeze male wages rather than to significantly increase female wages. Employers are only required to make adjustments 'by an amount that is not less than the lesser of ... 1 percent of the employer's payroll' or 'the amount required to achieve pay equity' (s. 13[5]), an amount that may become a ceiling rather than a floor for women's pay increases. In any case, if the total wage allocation remains virtually unchanged after pay equity, men may eventually lose in terms of their future wage gains. Moreover, the reliance on job evaluation puts pressure on both women and men to demonstrate that their work is relatively more valuable and more skilled, and involves more effort and responsibility along with poorer working conditions.

Similarly, the reliance on job evaluation may serve to separate women from each other, encouraging women to demonstrate that their jobs are more onerous or more skilled than those of other women. In addition, the reliance on employers and establishments as the basis for the pay equity plan may serve to increase pay differences among women. Some women will find comparators within their establishments, will successfully establish their equivalent worth, and will win pay increases. Some women, doing the same job in a different workplace, where there are no comparators, where they have a job-evaluation scheme that fails to establish their equivalent worth, or where the number of employees is too small to require a pay equity plan, will find themselves with no increase in pay.

Ontario nurses provide a case in point. The Ontario Nurses' Association, representing the majority of employed nurses in the province, has negotiated a standard pay scale for all their members, regardless of the institution that employs them or the specific nursing area in which they work. Nurses in large urban teaching hospitals may well find a male job class that earns more money but is rated on a job-evaluation scheme as having equivalent or less worth. In contrast, nurses employed in small rural hospitals, in homes for the aged, in clinics, or in public health are much less likely to find comparators or to qualify under the act. The result may be significant gains for some nurses and no gains for others. Moreover, the kinds of job-evaluation scheme currently in place emphasize the visible and specific skills, effort, responsibility, and working conditions women face. Such schemes may serve to indicate that some nurses, such as those facing obvious pressures and complicated technology in intensive-care units, are more valuable than others. Thus the evaluations may further separate nurses from each other (Armstrong 1988a, 1988b).

The involvement of unions in negotiations for pay equity plans may also serve to reinforce differences among women. The more powerful unions, with the greatest interest and skill in negotiating pay equity, in workplaces that offer comparators or where comparators can be negotiated through particular interpretations of the act, may well win significant gains for women. Women without unions are likely to have a plan imposed that offers little improvement, and to have few resources available to help them fight the plan. Those in small workplaces or without comparators may not even have this option.

The Ontario Pay Equity legislation, then, is most likely to benefit women who are already in the best-paid female jobs – those of mainly white, unionized women who work for large employers. Even within these groups, however, the impact will be uneven. The overall impact may be greater divisions among women.

But here, too, this need not be the case. The unions that are, by virtue of the act, involved in negotiations may use their position to test and stretch the act in ways that set precedents for other groups. They may use their technical expertise, along with the details of the act, to extend the coverage of the legislation to its limits and to establish a foundation for new strategies. The Ontario Nurses' Association, for example, has already done this in arguing successfully that the definition of the employer in *Haldimand-Norfolk* must be extended to include jurisdiction over the local police officers. Several unions have used the section of the act that calls for a job-evaluation scheme free of gender bias to reveal the complexity of women's work and to challenge the assumptions on which such schemes are based. This has been particularly important in cases before the hearings tribunal. The tribunal has ruled twice that consultants hired by employers to design their plans cannot intervene in the hearings process. At the same time, it has allowed expert witnesses to testify at length about the nature of women's work and about the problems involved in capturing this work through current job-evaluation schemes. Some unions are also involving their members in the development and critique of job-evaluation schemes, a process that can serve to empower these members. And the very resistance of employers to union complaints under the act may reveal the benefits employers gain from women's work, and those that workers gain from organizing themselves in unions.

The greater gains of women in strong unions may also be used to strengthen women in general. If these gains are used to help women outside unions understand that state legislation is not enough and that collective action is what leads to improvements, then the legislation can serve to extend the union movement. What is required is coordination among women from different workplaces and efforts by union women to help those outside their membership. Although unions have not always been on the side of women, we know that the wage gap is smaller in unions, and that countries with high rates of unionization have smaller wage differentials between women and men (S.C. 13; Burton 1987; White 1980, 1990).

Because pay equity bases comparisons on wages and benefits as well as on the structure and content of jobs, it opens up the possibility of access to a wide range of information previously kept confidential. Managers have traditionally kept such information as secret as possible, precisely because it is a basis of power. Both union and non-union groups can use this information to expose inequity and to develop strategies that go beyond the limits of the legislation.

Legitimation and Profit: The Role of the State

There can be little question that, in responding to the Equal Pay Coalition's demand for action, the state tried to create legislation that would appear to solve the problem once and for all but would also appear to respond to employers' concerns. The exclusion of small business, the definitions of 'employer,' 'establishment,' and 'job classes,' and the requirement that comparisons be made first within bargaining units, along with other technical details in the act, have limited the impact of the legislation (Armstrong and Armstrong 1990a; Lewis 1988; Warskett 1990).

But while the strategy has been successful in preventing many employers from paying out to women, it has backfired on the state in a number of ways. The effort to restrict the impact of the legislation has increased enormously the costs to employers of developing a pay equity plan. The complexity of the act has invited different interpretations and has resulted in a multitude of expensive cases ending up before the Pay Equity Tribunal. Appearances before the tribunal not only cost the employer time and money, they also cost the employer information. A feature of the tribunal hearings is that employer strategies and data are subjected to union and public scrutiny. Moreover, disputes before the tribunal offer union and non-union employees the opportunity to present their own cases for women in a public forum, with their alternative assumptions and interpretations given equal time. The impact of this forum may be far greater than any of the planners intended.

Furthermore, the very unevenness of the impact may be detrimental to employers. Some are finding themselves with expensive bills for job evaluations and hearings as well as for large pay-outs to women. At the same time, other employers, even those engaged in the same kind of work, may get away with few if any costs, and no pay equity payments.

Unlike legislation such as the minimum wage, the act does not equally apply to all, and therefore interferes more with competition and that level playing-field than would be the case with more systematic and universal legislation.

The state could go two ways in responding to these problems for employers. It could, as a number of employers and politicians have suggested, simply cancel the legislation and remove equal pay from the agenda. Doing so, however, would still leave those who have already increased wages with expensive settlements. The alternative would be to develop a simpler and more universal strategy to raise the wages of all those who do women's work for women's wages. The state could, for example, use one institution as the prototype for all jobs and determine an across-the-board increase for all employees who do this kind of work. The specific direction the state takes will depend, to some extent at least, on women's strength and on the nature of their demands.

Contested Terrain

Any legislation is limited by the reality of the democratic process in terms of its potential to transform the nature, conditions, and allocation of women's work (Armstrong and Armstrong 1990b, ch. 7). This legislation is additionally limited because it has a host of particular flaws that were designed to restrict its impact. But unlike employment equity legislation, for example, pay equity legislation does not focus primarily on reallocating individuals, on shuffling the occupants of the same old jobs. Because it deals only with who does the job, legislation such as employment equity has little potential for challenging the conditions and relations that keep large numbers of people doing unrewarding work, or the hierarchical organization of that work. This pay equity legislation is not based on individual solutions. Instead, it requires responses for women as a group rather than for women as individuals, and it requires that some women, at least, be involved in determining the necessary response. It thus could challenge much more than what individual people are paid and could lead to a questioning of not just the allocation but also the structure and conditions of all work. Whether or not this potential is realized is not predetermined.

The point is not that there are good and bad parts of the act. Rather, the various aspects of the act are contradictory in themselves. Women may emerge from dealing with this legislation to find themselves more divided than before and with very little money to show for the effort.

At the same time as the act creates the possibility for this scenario, however, it also creates the opportunity to move beyond the specifics of the act to make both short- and long-term gains for women. Neither of these developments is built into the act. The outcome will depend on our ability to use these contradictions to move beyond the legislation by using the legislation for women's ends.

NOTES

1 Although the Pay Equity Act (S.C. 1988, c. 32, s. 7) states that 'every employer shall establish and maintain compensation practices that provide for pay equity,' it does not set out compulsory payment amounts after the first settlement period. It seems unlikely that, without this pressure, pay equity negotiations will, in fact, be seen as a continuing process.
2 This case has been made repeatedly by expert witnesses who have appeared before the Ontario Hearings Tribunal in the cases where the Ontario Nurses' Association is challenging the plans used by the Regional Municipality of Haldimand-Norfolk and Women's College Hospital.

6 Pay Equity Challenge to Collective Bargaining in Ontario

Patricia McDermott

Ontario's Pay Equity Act,[1] which came into force in January 1988, presents some fundamental challenges to the province's industrial-relations system. There are many legal, theoretical, and practical questions that remain unanswered about the relationship between this new legislation and a forty-year-old labour-law jurisprudence. It is likely that the assumptions and practices that have shaped the relations between unions and their employers for decades will come into conflict with the goal of equitable pay practices. Our discussion of the relationship between pay equity and collective bargaining will begin with a brief overview of this complicated legislation.

The Pay Equity Act places an onus on all public-sector employers and all private-sector employers with ten or more employees in the province[2] to 'redress systemic gender discrimination in compensation for work performed by employees in female job classes.'[3] If there is a union present, the entire pay equity process discussed below is negotiated between the union and management.[4] Even the initial steps of identifying the employer and the 'establishment'[5] are to be decided in 'good faith' negotiations.[6] If there is no union present, the employer goes ahead and develops a pay equity plan, which subsequently becomes open to complaints from employees. It is interesting to note that complaints to the Pay Equity Commission, from either unionized or non-unionized employees, can be anonymous.[7] This is indeed a unique feature of the act that could put pressure on both employers and unions to gain the support of the employees affected by the plan before proceeding.[8]

The first step that has to be undertaken before the pay equity process begins is the identification of both the employer and the establishment. Although the Pay Equity Act does not include a definition of employer, this is not likely to be a major problem in unionized workplaces since identifying the employer has already been done during the certification process under Ontario's Labour Relation Act.[9] Although the employer will, for the most part, be the same for the purposes of both collective-agreement and pay equity negotiations, problems could arise about the employer's status in the collective-bargaining arena that will significantly affect the pay equity process. For example, applications about whether an employer is a 'related employer'[10] for such purposes as accessing a so-called deeper pocket in situations of bankruptcy, and especially a decision about whether an employer is a 'successor employer'[11] when a business is sold, would have a direct impact on the pay equity process. There has already been a case decided that suggests that Ontario's Pay Equity Hearings Tribunal will be quite flexible in defining 'the employer' for the purpose of pay equity.

It should be noted that there will also be situations that raise questions about the status of the bargaining agent that will affect the pay equity process. For instance, certification[12] and decertification[13] applications, as well as bargaining-unit merges that result from the sale or purchase of a business or the combining of two unions,[14] could operate to alter the dynamics of both employer-initiated and negotiated pay equity plans, particularly if the plans have not yet been signed and posted.

The Pay Equity Act includes a rather unusual definition of 'establishment.'[15] Essentially, it is a geographic definition that is based on the division of the province by the Territorial Divisions Act. Thus, any city, including the entire Municipality of Metropolitan Toronto, is considered *one* establishment, and all of the employees of an employer within such a 'geographic division' are in one establishment and potentially covered by one pay equity plan. There is also a provision in the legislation that allows employers to expand the definition of 'establishment' to become much larger units, but they cannot reduce the establishment to a smaller size than that set out in the Territorial Divisions Act.[16]

The scheme of the act requires that a pay equity plan be negotiated for each bargaining unit in an establishment. These negotiations will decide what definition of the establishment is to be used for the purposes of each bargaining unit's pay equity plan. This decision can be important for both the employer and the bargaining agent because an expanded definition could introduce more beneficial male comparators for female job classes in the bargaining unit, consequently costing the employer more to achieve pay equity.

Once the definition of establishment has been agreed upon, the next major items that must be negotiated are the 'job classes.'[17] Female job classes are those that have 60 per cent or more females, male job classes, those with 70 per cent or more males.[18] When the female and male job classes are identified, each job class is assigned a value by 'using a gender-neutral comparison system'[19] that is to be based on the four standard factors used in job-evaluation methodologies: skill, effort, responsibility, and working conditions.[20] Next, the 'job rate,' which is defined as the highest rate of compensation for the job class, and includes both salary and benefits, is established for each male and female job class.[21]

When the evaluations have been done and the job rates calculated, each female job class seeks a male job class that has 'equal or comparable value.'[22] When one is located, the female job class is entitled to the job rate of that male job class.[23] In other words, each person in the female job class receives as an adjustment the difference[24] between the female and comparable male job rates, no matter where they are located on the salary grid.[25] An adjustment schedule is established and the employer must make available 1 per cent of the province-wide payroll annually to accomplish the equalization of all the female job classes that need adjustments.[26]

The comparison process occurs within the bargaining unit first, but, if no appropriate male comparator is found, continues 'throughout the establishment.'[27] The bargaining agent and the employer must agree about the definition of 'establishment' to which this phrase refers. Pay equity plans are documents that include: a definition of the establishment; all of the job classes 'that form the basis of the comparison'; a description of the 'gender-neutral comparison system'; the 'results of the comparisons'; and any 'differences in compensation'[28] that an employer argues should be 'exclusions from determination.'[29] The plan must also describe how the adjustments in the female job classes will be made and must give the date of the first adjustment, which cannot be later than a fixed date set out in the act.[30] This plan, which is to be negotiated 'in good faith,'[31] is signed by both parties and then posted by the employer 'in prominent places in each work place for the establishment to which the document relates.'[32] Employers are also required to provide a copy to the bargaining agent representing the employees affected by the plan. It is unclear precisely what 'describe the gender-neutral comparison system' means. Does it simply mean a brief description of the plan or does it require the inclusion of factors weights and the methodology used to evaluate jobs? Also, it is not clear what 'set out the results of the comparisons carried out' implies. Whether the precise job-evaluation scores are necessary and whether the male comparators need to be included, along with their evaluations, are two more uncertainties.

It appears that employers are to keep paying matched pairs the same compensation, since section 7 of the act states that employers 'shall establish *and maintain* compensation practices that provide for pay equity.' It also seems that the employer is able to stop such payments, once pay equity has been achieved, only by proving that the difference in compensation between the female and the male job classes is 'the result of differences in bargaining strength.'[33] If compared job classes are within the same bargaining unit, this argument could not be made since, one assumes, both job classes would have the same bargaining strength as represented by their union.

Small Employers

The above so-called proactive process of developing and posting a formal pay equity plan is mandatory only for public-sector employers, regardless of size, and private-sector employers with at least 100 employees.[34] Employers who had, on average, from 10 to 99 employees during 1987 are not required to post a pay equity plan.[35] Under part III of the act, employers with 50 to 99 employees are allowed to 'maintain compensation practices that were in existence in the employer's establishment immediately before the effective date' (which was 1 January 1988) until 1993, while those with 10 to 49 have until 1994 to make changes.[36]

The provision that small employers may maintain their compensation practices is modified by the following clause: 'a compensation change that is the same in percentage terms for female job classes in the establishment shall be deemed not to be in contravention of those subsections [s. 7(1) and (2)] even though the change is different in dollar terms for a female job class than for a male job class.' Subsections 7(1) and (2) referred to above state that every employer 'shall establish and maintain compensation practices that provide for pay equity' and that no employer or bargaining agent shall agree to a compensation practice that violates the act. So, what precisely does section 21 mean? It seems that this section allows employers to pay those in female job classes the same or a higher percentage increase in compensation as to those in male job classes during the five- or six-year 'transition period.' If employers want to pay any male employee a higher percentage increase during the transition period it would appear that they, as section 21 indicates, must have decided on the 'establishment,' identified male and female 'job classes,' and calculated the 'compensation' (wages and benefits) for each job class.[37] Having done this, how do they then comply with section 21? Perhaps they could demonstrate that there are no female job classes? If there are both female and male job classes, it would be difficult to justify, without engaging in an evaluation process, paying any male job class a greater percentage increase than a female job class.

Small employers may voluntarily opt to post a pay equity plan but are not required to do so until 1992 or 1993, again depending on their size.[38] What if an employee in an establishment that has between 10 and 49 employees complains that, during the five-year period between 1988 and 1992, the males in the establishment received a higher percentage increase than the females? Could an employer simply say that he or she is planning to engage in a proactive plan under part II that does not have to be posted until 1993?

As far as collective bargaining is concerned, small employers must notify the bargaining agents of their intention to engage in a negotiated pay equity plan,[39] but the act does not state when they have to be notified. Also unclear is what happens if the employer decides not to develop a negotiated pay equity plan. It seems that the bargaining agent is thus not involved in the decisions about the definition of establishment, job classes, and the rate of compensation – all of which can significantly change the impact of the act.[40]

Even such critical issues as what small employers must do when the transition period ends in 1994 are not spelled out in the act. Are they then required to prepare a pay equity plan or do they only become subject to complaints under section 7? Also, if a complaint is launched at this point, would the requirement that all employers 'establish and maintain compensation practices that provide for pay equity' not mean that a pay equity plan must by then have been prepared, since the act defines pay equity as a process whereby job classes are identified, evaluated, and compared?[41]

'Normal' Bargaining and 'Pay Equity' Bargaining

One of the most important decisions about the pay equity process has been whether the negotiations over a pay equity plan should take place during the legally open period during which the Ontario Labour Relations Act allows for bargaining a new collective agreement or take place separately from normal collective-agreement bargaining. Ontario's act is silent on this issue. It is interesting that Prince Edward Island's pay equity legislation for the provincial public service explicitly states that pay equity bargaining is to be 'separate and apart from the normal negotiations conducted for the purpose of negotiating a collective agreement.'[42] Manitoba's pay equity legislation for the public service does not contain a provision requiring that pay equity negotiations be conducted separately;[43] however, since all of the bargaining agents for an employer must jointly bargain a single pay equity plan, it is necessary that pay equity negotiations be separate from normal, collective-agreement bargaining.[44]

In Ontario, it would seem that the option to combine pay equity negotiations with normal collective bargaining could be prohibited if a collective agreement is in place that has two or three more years to run, but the parties, as required by the act, have to negotiate a pay equity plan.[45] It may be possible that an agreement could be opened mid-term to negotiate pay equity if the parties both agree to such a process and jointly apply to the Ontario Labour Relations Board for consent to terminate the agreement.[46] If both parties do not consent, however, the contract cannot be terminated, and pay equity would have to be done outside the normal collective-bargaining process.

If negotiating pay equity as part of normal collective bargaining is possible, it is not clear whether the bargaining agent gains the powerful tool of the strike during the negotiating process. Given that the act sets out a procedure to resolve disputes arising over the plan, it may be that the union will be prohibited from striking over pay equity. If it does engage in legal strike action as a result of a breakdown in negotiations over pay equity, it is possible that the union would be found not to be bargaining in 'good faith'[47] once the Pay Equity Commission resolved the dispute via an order.[48] Also, if pay equity were merged with normal collective-agreement bargaining, the pay equity plan may have to be ratified by the members of the bargaining unit, if requested by the employer[49] or if required by the union constitution, in order to avoid both bad-faith bargaining and unfair-representation[50] charges under Ontario's Labour Relations Act.

Perhaps the most important provision in the Pay Equity Act with respect to collective bargaining is section 13(10), which states that a pay equity plan that is negotiated by the employer and the union 'prevails over all relevant collective agreements and the adjustments to rates of compensation required by the plan shall be deemed to be incorporated into and form part of the relevant collective agreements.' One assumes that 'all relevant collective agreements' in this clause refers to adjustments being incorporated only into those agreements that contain wage rates for female job classes receiving pay equity adjustments and not into the agreements containing wage rates for comparable male job classes.[51] Precisely how these 'adjustments to rates of compensation' will be incorporated into a collective agreement is unclear. It may be that whether pay equity negotiations are part of normal collective bargaining or not, the adjustments that are owing to female job classes would replace the job rates for those classes that have been negotiated during the normal bargaining process.

One practical problem that will emerge when trying to incorporate adjustments to rates of compensation into a collective agreement is that collective agreements do not contain 'rates of compensation' but instead have 'wage rates' and separate benefit provisions that are not costed for each individual. Although 'compensation' is defined in the Pay Equity Act as including both a wage and a benefits component,[52] 'rate of compensation' is not a defined term, but is used only in the course of defining 'job rate' as the 'highest rate of compensation.' So, when incorporating the adjustment into the collective agreement, is it simply a matter of adding the dollar value of the adjustment to the wage rate for each person in the female job class?

Since it is likely to take at least four of five years to achieve pay equity,[53] what happens when the job rates of the male comparators in another bargaining unit increase as a result of normal bargaining *before* the pay equity process is complete? Do female job rates pegged to these increased male job rates now have what could be seen as a 'new target'? Furthermore, what is the status of normal collective bargaining for female job classes both during pay equity negotiations and especially after it has been established that some of these female job classes are entitled to a pay equity adjustment? Such basic questions remain unanswered both in the act itself and in the Pay Equity Commission's *Guidelines*.

It is important to note that the so-called internal relativities established in negotiated wage grids as well as the hierarchical relationship between various job classes could be altered by the pay equity evaluations. For example, job class A that made more than job class B under the collective agreement could, after pay equity adjustments have been calculated, make less than B. Since it is not possible to know in advance how dramatic the results of a 'gender-neutral' evaluation will be, it would perhaps be best to undertake the pay equity process first, and then engage in normal collective bargaining to bring upset internal wage relativities into harmony. In doing so, however, a feminist litigant would insist that this not be done in such a way as to return the wage relationship to the gender-biased status quo.

As mentioned, female job classes must first be compared with male job classes within their bargaining-unit plan. If no appropriate comparator is found, a search can be made 'throughout the establishment.'[54] Thus female job classes in one bargaining unit may end up being compared with job classes in another bargaining unit or with job classes outside any bargaining unit. Similarly non-union female job classes could be matched with male comparators that are within bargaining units. Given the extensive segregation of our labour market and the comparatively low rate of unionization of women workers in Ontario (about 22 per cent for the private sector: Ontario, *Green Paper* 1985, 39) it is likely that many, if not most, unorganized women will be seeking comparators among male job classes in bargaining units. The result of such comparisons could be that non-unionized female job classes become entitled to the job rates of unionized male job classes. These union/non-union comparisons could be perceived as unfair in that people not in unions become entitled to wages and benefits[55] that have been bargained for, and even struck for, by those in bargaining units. One must keep in mind, however, that there have been many barriers to women becoming unionized. Some of these have to do with established unions not actively organizing service-sector jobs where women predominate. There have also been difficulties in getting a first collective agreement (Forrest 1986). Whether or not these barriers justify the process of giving unorganized female job classes the wages and benefits of organized male job classes is an open question.

Bargaining Strength and the Value of Work

As mentioned earlier, *after* pay equity has been achieved in an establishment, an employer may argue that job rates that have been pegged together for the purpose of pay equity may be separated on the grounds of 'bargaining strength.'[56] This claim, of course, is more likely to be made in regard to male-dominated bargaining units than to female-dominated units. What is strange about this provision is that past bargaining strength is essentially ignored by the act, whereas future bargaining strength is honoured. One wonders what policy is being fostered by this legislation. Why can an unorganized female job class become entitled to the wages and benefits produced by the bargaining strength of a male-dominated union? Is the legislative intent to encourage those in female jobs to employ more bargaining strength to maintain equitable wages? Is it a 'one-shot' chance for some female workers to catch up after which they are 'on their own'? Such a scheme appears to be contrary to the requirement in the act that pay equity be 'established and maintained.'[57]

The ambiguous stance the Pay Equity Act takes on the issue of bargaining strength is further complicated by the explicit assumption to male job classes on the basis of the 'value' of their work that can be measured by a job-evaluation scheme. Since it is acknowledged that bargaining strength may play a role in eventually paying certain male job classes more, even though they would theoretically 'not be worth it' according to the job evaluation used, surely this is proof that bargaining strength, and not 'measurable worth,' was at least partially responsible for existing male wage rates.

Ignoring past bargaining strength, while accepting that job worth can be measured by job evaluation employing the four factors of skill, effort, responsibility, and working conditions, is to suggest that some male job classes are 'overpaid.' No doubt, pressure will be applied to red-circle male job classes that produce a low 'value score.' It is also likely that employers will argue during wage negotiations that having to pay female job classes the same wages and benefits will invariably mean lower settlements for male job classes generally. Such trends may cause a growing 'gender gap' in the labour movement over the issue of pay equity.

The legislation places a great deal of faith in the ability of 'gender-neutral' job evaluation to capture the value of work, while literature on this topic would suggest that such faith is unwarranted. For decades, job evaluation has primarily been an employer-initiated process that many unions have either actively resisted or passively allowed – only to subject them to extensive policy and reclassification grievances.[58]

The theory behind Ontario's Pay equity legislation is essentially to give the 'market value,' as established by men's work, to those doing equally evaluated women's work. An important assumption is made that the market does not operate to equitably set the wages for women's jobs in the same way that it does for men's.[59] For example, in answer to the question 'Doesn't pay equity ignore market forces?' one of Ontario's Pay Equity Commission's *Guidelines* responds: 'Pay equity emphasizes *job content* as the basis of which the pay for female-dominated jobs should be determined ... Pay equity does not disregard the market for male-dominated and gender-neutral jobs: it only addresses inequities within the company.'[60]

For the most part, job-evaluation systems have been used by employers, primarily in non-union settings, to ensure that their wages remain competitive with market rates and also to maintain internally acceptable wage 'relativities' among employee groups. They have also been used, again in non-unionized workplaces, to evaluate employee performance and establish individualized compensation relationships rather than ones based on collective bargaining. Unions have largely fought performance evaluation and, indeed, since pay equity is interested in evaluating 'the job, not the person,' this aspect of job evaluation has no role whatsoever to play in the pay equity process.

Given the traditional uses of job evaluation, one could argue that it is an inappropriate mechanism to employ in the collective-bargaining context. There has been long-standing resistance to job evaluation by unions, who have deliberately developed strategies to increase their wages and benefits that have emphasized bargaining strength. That is not to say they have refused to negotiate wages within the framework of the employee' classification system that has used job evaluation; however, most bargaining agents have declined involvement in the construction of such systems and, as mentioned, have had input into classification primarily via the grievance process. Since the required compensation adjustments and the pay equity plan have become part of the collective agreement, there may be an option open for bargaining agents to exercise minimal involvement initially and become more active via grievance arbitration. However, it is not clear whether the members of a bargaining unit have the right to grieve details of the pay equity plan. After all, their union negotiated and signed the plan in order for it to become part of the collective agreement. It is certainly possible that an arbitrator would not find the matter a proper subject for arbitration. If female members of a bargaining unit felt that their male union leadership 'sold them out' during pay equity negotiations, it may be possible, as will be discussed, that they could take a complaint to the Pay Equity Commission and possibly even the Ontario Labour Relations Board.[61]

During pay equity bargaining, for the first time many unions in Ontario became involved in selecting a job-evaluation system. Given the penalties that could be forthcoming for non-compliance,[62] it may be that bargaining agents and employers will feel they have little choice but to negotiate which job-evaluation system should be used and proceed with the comparison process set out in the act. There are also likely to be negotiations about the status of job-evaluation results. For example, the employer may want the union to accept red-circling if 'overvaluation,' particularly of men's jobs, is revealed by the job-evaluation process. Although noting in the act suggests that accepting red-circling is necessary, job-evaluation systems have traditionally created new internal relationships among jobs that have resulted in some degree of red-circling. This issue is undoubtedly being carefully negotiated by the union, and it will indeed be interesting to see how the Pay Equity Commission's Hearings Tribunal settles this matter.

If the job evaluation does have a role to play in the pay equity arena, it is one in which it guides and supports negotiations at the bargaining table, rather than one in which it directs precise wage settlements. In the United States some well-known pay equity studies have been commissioned by unions to assess both the undervaluation of women's work and how the bargaining agent has represented their female members.[63] The studies are undertaken to encourage bargaining strategies directed at achieving equitable pay and not to bind the union and employer to a scheme of matching male and female job classes.

In Manitoba the public-service pay equity job-evaluation exercise did not involve a direct transfer of evaluation to the wage-setting arena, but operated only to guide the bargaining process. The Manitoba scheme requires all the unions of each public-sector employer to jointly bargain one plan. This necessitates that the process take place outside the context of normal collective bargaining. Here is a description of the role that job evaluation played in the Manitoba government's public service setting: 'We had agreed we were not involved in a mechanical or rigid "pay for points" exercise. There is no magic formula which can be fed into a computer to spit out solutions. Rather, we viewed the rating exercise as a means to give us the information on our gender-dominated classifications. That data then served as guidelines to the negotiating teams who bargained the adjustments' (Ellis-Grunfeld 1987, 231).

Scope of Bargaining a Pay Equity Plan

Whether negotiated with normal bargaining or not, it is unclear what type of pay equity plan will be acceptable under the terms of Ontario's Pay Equity Act. For example, does a plan have to be based on job comparisons, or can it be a system designed to raise the base rates of entry-level positions? Or, is it necessary to use the factors skill, effort, responsibility, and working conditions as required in the act?

Although it appears that bargaining pay equity plans are 'deemed to have been approved by the Commission'[64] once such a plan has been signed by the parties, individual members of the union may have the right to complain about it. It may, for example, be possible for them to launch a complaint against the union, alleging that it has breached the 'duty of fair representation'[65] because the bargained pay equity plan did not provide for an evaluation and comparison process as required by the Pay Equity Act. The likelihood of this type of complaint would undoubtedly increase if the pay equity plan was not ratified by those in the bargaining unit.

An individual or group of unionized employees may also have the right to complain by using section 22(1) to charge that the negotiated pay equity plan does not comply with the procedures clearly set out in the legislation. There is, after all, no provision allowing bargaining agents and employers to opt out of the operation of the act because of an agreement in which the issue was dealt with during collective bargaining.[66] Furthermore, it could also be argued that, according to the act, the parties shall not 'agree to a compensation practice' that would interfere with the establishment and maintenance of pay equity.[67] It should be noted that the achievement of pay equity in the legislation is specifically described in terms of job rates, job classes, and comparisons: 'For the purposes of this Act, pay equity is achieved when the job rate for the female job class that is the subject of the comparison is at least equal to the job rate for the male job class in the same establishment where the work performed in the two job classes is of equal or comparable value.'[68]

Given such precise language, it is unlikely that an alternative route can be taken to pay equity. Since it appears that a single disaffected unionized employee may be able to launch an anonymous challenge to the pay equity process, neither employers nor bargaining agents would be likely to risk undertaking a system of achieving pay equity that differed from the scheme in the act, unless they knew such deviation was considered acceptable. This question, of course, can be resolved only by the Pay Equity Commission's Hearings Tribunal.

Conclusion

As we can see, there are many legal, political, and technical issues that remain unresolved under Ontario's Pay Equity Act. Some of these issues are fundamental and touch on a bargaining agent's main role: negotiating wages. One could argue that this statute was drafted with little thought given to how it would operate, not only with current labour legislation, but, indeed more important, with long-standing traditions and practices in collective bargaining. The proof, of course, of whether pay equity legislation is effective will be through a thorough assessment of the wage patterns before and after the implementation. In such an assessment, careful attention must be given to whether there is actually more money being paid out in wages by the employer. If pay equity, at best, proves simply to be a redistribution of wages from those doing men's work to those doing women's work, it will have to be addressed politically and in the collective-bargaining arena. If, at worst, pay equity leads to a rationalizing and equalizing of wages in a way that actually *reduces* wages, the potentially serious conflict between male and female workers must be solved by focusing on strategies that emphasize wage solidarity.

NOTES

1 Pay Equity Act (PEA), Statutes of Ontario, Chapter 34, 1987. Hereafter cited as PEA
2 PEA, sections 11 and 18
3 PEA, section 4(1)
4 PEA, section 14
5 The term 'establishment' is defined in a rather unusual manner in the act. It means 'all employees of an employer employed in a geographic division.' A 'geographic division' is a unit established by Ontario's Territorial Divisions Act and does not coincide with the standard notion of workplace. The Territorial Divisions Act simply divides up the province into counties, territorial districts, or regional municipalities. Employers and unions may agree, for the purposes of the pay equity plan covering the bargaining unit, to expand the 'establishment,' but they cannot agree to reduce the size to a smaller unit.
6 PEA, section 14(2)
7 PEA, section 32(4)
8 The extent to which those in unions can complain about a plan that has been negotiated by their bargaining agent is unclear. This issue will be discussed later.
9 Labour Relations Act (OLRA), Revised Statutes of Ontario, 1980, Chapter 228; as amended by: 1983, Chapter 42; 1984, Chapter 34; 1986, Chap-

ters 17 and 64, s. 23. Hereafter cited as OLRA. Note that, although we are primarily referring to bargaining units under this statute, the comments would similarly relate to most other public-sector labour legislation in the province.

10 OLRA, section 1(4)

11 OLRA, section 63

12 OLRA, sections 5, 7 and 8

13 OLRA, sections 56, 57, and 58

14 OLRA, section 62

15 PEA, section 1, for the definitions of both 'establishment' and 'geographic division'

16 PEA, section 14 and 15

17 The term 'job class' is defined in PEA, section 1, as those positions that have 'similar' duties, responsibilities, qualifications, and recruiting procedures; and 'the same' compensation schedule, salary grade, or range of salary rates.

18 There is some flexibility in the identification of job classes since the act allows consideration to be given to both 'historical incumbency' and 'gender stereotypes of fields of work.' See PEA, subsection 1(5).

19 PEA, section 12

20 PEA, section 5. It is interesting to note that these four factors are also used in the 'equal pay for equal work' provisions of Ontario's Employment Standards Act, Revised Statutes of Ontario 1980, Chapter 137, Section 33.

21 In section 1 of the act, the term 'job rate' is defined as 'the highest rate of compensation for a job class.' The term 'compensation' is also defined and refers to 'all payments and benefits' that 'entitle the person to be paid a fixed or ascertainable amount.' Thus, there may be negotiations over how this figure is to be calculated.

22 PEA, section 6

23 PEA, section 6

24 PEA, section 9(3), states that, when a female job class is entitled to an increase, 'all positions in the job class shall receive the same adjustment in dollar terms.'

25 Note that no one has to be actually earning the job rate; however, it has to be a potentially available to each person in the job class.

26 PEA, sections 13(4) and (5)

27 PEA, section 6

28 PEA, section 13

29 PEA, section 8

30 PEA, section 13(2)(e)

31 PEA, section 14(2)

32 PEA, section 1(2)

33 PEA, section 8(2)

34 Part II of the PEA

35 Part III of the PEA

36 PEA, section 21(1)

37 See PEA, section 1

38 PEA, section 10(c) and (d)

39 PEA, section 20 (1)

40 It appears that this is the case because the act explicitly states that, if the employer is going to negotiate a pay equity plan, he or she must notify the bargaining agent, while the act is silent on how the job classes and so on are decided. See PEA, section 20

41 See PEA, sections 4(2) and section 6

42 Prince Edward Island's Pay Equity Act, section 13(3)

43 Manitoba's Pay Equity Act, Chapter P13, R.S.M., 1985

44 Such would be the case simply because all of the collective agreements with one public-sector employer, such as a university, hospital, or school-board, would not conclude at the same time. Furthermore, the Manitoba act does not require, as Ontario's does, that the necessary compensation adjustments be built into the collective agreement.

45 PEA, section 10

46 Section 52(3), OLRA, Chapter 228, R.S.O., 1980

47 PEA, section 14(2)

48 The dispute may not be resolved until the Pay Equity Hearings Tribunal decides on the matter, since both parties have the right of appeal to the tribunal from orders of a commission's review officer. See PEA, subsections 23(4) and 24(6).

49 OLRA, section 40. It should be noted that the minister of labour can also, on the grounds of 'public interest' direct that a ratification vote be taken. OLRA, section 39.

50 OLRA, section 68

51 This is not clear since the matter is complicated by the notion of 'bargaining strength,' which we will discuss later. Since bargaining strength can be used by employers to argue for the separation of matched male and female comparators once pay equity has been achieved in the establishment, one wonders what happens *before* pay equity is achieved. Can the matched job classes be separated by normal bargaining?

52 PEA, section 1

53 This estimate is based on the experience in the United States and Manitoba. Manitoba, for example, legislated the completion date for adjustments to be four years from the beginning of the adjustment period. The Ontario government has also estimated that pay equity in the public service would take approximately four years.

54 PEA, section 6(5)

55 The definition of 'job rate' in the act includes both wages and benefits. See PEA, section 1.

56 PEA, subsection 8(2)

57 PEA, section 7(1)

58 The notable exception that is regularly mentioned in the literature is the United Steelworkers of America's long-standing involvement with the joint union-management job-classification system called the Co-operative Wage Study.

59 The classic example of this, of course, is nursing. Despite a serious, long-term shortage of nurses, the wages in nursing have not risen proportionately.

60 See the Pay Equity Commission, 'Pay Equity Implementation Series #1,' Toronto, March 1988, p. 1:7.

61 This would take the form of a 'duty of fair representation' complaint under section 68 of the OLRA.

62 PEA, section 26

63 For example, see the often-cited study done for a public-sector union in 'a large industrial eastern state': David Pierson, Karen Shallcross, and Russell Johannesson, 'A Policy-Capturing Application in a Union Setting,' Helen Remick, ed., in Comparable Worth & Wage Discrimination (Philadelphia: Temple University Press, 1984), pp. 118–37.

64 PEA, section 14(5)

65 Section 68, OLRA; this phrase is actually in the margin note of the section.

66 Such a provision, for instance, is contained in the federal Labour Relations Act, concerning the issue of technological change.

67 PEA, subsections 7(1) and (2); see note 1.

68 PEA, section 6(1)

PART THREE

The Politics of Implementation

7 What Counts as Skill? Reflections on Pay Equity

Jane Gaskell

Much of the ideological power of pay equity lies in its promise of a process that substitutes objectivity for politics, technical expertise for power relations. A pay equity committee judges the worth of a job by assigning points on an agreed-upon scale. Numbers seem objective and neutral. The scale is based on criteria that are shared within the committee and can be communicated to the sceptical. Where collective bargaining, the market, and employers' decisions have demonstrably disadvantaged women, a technical process that insists on 'unbiased' assessments of the characteristics of jobs, and, therefore, of their worth, seems enormously promising.

But is the promise real or illusory? Can employers, or management consultants, or even teams of workers and managers, come up with assessments that are not biased? Can assessments of jobs be done objectively, without a political point of view implicit in the analysis? The simple answer is no. Any rating scale, any determination of job value is based in judgments that can be politically contested. The job-evaluation process involved in pay equity looks like a technical process, but it is a political one.

This kind of argument is not a new one for feminist analysis. Revealing the hidden ideological underpinnings of 'objective assessments' has been grist for the feminist academic mill. Feminist scholarship has continually pointed to the ways in which what have been described as taken-for-granted, neutral, and objective judgments are actually partial, if not completely wrong and misguided. Feminist analysis has shown that what has been taken as objectivity and political neutrality has too often been simply what powerful males think and say. 'Subjectivity' and 'politicization' enter in when someone with less power raises questions. This general lesson applies to the determination of pay equity.

Pay equity committees are asked to evaluate jobs on the basis of four criteria – skill, effort, responsibility, and working conditions. My academic work has been directed at one of these issues, the historical and social processes that have shaped our evaluations of skill. My argument, in short, is that there is no one correct, objective version of how much skill is involved in doing a job. In making statements about and evaluations of skill, we stand in our historical time and place, in our culture. We stand in traditions of thought that have been thoroughly dominated by men. And we come face to face with basic questions of value, of power, of women's place in the world. When people overlook women's skills, devalue them, give them low ratings, it is not a technical glitch, but a reflection of the status and power women have not had in the world.

Women have not had the power to insist upon the recognition and value of their skills in the workplace. Their lack of ability to define their work as skilled is not simply something that has occurred in people's heads, but is a social process that has had institutional consequences in relation to educational qualifications and opportunities for vocational training, as well as in relation to wages.

The ways this works are various. Women's skills have often been considered part of their femaleness, and therefore not to be counted. Being polite and helpful and 'attractive' in particular ways are learned, but considered personality, not skill. Many of the things that women do at work tend to be taken for granted in this way, and not seen as skills.

When skills are recognized, evaluating their relative complexity and worth is equally complicated. Are technical skills more valuable or more complex than social skills? What is the relative importance of the ability to manage social interaction, the ability to put up with routine tasks, the ability to analyse problems? Do supply and demand determine the value of a skill, even if they do not determine the value of a job? Is it a question of how well the enterprise could function without a particular skill? Can we measure the use-value and the exchange value of a skill? Different things will count in different circumstances. Different people will count different things.

The question of learning time as a measure of skill is also much more ambiguous than it appears. A job that takes longer to learn appears to be more skilled. But whose learning time, under what circumstances, should we take into account? The actual length of time someone is required to attend a training program to get a credential is likely to be different from the amount of time it actually takes anyone to learn the job.

The process of evaluating skills is a highly political, contextual, and ideological one. 'Skill' is a category that gives status and importance to work in common parlance and in wage negotiations. Skill categories are ideological categories, used to justify and challenge existing hierarchies at work. Indeed, some would argue that skill designations are nothing more than power relations expressed in the language of skill. The more important, highly paid, powerful work must by definition be more 'skilled.' We treat mental work as more skilled than manual work, reflecting the power managers have over manual workers. Characteristics of powerful positions – autonomy, supervision of less powerful workers, making judgments for others – are what we count as higher-order skills. Our ideas about skill are continually constructed and reconstructed in the politics of the workplace. Attaching numbers to it does not change this fundamental fact.

Skill and Pay Equity

A pay equity policy using the most conventional definition of skill would increase women's salaries substantially. We have seen a few settlements that do this, and some data on the labour force indicate why. Years of education and training is perhaps the simplest and most conventional indicator of skill. Women in the labour force have more education than men in the labour force, even though women are paid much less (Picot 1980; Gaskell 1982; Boyd 1982). If women were paid for their education as much as men are paid for theirs, women would be much better off.

When more complex measures of skill are used to compare men's and women's occupations, we continue to find that women are paid less than men for the same skills. Women earn less than men, when their jobs have equivalent requirements for education, experience, skill, and working conditions (Oppenheimer 1970; Englund et al. 1988). Several studies have found that the percentage of females in an occupation depresses wages even after measures of skill demands, as described in the *Dictionary of Occupational Titles*, are controlled (McLaughlin 1978; Englund and McLaughlin 1979; Treiman and Hartman 1981; Englund and Norris 1985). Englund (1982) concludes, based on these ratings, that 'females actually have an advantageous occupational skill distribution on balance,' meaning that the skills women are more likely to have (social and literacy skills, by and large) are skills that in the labour force as a whole tend to be rewarded with higher wages than the skills men have (physical strength, in particular). This advantage is offset by the combination of extreme occupational segregation and the depressing effect on wages of the concentration of women in an occupation.

This analysis is immensely valuable in showing that one major problem for women is in the way conventionally recognized skills are rewarded at work. With the same education and official skill level as a man, a woman gets paid less. Occupations that employ a large number of women pay less for the same skills than do occupations that employ a large number of men. This is the argument for pay equity, and it is a powerful one.

The question that arises in this kind of analysis is whether by controlling for skill we are controlling for another variable that is biased against women, so that the fact of controlling for it underestimates the amount of discrimination, explaining it away when it should continue to be the focus of attention. Will this kind of analysis justify gender inequalities that remain after pay equity committees have ruled on how jobs are unequally skilled? As Englund puts it,

regression analysis can tell us the relative returns to the job characteristics of heavy lifting and finger dexterity. Employers may pay a premium for heavy lifting rather than painstaking finger dexterity precisely because heavy lifting is done by men and finger dexterity is more often required in women's jobs. But a method that puts variables tapping finger dexterity and lifting into a regression to tap whether they are part of the policy of wage setting will not count pay differences between predominantly male lifting jobs and female jobs requiring finger dexterity as discriminatory. That is, the coefficient on sex composition ... will be determined net of the effects of these differences. (1985 p. 638)

If a skill is valued because it has been associated with men's work, and if we are not critical of these traditional judgments, gender inequity will get built into wage rates more securely than ever.

Does controlling for 'skill' really control for discrimination? This is the nub of the argument, and one that needs to be carefully considered before we allow that skill ratings are a legitimate way to determine wages. Pay equity policies would have us take 'skill' as a legitimate criterion for judging differences in the wages attached to jobs, and there is evidence that this practice would benefit women. The further question is whether by accepting existing notions of skill as legitimate criteria for differentiating among jobs, we aren't explaining away some of the problem. For, as I have argued above, skill is not an easily identified and quantified characteristic of a job, which can unproblematically be rated on a scale from one to ten and entered into an equation.

What Counts as a Skill?

In the sociological literature, Braverman (1974) has been an important stimulus to rethinking what counts as skilled or unskilled work. He points out that, according to census categories, work today is considerably more skilled than work a century ago. The census mirrors the assumption that life today is more complicated, as technology is more complicated, and that people have obtained more education in response to the requirements of the more complex jobs they do. 'The idea that the changing conditions of industrial and office work require an increasingly "better trained", "better educated" and thus "upgraded" working population is an almost universally accepted proposition in popular and academic discourse,' he wrote in 1974 (p. 424).

Braverman notes that working with machines was what originally set skilled factory workers apart from unskilled labourers in the U.S. census. As an extension of this line of thinking, the census classified drivers of motorized vehicles as skilled and drivers of horse-drawn vehicles as unskilled. But Braverman comments,

in the circumstances of an earlier day, when a largely rural population learned the arts of managing horses as part of the process of growing up, while few as yet knew how to operate motorized vehicles, it might have made sense to characterize the former as part of the common heritage and thus no skill at all, while driving, as a learned ability, would have been thought of as a 'skill'. Today, it would be more proper to regard those who are able to drive vehicles as unskilled in that respect at least, while those who can care for, harness and manage a team of horses are certainly the possessors of a marked and uncommon ability. There is certainly little reason to suppose that the ability to drive a motor vehicle is more demanding, requires longer training or habituation time, and thus represents a higher or intrinsically more rewarding skill. (p. 430)

Census categories reflect common ideological assumptions and patterns of informal learning abroad in the land – assumptions that, as technology gets more complex, jobs get more complex; that, as education levels increase, the jobs workers do become more skilled; that everyone can drive a car. What we take to be a noteworthy skill is fundamentally shaped by what is taken for granted in the society, what the social context is, where and how we learn to do something.

Having pointed out that the government classification system does not accurately describe skill levels, Braverman reverts to his own definition of skill, although he has difficulty describing it in one phrase. He sees skills as 'traditionally bound up with craft mastery,' and, as he indicates above, tied to training time and the 'commonness' of skills. He assumes this definition is shared with his readers and validated by common sense. He is uneasy with 'relativistic or contemporary notions' (p. 430) of skill that degrade the concept by having it refer to those 'able to perform repetitive tasks with manual dexterity.' His political concern for craft workers (he was a coppersmith, pipe-fitter, and sheetmetal worker, among other things) shapes the way he begins to think about skill himself. He points to craft skills, not to the interpersonal and social skills involved in being a waitress or a receptionist. His experience shapes his perceptions – understandably. None of us can avoid it.

Braverman's analysis of the shifting definition of skill suggests the importance of inquiry into the social processes involved in producing the shifting skill labels. He did not explore gender issues, but others have. Margaret Mead wrote, 'One aspect of this social evaluation of different types of labour is the differentiated prestige of men's activities and women's activities. Whatever men do – even if it is dressing dolls for religious ceremonies – is more prestigious than what women do and is treated as a higher achievement.' Being treated as a 'higher' achievement can easily translate in a more scientific world, into being considered a 'higher' skill. Mental labour is more prestigious than manual labour. Science is more prestigious than caring for children. Giving directions is more prestigious than working out what they mean and following them closely. It is not clear that one is more difficult than another. These are cultural values. Things associated with dominant values and with power are counted as higher skills.

Phillips and Taylor (1980) have pursued this argument in relation to men and women: 'The classification of women's jobs as unskilled and men's jobs as skilled or semi-skilled frequently bears little relation to the actual amount of training or ability required for them. Skill definitions are saturated with sexual bias. The work of women is often deemed inferior simply because it is women who do it. Women workers carry into the workplace their status as subordinate individuals and this status comes to define the work they do' (p. 79).

Judgments about women's skills are affected profoundly by the social context, by social cues that give them meaning. A secretary may be composing letters and running the office, but, because she is 'only' a secretary, the skills involved cannot be too complex. Phillips and Taylor would allow the amount of 'ability' required to legitimately differentiate among skill levels. But the same social processes mean that judgments of ability will be 'saturated with sexual bias.' Regression equations are able to show which abilities are rewarded most highly by employers today, but to build a politics on these judgments is to accept employers' existing practices as a standard for equity.

Providing an account of a worker's abilities is not a neutral descriptive process. The terms of the account are highly conditioned by the social context in which it takes place and by the social purposes to which it will be put. Labelling and valuing particular abilities involves an ongoing historical struggle between workers and employers, and among different groups of workers.

And women have not fared well in these struggles. Barrett (1980) argues: 'Women have frequently failed to establish recognition of the skills required by their work, and have consequently been in a weak bargaining position in a divided and internally competitive work force ... we need to know precisely how and why some groups of workers succeed in establishing definitions of their work as skilled' (p. 166).

This more thorough-going recognition of the social and political content of skill categories is one feminists must embrace. To revalue women's skills involves seeing the ways that our knowledge and abilities have been taken for granted. It involves fighting for the revaluing of women's work, because it is important and necessary work.

Education as Skill

Views of skill are based not only in abstract constructions of what we value and what we take for granted. They are based quite concretely in the length of educational preparation required for a job. More educated workers are more skilled. Workers who have spent longer in training programs are more skilled. Questions of value are given a material form in educational requirements and training programs.

The *Canadian Classification and Dictionary of Occupations* (CCDO) (1971) is the state's attempt to systematically 'classify and define occupational activity in the world of work.' It expresses the skill level of a job partly in terms of general educational development (GED) and specific vocational preparation (SVP). GED measures the levels of numeracy, literacy, comprehension, and reading skills necessary for performing a job. While it is described as 'not identical with the number of years of schooling required,' it is 'assumed to result from participation in the education system.' The SVP, which is closely correlated with the GED rating, is based on the 'time necessary for acquiring specific skills.' This measure is estimated from time in 'vocational training, apprenticeships, in-plant and on-the-job training, as well as from experience in other occupations.'

Even those who point to the ideological content of skill ratings (Braverman, Phillips, and Taylor) tend to rely on time spent in training as a legitimate way to differentiate between skilled and unskilled work. Time is a useful measure for administrators, labour negotiators, or social scientists trying to come up with ratings, as it can be turned into a number and used to compare things that are actually quite unlike. Time becomes a mode of exchange of value, like money, and it creates the same problem of losing sight of what it actually represents and how it is produced. Thus, time in training is turned into skill ratings, reifying skill into a undimensional 'thing.'

Taking training time as a sign of skill assumes that the length of training depends on the difficulty, complexity, and breadth of understanding necessary for performing the work. There is a long tradition in the sociology of education that treats skill in just this way, as something accumulated through years of formal education and justifying a claim to a higher-paying job.

But Braverman for one points out that increased educational levels cannot be used as a measure of skill upgrading in the work-force. 'A complete picture of the functions and functioning of education in the United States and other capitalist countries would require a thorough historical study of the manner in which the present standards came into being, and how they were related, at each step of their formation, to the social forces of the society at large. But even a sketch of the recent period suffices to show that many causes, most of them bearing no direct relationship to the educational requirements of the job structure, have been at work' (p. 437).

Changes in labour legislation, in the unemployment rate, in state investment in educational institutions, and in employers' use of education as a screening device are among some of the important factors that have increased the educational levels of workers. None of these means that the skill levels of jobs have changed.

How are we to determine the amount of training 'necessary' to an 'adequate' performance of a job? Some people learn faster than others. Some employers are more demanding. Some people will already know a lot of what they need, because they have picked training up informally. The length and form that training will take are decided through political and economic struggle. Collins (1979) comments: 'The "system" does not "need" or "demand" a certain kind of performance; it "needs" what it gets, because "it" is nothing more than a slip shod way of talking about the way things happen to be at the time. How hard people work, and with what dexterity and cleverness, depends on how much other people can require them to do, and on how much they can dominate other people' (p. 54).

Lots of different kinds of training will do to prepare people for their jobs. No single version is 'necessary.' What training programs do do is control the supply of labour and certify its skill. Turner has argued that workers are considered skilled or unskilled 'according to whether or not entry to their occupations is deliberately restricted and not in the first place according to the nature of the occupation itself' (1962, 184). Barrett (1980) echoes this observation: 'Training and recruitment may be highly controlled and skill rendered inaccessible for the purposes of retaining the differentials and privilege of the labour aristocracy' (p. 168).

Collins (1979) documents how some groups have successfully struggled to restrict entry through educational requirements, while others have not. Doctors and engineers were able to insist on university preparation for their work; nurses, child-care workers, and carpenters were not. Tool-and-die workers were able to maintain their apprenticeships on the job; clerical workers were not. Women's occupations – child care and clerical work, for example – are much more likely to be open to people with a wide range of educational and vocational backgrounds, and therefore to be treated as unskilled occupations. Women have not had the political might to keep wages in their occupations up by restricting entry to a narrow band of suitably credentialled workers.

There is evidence that many of the skills learned at school or in formal training programs have little direct importance on the job (Berg 1970; Hall and Carlton 1977). Educational attainment may act as a 'signal' or a 'screen,' without imparting any necessary skills (Spence 1973). The time training takes can vary for the same job, depending on which country a worker is in, or which employer she works for. Requirements for training change when the actual skills involved in the work do not. The training of teachers is an example. It has increased over the years as the demand for teachers eased and as the general educational levels of the population went up. Changes in the skills 'required' for a classroom have been produced by social changes extending well beyond the 'needs' of children.

The provision of on-the-job training is also negotiated. Women have been less able to get formal training after they are hired, as they are assumed to be short-term workers. If employers believe that women really belong in and will therefore return to the home, investment in their training is considered wasteful. As a result, women must often pick up skills in more informal ways, on the job or in the family. Opportunities for mobility through education are not built into their jobs. The difference between advancement and training opportunities for secretaries (women) and for general-purpose clerks (men or women) is the most obvious example.

In other words, the correspondence between schooling requirements and work demands need not be very strong, and certainly does not need to be based on 'skill.' While there undoubtedly are instances where training does develop necessary skills, this must not be assumed to be the case. The form that specific skill training and vocational education will take has been one of the major areas of struggle, within the public-school system as well as in the workplace and in state-run training programs.

And it is clear that training for women's work is organized in ways that are different from training for men's work. Women have been less able to insist on licensing and regulation of training, and have been less able to get on-the-job training (Wolf and Rosenfeld 1978). Rather than being an indication of skill differences in men's and women's jobs, these differences reflect the fact that the jobs have been filled predominantly by one sex or the other.

An Example: The Skills in Clerical Jobs

I will briefly illustrate some of these issues with reference to clerical work. Clerical work is an interesting example because, today, it is an overwhelmingly female occupation. It accounts for the employment of about a third of the female labour force. Secretary, typist, and receptionist are some of the jobs most fully identified with women. Yet the skills involved in these jobs are unclear, unrecognized, and learned haphazardly. Entry into the occupation is unregulated and unstandardized. Paying for existing educational levels, skills, and training would clearly help many women who work in clerical jobs achieve higher pay. But to recognize the worth of clerical jobs would entail more than this. It would entail recognizing the complexity and importance of the tasks that are done.

a) Historical Issues in Clerical Work
Clerical occupations were overwhelmingly male at the turn of the century; thereafter they rapidly became female. This transition offers an opportunity to see some of the discussions that took place as the general category 'clerical work' changed its relative wages, status, skill designation, prospects for advancement, and educational requirements.

The class position of clerks in the last half of the nineteenth century was marginally bourgeois. Incomes were higher than for blue-collar work (Lowe 1982; Coombs 1978). Relations between employers and clerks were based on considerable autonomy for the clerk. 'The only way to be sure that a bookkeeper or clerk had tallied a column of numbers accurately was for the employer to repeat the task himself,' Davies (1983, 21) points out. An apprenticeship system offered possibilities for promotion and responsibility, although there was a good deal of variation in how this worked.

Nineteenth-century employers and clerks saw little value in formal business training in the public schools, approving experience as the best teacher (Atherton 1952). But some schooling was useful, and the school curriculum was tailored to the expectation that many students would go into business positions. Lockwood (1958, 20) quotes the following requirements for a clerk in London in 1878: 'A little instruction in Latin, and probably a very little in Greek, a little in Geography, a little in Science, a little in arithmetic and bookkeeping, a little in French, with such a sprinkling of English reading as may enable a lad to distinguish Milton from Shakespeare are considered enough.' These requirements reflect the secondary-school curriculum of the time. Bookkeeping and penmanship were central to a public-school education.

In the late nineteenth century, office work expanded rapidly. As it expanded, jobs were differentiated, supervision was increased, working conditions and rewards deteriorated, and significant parts of the work were feminized. In Canada, the number of clerical workers more than doubled, from 2 per cent of the workforce in 1891 to 5 per cent in 1901, and in 1911 almost doubled again, to 9 per cent. The percentage of clerical workers who were women rose from 14 per cent in 1891 to 22 per cent in 1901, and to 33 per cent in 1911 (Lowe 1980).

Around the turn of the century, the typewriter introduced a new technical skill into the office. It was not immediately clear what its status was. Who would learn typing, and how would its relationship to the rest of the jobs in the office be worked out? Possibilities we no longer consider were quite plausible at the time. An advertisement from Shaw's Business School in Toronto in 1902 maintained that stenography was appropriate for men as a stepping-stone into management positions: 'To young men we wish to place special stress upon the excellent opportunities presented to them in the work of a stenographer. It is not only a congenial and profitable occupation in itself, but the intimate acquaintance with the business which they must necessarily acquire is very often the means of securing rapid promotion to positions of greater responsibility and trust.' And typing, said Shaw's, 'may well be considered a necessary qualification of every aspirant for a position in the commercial field' (Shaw College 1902).

Even when stenographic skills became identified with a distinct group of female office workers, their relative 'skill' status was not immediately clear. Lowe (1980, 377) comments on the potentially advantageous position of stenographers: 'Mechanization afforded considerable socioeconomic status and craft like work to a select group of female clerks. Early stenographers closely approximated the ideal of craft work, as evident in the range of their skills and their greater mastery and control over the work process.'

Stenographers earned relatively high wages to begin with, substantially more than teachers and industrial workers (Lowe 1982; Coombs 1978; Marks 1984, 45). It was pointed out in an advertisement aimed at women from Hamilton Commercial College in 1885 that stenographic positions 'require less arduous work and are better paid than teaching in public schools' (Marks 1984). In 1892, Brockville Business College pointed to examples of teachers who had taken their courses and become stenographers at wage rates double what they earned as teachers (Marks 1984).

However, as we know, wages for typists and stenographers fell relative to those for other workers, and the jobs became identified with women. In 1891, 65 per cent of typists and stenographers were women. By 1901, this proportion reached 80 per cent; by 1911, 85 per cent; and, by 1931, 95 per cent (Marks 1984). The skills involved in the work were revalued downwards. An ambiguous situation was given a clear meaning, which we now take for granted. Typing and secretarial work are low-level skills.

The process of defining skill took place in some very concrete economic, social, and political conditions. Women competed in a segmented, lower-paying labour market. Women were considered less suitable for management and for training because of their gender and their primary location in the family. Women were not well organized into unions. Hiring policies and guidelines for promotion and training explicitly disadvantaged them. The civil-service commission became alarmed at the potential deterioration in the number of training positions for men, and limited women to the third (lowest) category of clerical positions, whatever their examination results (Archibald 1970). Thus gender, not skill, was built into the very shape of the clerical hierarchy as it emerged. Women's skills were explicitly discounted because women had them.

Despite the official relegation of women to low-level, less 'skilled' positions, women continued to perform duties that went well beyond their job descriptions. Marks (1984, 83, Table 3) calculates that one-third of the women employed as stenographers and typists in the Ontario government were performing executive or supervisory work, either in combination with their clerical tasks or alone, between 1895 and 1911. The lack of collective organization of clerical workers meant they were unable to insist on having this fact recognized, or to restrict entry and exert much influence on the form of training that emerged.

For changes in training took place alongside changes in the definition of the work. Formal clerical training expanded dramatically in the last half of the nineteenth century. Private business schools offered credentialling for all, a process that quickly devalued the training they provided. Although the Business Education Association was founded in 1896 to combat abuses, it was too late to reverse the pattern of offering business training of variable quality to all who wanted it and could pay.

Public-school education for the office also expanded rapidly. At the turn of the century, the course of studies in the public high school was differentiated so that commercial education became a separate, lower-status program, a program teaching typing and stenography to young women headed for office jobs. Clerical knowledge moved from being mainstream, part of everyone's education along with Latin, to being part of a lower-status curriculum. Although industrial education was also separated out in a lower-status program, it bore quite a different relationship to labour-market entry. In order to qualify for a job in carpentry or sheet-metal work or drafting, a young man had to go through a formal apprenticeship, a combination of on-the-job experience and specific education controlled by employers and unions.

Clerical training developed progressively lower status as it was feminized and expanded. This was contended, not predetermined, but women were not able to insist on the recognition of their skills. Today we live with institutions that were formed through these struggles, and continue to communicate the low status of clerical skills.

b) Contemporary Versions of Skill in Clerical Work

Today, clerical work remains an area where skills are not recognized, where women experience the disjuncture between what they do and what others see. Pringle (1988) notes that secretaries are defined more by who they are (women), and by their relation to a boss (helpmate and subordinate), than by what they do. There are few agreed-upon job definitions, few clearly defined skills, few agreed-upon training requirements, and few ladders out of the job into more responsible positions, even though unions have increasingly addressed these issues. The extreme variability in jobs broadly labelled 'clerical' also contributes to the struggle around the meaning of the work, a struggle that is contested by workers, educators, and employers.

Comments like these from clerical workers express their sense of being undervalued in a variety of ways:

I don't think a lot of people realize that a lot of work done in offices isn't done by the boss ... most of it is done by the staff and everyone doesn't look at it that way.

A man [manager] was hired at one time who had no experience, and he got twice as much wages as I did. You know I had to train him. And it really got under my skin.[1]

The skills, the knowledge, the language abilities that are necessary in clerical jobs provide the motivation for these women to engage in further education. But their frustration is that their skills are not visible to others, and are not rewarded by high wages or respect in the office. They may need better language skills than the boss because they must fix his grammar, and they may have more knowledge of how the office runs, so they show the boss what to do, but theirs remains a job that is not perceived as skilled.

The training for clerical work remains unregulated. Some employers will prefer and hire clerical workers with university degrees, while others prefer and hire women with less than high-school diplomas. Some educators will argue that a single typing course is enough, if combined with general academic skills, while others stress the necessity of elaborate programs of training in accounting, dicta-typing, shorthand, computer technology, and office practice offered at a community college. BAs in secretarial science are offered at a couple of universities in Canada, indicating that one might construct the training requirements as quite elaborate. But, for the most part, clerical training is short, even while the skills involved in the job are many.

In order to prepare women for a job that can be quite complex within the terms of a short training program, instructors must admit into training women who already know most of what they need to know. Clerical training gets women to quickly recognize, label, polish, and feel confident in skills they already possess. Neither the resources nor the time are available for teaching what needs to be known.

In a twenty-six-week government-sponsored clerical-training program I studied, students who had already worked as clerical workers were chosen as students. The instructors instituted a screening interview, and made grade 12 completion a requirement for students. Applicants were chosen if they were emotionally secure, well dressed, used the English language correctly, and already had basic clerical skills, most importantly typing. Some had university degrees. The instructors were worried about this phenomenon, pointing out that the women most in need of training were not getting it, but the structure of the situation made such selection procedures necessary.

The curriculum centred on life skills and work experience. The technical skills were at a very introductory level – more advanced skills were seen to be necessary for the work, but would have to be learned on the job. The students spent time on typewriters upgrading their typing speed. They also learned Multi-Mate, a software program for personal computers that gave them an idea of what word processing was all about. There were no accounting courses taught, no spread-sheet or data-base-management programs, no other word-processing packages. There was no dicta-typing; no shorthand; no basic grammar, spelling, or arithmetic.

In other words, successful clerical training, at least in short-term programs, depends on students having already informally learned the skills that the training is meant to impart. Training can be short because it depends on everywoman's skills. More advanced technical training is not provided, a phenomenon that reconfirms the notion that clerical workers lack skills and allows the government to continue to underfund women's training.

What was taught in the program also speaks to the construction of clerical skills. 'Life skills,' including dress codes, were taught because they would have an immediate pay-off in an interview, because they mattered to employers. What is taken for granted is femininity must be taught. It is not natural. It is a 'skill.'

In the class on dress, clear rules were adduced. 'Buy fake pearls that are knotted in between the pearls and don't have too high a gloss; Buy beige. It's boring as hell, but it goes with everything.' But, at the same time, the contextual discussion was fairly sophisticated. 'Whatever I'll tell you today, someone else will tell you something else tomorrow' (and, later, as the students make clear the variety of their actual work situations), 'It all comes down to, you'll have to figure out what your interviewer will be like.' In other words, figure out the social relations of the office and conform in ways that recognize your social position.

The objective of the class was described as 'to identify a professional look ... Women don't know how to dress. Men do ... There are things your mother never told you, the best things to wear to get ahead in business.' The discussion was interspersed with scientific findings: '75% of women from Harvard thought their appearance was important in getting a position.' Through looking at pictures of men and women, students were encouraged to examine critically the meaning of various styles of clothing, what clothes say.' 'The jacket puts the woman at the top. Jacket is a mantel of authority. Men know it. They put it on when they see a client. A sweater is textured. It says touch me, it seems more friendly.' As the class goes on, each look is critiqued for how powerful it makes the woman appear. 'I think it's a very successful look. It says money. Off white or cream. Only the rich can afford to have them dry cleaned. Pearls are quite successful';'Fake it till you make it. Dress like where you want to go, but never more than the boss.'

There is a gender code that must be learned. Sexuality must be controlled, but cannot be denied. The discussion of dressing like or for men included the following comment: Student: 'We don't want to look like them, but they are the ones that hire you. You need to understand them.' The problems with dressing like a woman were that 'there's nothing that will put you down in authority more quickly than a little pink sweater. You look like a housewife.' Long hair is too 'counter culture,' and yellow is 'not a power colour.'

The description of this class provokes laughter from many of the educators to whom I have described it. These skills are not skills that are valued and respected and put in most curriculum outlines. But these are skills the women wanted, felt they needed at work, and would be hired because of. The instructors, who had a good deal of experience with placing students, agreed that the ability to dress appropriately was an absolutely critical skill, a skill women are expected to have and punished for not having. How should these skills be valued? The answer depends on who is asked.

Another point in the training program where the social construction of skill becomes explicit is in constructing a résumé. The instructors pointed out that the résumé is a way of communicating to employers what you can do. It 'is the packaging for you – you're writing a real box package – making it appealing. The purpose is to sell yourself.' The instructors advised women to highlight skills on their résumés, to thereby construct themselves as skilled workers. The résumé was a place where they could decide what counted as a skill, and where they could communicate their competence using a frame of reference that suited them. The instructors showed students how to 'trick,' as they put it, employers into seeing them as skilled. As the instructor explained, 'We try to show that everything that they've been doing in their life, the things they are dismissing as just housewifely chores, are all really skills that they've learned and that they can help make a contribution in the business world.'

In class, the instructor explained, 'We do skill right up front, not education but skills – that's a functional résumé ... we'll forget about chronological résumés here. In traditional application forms they want you to list your work, starting from the most recent. It makes me freeze.' Student: 'That's what Canada Employment wants you to do.' Instructor: 'Well, we're going to trick them – assemble it so that the gaps don't show ... Because you have so many skills – look at all the ones you've got. I'm impressed ... Look at page 15, we're going to use some of these words. They've been designed by experts – action words that people can hang on to ... Most words are "ing" words. A résumé is not in past tense.'

Instructor: 'With skills, what you list you don't have to be paid for it ... in a functional résumé your skills are what you've been paid for or not. You did the work, you had the skill. In the last group one woman ran her husband's trucking business for twenty-five years while her husband was out on the road. Never got a penny. But she had to do invoices, phoning, contracting. Doesn't matter if you've been paid or unpaid – doesn't connect with traditional paid employment.'

The skills that the instructors particularly encouraged the women to recognize, value, and write down were social skills.

Student: 'What are interpersonal skills?' Instructor: 'Counselling, interviewing, dealing with people all day. A lot of secretarial work is interpersonal – handling complaints, conferences, handling people is distinct from technical ... Dealing with people is one of the hardest things to do. Those who go to management school – it's all people skills. The reason why women are doing well in the workplace is that they have good people skills. Don't forget the interpersonal – like handling complaints.' Student (indicating here that she is getting the idea of 'packaging' her skills): 'Handling is not a good word.' Instructor: 'What else could we use? Dealing? – mediating is a good word.

'Interpersonal skills – there are thousands of women who can type and use word processors but if they are being difficult or get in cliques —'

What is the value of these skills and abilities? There is no simple answer to these questions, but it is important to see them as questions. Too often knowledge of dress and social graces are taken for granted as personality characteristics. Their association with women makes them lose value. Sitting in these classrooms makes one aware of how the skills are learned and how they are taken seriously by women returning to the labour market. They should be recognized as we struggle over our assessments of skill. They will be recognized only if the women who do the work are able to insist on their importance, their scarcity, and their value.

Conclusion

The process of defining and valuing the skills necessary for a job is a complex one that is based in someone's point of view. It has rarely taken the point of view of women workers. The devaluation of women and their work has shaped the assessment of women's skills, and affected the kind of training women receive for their work. Training programs symbolize skill and restrict job entry. Women workers have not been able to insist on long and regulated training programs. They have not been able to insist that on-the-job training be provided.

Any processes that hope to produce pay equity must make the politics of skill attribution explicit, and abandon the idea that skill is an objective criterion to which we can appeal to get away from politics, power, and struggle. Can pay equity legislation be used to raise consciousness about women's skills and training at work? Can it be used to show women that their skills are important and real, and that they can legitimately make demands based on them?

The answer probably depends on how pay equity is implemented, how it is discussed by unions and employers and lawyers and all of us. The requirement of pay equity committees means that the question of what skills are required at work must be confronted and discussed. The terms in which this discussion takes place are critical. If the discussion simply leads everyone to discuss where on a taken-for-granted scale of value their own job fits, the politics of pay equity will consolidate in the workplace a version of skill that was arrived at with little input from women. If the scales themselves are discussed and re-evaluated, there is an opportunity for a fundamental revaluing of women's work.

There seems to be preliminary evidence that both processes occur. Women do sometimes discover that they have skills they had never thought about, and they force employers to recognize it too. But sometimes, the process can confirm for women their place at the bottom, and legitimate ways of valuing that obscure women's skills. Pay equity has no single necessary outcome. In can have one effect in one workplace, and another next door. What will happen will depend on how we all engage the process, and over time perhaps we will see its ideological impact on all of us.

NOTES

1 These comments are taken from transcripts of interviews with women in clerical-training programs in Vancouver. The research was funded by the Social Sciences and Humanities Council of Canada under grants number 410-83-0535 and 410-85-0356.

8 Pay Equity Implementation: Experimentation, Negotiation, Mediation, Litigation, and Aggravation

Lois Haignere

This essay draws on my experiences working in implementation of pay equity in Canada and the United States. Fortunately, or unfortunately, the problems that beset us in pay equity implementation appear to be widely applicable. The six problems I outline are in no way exhaustive. They are simply important problems I have encountered in my role as a consultant and implementor.

Losing the Baby in the Bath-Water

A common problem besetting the pay equity implementation process is losing sight of the basic goal. The goal of pay equity reform is to pay those in traditionally female jobs what they would be paid had their work been done traditionally by men. We cannot know for sure what that figure would be, but in the implementation of pay equity we should make our best guess.

Problems occur when we take on 'excess-baggage objectives.' The players in the implementation process commonly have objectives that are pertinent to their needs. Sometimes these objectives that are so fundamental in their eyes that they become one-in-the-same with the goal of pay equity.

Management may come to believe that pay equity requires a complete overhaul of the existing classification and compensation system. Or, personnel administrators may consider it impossible to do pay equity unless certain traditional administrative procedures are continued. They may believe it is crucial to continue to use a familiar set of factors and weights or to have supervisors approve incumbent job-content information. A union may see gathering all the job-content information on work done by their members as the primary objective. Or they may want to maintain an existing centralized 'one-title-fits-all' system rather than breaking down job titles into different levels of skill and responsibility. Examples like these are usually stated objectives and, therefore, easier to deal with than the many unstated objectives. Some unions, for instance, worry about getting locked into a point-factor-system poltergeist that will come back to haunt future negotiations. Others may consider it more important to keep male-member blood pressures down than to elevate the pay for traditionally female jobs. Management may have an unstated objective of maintaining an existing salary relationship between management and non-management titles. Both union and management policy makers frequently have an unstated objective to minimize change.

When objectives like these replace the goal of making a best guess and paying accordingly, they gum up the implementation process. They may be desirable objectives, depending on the setting, but their importance should be measured against the ultimate goal. Will they contribute to ensuring that we have the best guess, or are they 'excess baggage' that will prolong or even totally subvert the implementation process?

Fitting the Disease to the Treatment

When the bottom line is predetermined, i.e., the money available for implementation is already established, the goal of removing sex bias from pay is likely to be replaced with making sure that the amount of bias found fits the amount of money available. In other words, the pay equity disease has to equal X dollars because X dollars is what we have to treat it.

In New York State, 1 per cent of payroll over three years (a total of 3 per cent) was allocated for pay adjustments, including pay equity through union/management contracts. The implementation team's focus was to make the price tag fit. This team was made up of mid-level managerial employees. It was controlled jointly by the highest officials of the Budget, Civil Service, and Employee Relations departments. Before the team began its work, a market study was completed. This study showed that the state was paying above market for college- and university-educated professionals but below market for clerical and institutional care-giving positions. When the implementation team finished creating its factor and weight system for evaluating New York State's 7,000 job titles, the necessary adjustment not only fit the less than 3 per cent of payroll price tag, but, amazingly, also just happened to be in a direction that corrected for the problems found in the market study; in other words, the adjustment minimized increases for university-educated professionals and increased the below-market salaries.

Evans and Nelson (1989a, 155), in reporting on the implementation of pay equity in the Minnesota local jurisdictions, note that, as the cost of implementation rose, cost-containing mechanisms were used at the expense of the reform. One such mechanism was to use a pay line that was not adjusted for the existing discrimination against women's wages. This line was produced by using a scattergram that included female-dominated job classes and their existing undervalued salaries without statistically correcting for the undervaluation.[1] Another costly cost-containment mechanism was to use a corridor around the pay line, which meant that a female-dominated job class had to be substantially below the average salary of male-dominated classes before it would receive any pay equity increases. These corridors can be set so that only 2.5 or 5 per cent of the female-dominated classes receive adjustments. Lump-sum payments were also used by local jurisdictions in Minnesota instead of adding the pay equity increment to the base salary.

In Manitoba, the amount specified for treatment of the pay equity problem was 1 per cent of payroll for four years. This may have been a reasonable estimate of costs for most public-sector employers where female-dominated job classes constitute less than half of the workforce. But, in the health-care sector, female-dominated classes constitute 80 per cent of the workforce. As a consequence, pay equity adjustments for employees in the Manitoba health-care sector were put on hold for almost two years until the policy makers forced the pay equity adjustments under their cost ceiling.

The implementation of the Ontario pay equity legislation added a new twist to the spectre of the bottom line. Policy makers in sites that had not completed their pay equity plans collected the pay equity plans of sites similar to theirs; for example, universities collect the plans of other universities and hospitals collect the plans of other hospitals. They used the 'precedents' set by these plans to define the procedure and costs they were willing to accept. At one site the managers refused to consider further adjustments to the point-factor system because those adjustments would raise the price of the pay equity adjustments at their institution above the pay equity adjustments that had been made at other similar institutions.

To return to my disease analogy, if we insist on a treatment plan dictated by the bottom line, I suspect that sexism in salaries, like most social diseases, will demonstrate its ability to develop resistant strains and new variations. We will be faced with another epidemic later, when untreated disparities have been exaggerated through percentage increases.

Questioning Values beyond Question

Deciding which job-content factors to include in a job-comparison system and how to weight each factor brings us face to face with our cultural value systems. This is a painful, confusing process. Our cultural values are diverse, and many existing monetary values conflict with other values. Is responsibility for budgets or equipment more important than responsibility for safety and human lives? Is exposure to heat or cold a more negative working environment than exposure to the chronically ill or severely retarded? Is managerial know-how more important than technical know-how? Can we dare to question long-held cultural assumptions?[2]

The pay equity reform itself questions the long-held cultural assumptions that women are second-class citizens and, by extension, their work is second class and can be paid for accordingly. To challenge this pervasive assumption, the Manitoba and Ontario pay equity laws require the use of gender-neutral job-comparison systems. So what does a gender-neutral factor look like anyway? Which of the common factors in most a priori point-factor systems are gender neutral? Do any of these factors favour the job content found in female-dominated job classes?

A simple test of correlation can tell you. To demonstrate that a factor captures the job content of female-dominated classes in a particular workforce, all you need to know is the percentage of women in each of the job classes and the number of points each class received from that factor. With this information you can do a simple correlation analysis between the points for the factor and the female percentage in each class. Positive correlations (correlations greater than about +3) indicate that the factor is measuring job content that is more prevalent in female-dominated classes than in male-dominated classes. A negative correlation indicates that the factor is more prevalent in male-dominated classes. Correlations around zero indicate the factor relates equally to both male- and female-dominated classes.

When we apply tests like these to most widely used traditional point-factor systems, we frequently find that all the factors are negatively related to female-dominated work. That is, none of the factors captures job content that is more present in traditionally female jobs than other jobs. How can we challenge the traditional systems if we don't know what to challenge them with? Even assuming that there are no political barriers and we can include any female-dominated work we want at the weights we want (a fantasy world), we still have two dilemmas: 1 / How do we know what female-dominated job content to include? and 2 / How do we know how to weight job content that has never been given a value before?

We have developed some ways of dealing with the first of these two dilemmas. However, currently there is very little information to help us with the second.

How can we know what job content of traditionally female classes ought to be included? One excellent way is to distribute a comprehensive closed-ended questionnaire to the workforce in question.[3] Another way is to consult one of several available lists of commonly overlooked female job-content items. Such a list can be found in Steinberg and Haignere (1987) or you may prefer the one on page 11 of the Ontario Pay Equity Commission's publication *How to Do Pay Equity Comparisons.* If the factor seems to fit wear it. It is better to include factors that may not be used in the job-evaluation process than it is not to provide a factor to the job evaluators that represents important job content of either the male or the female comparator job classes. This assumes, of course, that the factor is not already in the system.

From my experience, there are four notable categories of female-dominated job content that have been traditionally ignored by job-evaluation systems. I believe that all of these suffer from an association with the traditionally female roles. They are care-giving, exposure to communicable disease, laundry and food services, and information management.

By care-giving[4] I mean all of the classic bedside and first-line care roles traditionally filled by women in hospitals, nursing homes, schools, and institutions for the mentally ill or physically handicapped. However, I would also include care-giving to customers and the public (e.g., waitress, sales clerk, receptionist, motor vehicle clerk). In New York State our study showed that this type of job content was negatively weighted; that is, all other things being equal, the more a job class was required to do care-giving the less it got paid. The so-called implementation of pay equity in New York State did not change this (Steinberg 1987). This is the classic good-news, bad-news joke: the good news is they include care-giving as a factor; the bad news is they gave it a negative weight.

Being exposed to communicable diseases such as AIDS and hepatitis is not considered a hazardous working condition, whereas the possibility of falling off a ladder or of being injured by a machine is considered a hazard. However, before you work too hard on including 'Exposure to Communicable Diseases' in the 'Hazardous or Poor Working Conditions' factors, consider the weight given to these factors. Classically, they represent less than 5 per cent of the possible job-evaluation points.[5] This situation is one ramification of élitism in job-evaluation systems, an 'ism' that is far from illegal in either Canada or the United States. When jobs involve hazards such as being exposed to toxic materials and fumes, nuclear waste, x-rays, or communicable terminal disease, how much is that job content worth? What about laying hot asphalt, coal-mining, or garbage collecting? When we say, 'You couldn't pay me enough to do that job' how much is it worth to us to have someone else do it?

I believe that food- and laundry-service work suffers from association with the traditional housewife role. In the pay equity research studies with which I am familiar, food and laundry service job titles have been found to be among the most undervalued job classes. In many cases the incumbents of these jobs are not only women but minorities and, as often as not, part-time. Unions, even unions that have focused on pay equity for their clerical and professional bargaining units, may ignore the undervaluation of these jobs. The skills of running the machines involved – the mangles, steam trays, mixers, and washers – the exposure to poor working conditions and hazards, the service to the customer and the responsibility levels (special diets, etc.) – all are likely to be ignored. Why? Probably because women just naturally know how to serve food and do the laundry.

Information management, such as filing, data entry, and record keeping, is similarly associated with the clerical, office-wife, order-keeping functions that women are also genetically created to perform. A cartoon that illustrates this point features a help-wanted ad that reads: 'Wanted male experienced with complex information classification and data retrieval specialization, $10 an hour. Or, female file clerk, $5 an hour.' Most pay equity studies find substantial undervaluation of clerical workers but don't include this factor in the job-evaluation process. What if it were included and properly weighted?

That question brings us to the second dilemma mentioned above. How do we know how to weight job content that has never been valued before or has been valued only as 'women's work'? At one site recently, we were considering including an information-management factor in the job-evaluation system, but we had no idea what weight to give the factor. Should we give it the same weight as the lowest-weighted male job-content related factor, physical effort? On the one hand, this would seem to be a conservative weighting. On the other hand, it would raise the pay equity adjustments of a very large pool of employees, and the total price of pay equity would go up substantially. When there is no 'evidence' to show that it should be weighted higher and when some involved are against including this factor, what do you do? We need a comparable-worth study for our traditionally female job-content factors. What traditionally male-dominated job-content factors are of comparable worth?

The Travelling Used Job-Evaluation System Salesman

The Canadian pay equity legislation created a situation where everyone, unions and management alike, was looking for consultants with credentials. In terms of the number of sites and years of experience in applying point-factor systems, traditional management consultant firms have the sought-after credentials. However, these 'credentials' primarily relate to traditional classification and compensation, and not to projects where gender neutrality was an objective. Moreover, the primary goal of these consultants is to continue to sell the systems they are wedded to through long years of marketing. If they greatly alter their systems for gender-neutral pay equity purposes, can they continue to market them to management elsewhere? If they develop a new system just for pay equity, are they indicting their classical system?

In most cases, management consultants are willing to alter their systems in only minor ways. Acker (1989, 71–6) has provided us with an agonizing account of the struggles of the pay equity advocates on the Oregon Task Force to get Hay Consultants to alter their 'human relations' skills factor. She notes that the consultants and the state management objected to the idea of adding two levels to this factor because it would reduce the salary differences between management and non-management. Such a reduction would be consistent with the pay equity reform, since managerial classes tend to be male-dominated and most female-dominated classes are non-managerial.

The Oregon experience illustrates the incongruity in trying to bring about change in job-evaluation systems that were developed to keep things the same. A decade ago, the National Research Council of the U.S. National Academy of Sciences noted this incongruity. They studied the feasibility of using existing job-evaluation systems for assessing gender equity in salaries. They concluded: 'As we have shown, the factors and their relative weights are often chosen in such a way as to closely *replicate existing wage hierarchies*. For that reason, they can hardly serve as an independent standard against which to assess the possibility of bias in existing wage hierarchies' (Treiman and Hartmann 1981; emphasis added).

Many of the factors in traditional point-factor systems are focused primarily on measuring managerial job content. Factors that seem to be conceptually different, such as judgment/problem solving, accountability, initiative, and interpersonal skill, turn out to be strongly statistically related.[6] One reason is that many factor levels follow the bureaucratic structure of the organization. The top two or three levels may be attainable only by those who 'coordinate more than one unit.' The most skilled scientist or professional, perhaps one making decisions concerning the development of vaccines that could have impact on health world-wide, would be unlikely to obtain one of the top three steps in many judgment/problem solving/decision making factors. To do so he or she would have to be in a managerial position that makes judgments that serve 'to guide the organization as a whole.'

The highest factor levels for accountability, responsibility, and results of error factors are usually reserved for top managers by specifying a relationship with organizational policy making or errors by top executives. Isn't it possible that some errors made by those at the lower bureaucratic levels could be just as devastating as those at the higher levels? If a medical technician misinterprets a test, thereby causing the death of a patient, is this less important than a fiscal error made much higher in the bureaucracy?

I am not suggesting that there should be no factors relating to the bureaucratic structure. Managerial and supervisory job content logically relates to bureaucratic levels. The higher levels of these factors may legitimately be reserved for those who 'coordinate more than one unit.'

So, the travelling used job-evaluation system salesman, with his thirty- or forty-year-old system legitimized primarily by its long use in many sites, is a problem for pay equity implementation. To implement gender-neutral pay equity I believe we should be willing to begin with the job content of the traditionally female jobs and their potential comparators and build a factor and weight system that does not ignore any important job content on either side of the equation. Some of the more traditional job-content factors may be appropriate in some settings. But their wholesale adoption without consideration of the job content of the job classes being compared jeopardizes pay equity implementation.

The Ravages of Time

When meeting the deadline becomes the ultimate objective, the reform suffers. This is not to say that deadlines aren't functional. They are. Without them some people would never even start, let alone finish. Still, impossible deadlines invite short-cuts that follow the lines of least resistance, which are usually those that replicate the existing system. In the face of impossible deadlines, the advocates for the reform may work long dedicated hours only to become too burned out to resist those who just want to declare the job done. In Manitoba, meeting the deadline of the provincial legislation became so important that it largely replaced the goal of implementing pay equity. The Unified Health Care Organizations Pay Equity Task Force held many long, exhausting meetings to forge an agreement to meet the 30 September 1988 political deadline. Yet, it was August 1990 before Manitoba health-care employees received any pay equity increases. Then they received only the proportion allowed by the previously mentioned inadequate bottom line. Meeting the deadline was politically crucial, but fully implementing pay equity was not. Resist impossible deadlines. Don't make haste into the waste or providing the appearance that pay equity has been achieved, when it has not.

Loopholing

Originally I had planned to cover only five problems in this essay. However, after reading some of the pay equity plans submitted by universities in Ontario, I had to add this one. Some universities have truly taken the intent of the Ontario Pay Equity bill seriously. For instance, at one university all of the classes in the staff-association bargaining unit were matched to male comparators. The class with the greatest salary disparity was then used as representative for a group-of-jobs approach. Thus, all job classes got the same high increase. At the University of Western Ontario they used an approach that brought the female pay line up to the male pay line by giving every individual in a traditionally female job an annual increase of about $3,200.

Unfortunately, other sites appear to have aimed at the loopholes in the law. One site, for instance, treated almost every position, male and female, as a single-incumbent class. All were assigned job-evaluation points with a traditional job-evaluation system. They then chose a wide definition of 'similar,' i.e., plus or minus 7 per cent. This meant that a 14 per cent point band could be used to search for a male comparator with a lower salary. If one could be found within the band, then no raise had to be given. The combination of treating most male-dominated positions as single-incumbent job classes and the wide range in which a comparator could be found maximized chances of finding a lower-paid male job.

Needless to say, not many people got pay equity adjustments at this university. In all, twenty-eight 'classes' with a total of thirty-nine incumbents got salary increments. Twenty-four of these incumbents got hourly raises of six cents or less. The total for all pay equity salary adjustments at this institution was less than $52,200. Unfortunately, this so-called pay equity plan was noted by other institutions that had not completed their plans.

Conclusions

It is painful to highlight some of our biggest implementation problems. However, nothing is gained by sticking our head in the everything-is-okay, politics-as-usual sand. As pay equity advocates involved with real-life implementations, we are frequently caught between the purity-of-the-reform rock and the politics-of-the-possible hard place. We all know we make compromises. I suggest we directly address these dilemmas and develop some new 'old' adages to help us. I offer the following for starters:

1 Avoid losing the pay equity baby in the implementation bath-water. As you participate in the process of implementing pay equity, keep in mind the objective of arriving at the best guess as to how traditionally female job classes would be paid if they had been traditionally filled by men. *What we get is what we implement.*
2 Aim for an honest diagnosis of the full extent of the disease ignoring any 'cost ceiling.' You won't be able to apply treatment where you have found no illness. Remind all those involved that any undetected sexism is uncorrected sexism. Uncorrected sexism in salaries will be exaggerated over time through percentage increments. *Don't put off to tomorrow the pay discrimination of today.*
3 Challenge the lack of inclusion of traditionally female job content in

most classic job-evaluation systems. Insist on statistical tests to show whether or not a given factor or set of factors captures the work done in female-dominated classes. Design traditional female job-content factors. Figure out how to weight these factors appropriately. *If the factor fits weight it.*

4 Avoid the travelling used job-evaluation system salesman. Try to ensure that those who are assisting you have no vested interest in protecting existing salary relationships. Build a factor and weight system that does not ignore any important job content of traditionally female or traditionally male job titles. *Credentials are as credentials do.*

5 Put the reform before the deadline. *Better late than never.*

6 If you are fortunate enough to live in a jurisdiction that has pay equity legislation, don't rest on your legislated laurels. Look for the loopholes. Head off any attempt to make an end-run for them. *What we implement is what we get.*

NOTES

1 See Steinberg and Haignere (1987) for an explanation of how this not only minimizes pay equity adjustments, but also imbeds the bias in women's jobs so as to lower the pay of traditionally male and integrated job classes.

2 While I am dealing primarily with the cultural assumptions that relate to sexism, Treiman (1979) notes that there are even more basic and widely held assumptions that underlie salary setting. These say that jobs ought to be paid differently; that these pay differences should be based on job content; that particular kinds of job content ought to be rewarded more than other kinds; and that these kinds of job content can be accurately measured. As Treiman notes, the fact that these beliefs are 'taken for granted by most of the people professionally concerned with jobs and wages, and indeed probably by most Americans in general, does not make them any less value-laden' (1979, 35).

3 Closed-ended questionnaires are better than open-ended ones because they are easier to test for reliability and validity. The art of closed-ended job-content questionnaire development has reached new heights in Ontario where the Ontario Public Service, the University of Western Ontario, and Carleton University have each built on the earlier questionnaire was developed for the New York State study. These questionnaires are available.

4 It is important to distinguish care-giving from care-taking, which is frequently the name used for grounds-keeping, janitorial, and the mainte-

nance male-dominated world. As Isla Peters pointed out to me, it is the classic case of men doing the taking and women doing the giving.

5 In New York State, poor working conditions were negatively weighted before pay equity was implemented and to my knowledge still are. In other words, the more a job class requires exposure to poor working conditions, the less it gets paid.

6 Statistically analyses have been conducted that show that traditional factor systems have factors that are really statistically measuring the same job content. One example is a study that Willis & Associates commissioned of their own system (Milczarek 1980). This study found that three of the four major factors – knowledge and skill, mental demands, and accountability – were intercorrelated at the 0.95 level.

Any firm can easily assess its system to determine if some of its factors are measuring the same underlying dimension by using a common statistical technique called 'multiple regression.' Some interactions are to be expected. After all, some factors that related to pay are necessarily related to each other. For instance, the job classes that require higher education will tend to be those that involve higher levels of responsibility, and jobs that involve a high level of physical effort tend to be the ones with poor working conditions. However, there is a difference between some interaction and almost total overlap. There are statistical techniques that can create factors that are as independent of each other as the particular data set will allow. These techniques can help create point-factor systems that minimize redundancies.

9 Political Power, Technical Disputes, and Unequal Pay: A Federal Case

Rosemary Warskett

It is now well over twenty years since the Royal Commission on the Status of Women in Canada (1970) issued its report on women's inequality.[1] The commissioners' recommendation for equal pay for work of equal value (hereafter referred to as 'equal value') provided an important source of state legitimation for women's groups seeking ways to close the wage gap. Indeed, since that time, the equal-value approach to women's unequal pay progressively became the chosen strategy of feminists within dominant feminist groups such as the National Action Committee on the Status of Women (NAC).

Although the pursuit of equal value is the main approach adopted by liberal feminists since the early 1970s to address women's unequal pay, it has not escaped criticism. Questions regarding the meaning of 'value' were raised in the 1970s but largely went unheard (Ramkhalawansingh 1979). More recently, mainly as a result of the practical experience of attempting to implement legislation, some feminist activists and researchers have begun to question the consequences of applying the equal-value concept (Ballantyne 1988; Findlay 1987a; Lewis 1988; Warskett 1990).

There is a risk of oversimplifying the various positions in the debate, but below I am concerned to reveal the arguments for and against adopting the concept of equal value as an approach to women's unequal pay. I do not deal, therefore, with the question of how effectively and extensively equal value has been implemented in particular jurisdictions; for example, in terms of the efficacy of proactivity as compared to the complaint mechanism or in terms or how complete coverage is of sectors and groups. My main purpose in outlining the current debate is to focus on the concept of equal value and the general consequences of adopting it as a policy instrument for redressing women's unequal pay.

Those who are positive about the merits of equal value argue that it is a reform that promises to go some way towards revaluing women's work and eliminating the inequality inherent in women's substantially lower pay compared to men's. Comparing the content of jobs by evaluation procedures can work in women's favour even though traditionally constructed plans worked against women in the past (Remick and Steinberg 1984, 289). In other words, it is thought that job-evaluation plans can be transformed into gender-neutral systems that place a higher value on work traditionally performed by women, thus operating to raise women's pay rather than justifying their lower wages (Cornish 1986, 31–4). This can be achieved, it is argued, by selecting criteria in the design of job evaluation that 'maximize consistency and minimize bias' (Steinberg and Haignere 1985, 33). Gains, it is pointed out, can be made even when the evaluation system is defective (that is, not gender-neutral) simply by using the same evaluation plan and applying it consistently to both men's and women's jobs (Remick 1984b, 99; Millar 1989).[2] By reforming job evaluation, it is claimed, the tables can be turned in women's favour and much-needed money placed in their hands. The women's and union movements must, therefore, continue to pressure legislatures to introduce improved provisions to broaden both the mechanisms and coverage of equal value (Cornish 1986; Equal Pay Coalition 1988).

In contrast to these optimistic views of equal value and the potential it has for rectifying wage inequality, critics argue that it is neither possible nor desirable to compare and differentiate between jobs on the basis of job content (Lewis 1988; Mitchell 1988). The point is strongly made that the value of a job cannot be determined objectively and fairly. 'Value in the market place has meant value to the employer,' and therefore job evaluation is the tool whereby employers justify existing hierarchies and women's subordinate place within them (Mitchell 1988, 64–5). It is asserted that women's oppression is endemic to the system and cannot be addressed by minor tinkerings (Lewis 1988). Furthermore evaluation is ideologically based on the employers' standpoint of what is valuable in terms of the goals of the organization. It legitimizes the ideology that there should be class differentials on the basis of job content. Equal value, therefore, does not 'contest the notion that people's income should be determined primarily by where they fit in an occupational hierarchy'

(Brenner 1987, 457). Added to this is the problem of complexity. Job-evaluation techniques are thought to be so complicated that only the experts can understand what's going on. The end result is that women lose control of the process and become demobilized and depoliticized with regard to the issue (Ballantyne 1988). These problems led one critic to question why feminists continue to participate in the implementation of equal value at all (Mitchell 1988, 66).

Although all these critics raise very important questions about the nature of the equal value reform, thereby aiding reassessment and re-thinking about the meaning of value and the worth of job content, the way the debate is framed is ultimately inconclusive. Neither side really comes to a solid conclusion. This is seen when those who are among the strongest supporters of equal value point out paradoxically that where proponents push for 'feminization of the job content values in wage structure, they rarely succeed' (Steinberg 1988, 206). And when even the fiercest critics are led to give equal value minimum support when faced with legislative reality. For example, Debra Lewis in *Just Give Us the Money* (1988, 94) concludes that 'women must learn to use job eval-uation to the best possible advantage where it is required by legislation.'

Clearly, the debate is inconclusive because simply to focus on the advantages and disadvantages of the equal-value reform is to leave aside the historical realities women have faced over the last twenty years in fighting for equal pay. This essay is, therefore, an attempt to frame the debate in a different way by focusing on the way in which the power relations of gender and class intertwine and act to shape the strategies we form. It attempts, therefore, to move away from an ahistorical treat-ment of the choices women make in terms of how, where, and with what we will struggle. Strategic decisions regarding the contestation of unequal pay depend on political power – who has it and who has not – at any point in history. To abstract the debate from history is to ignore what is possible in the present circumstances, given past and present political realities. In other words, although women make their own his-tory they can do so only in the context of practices and meanings that are formed as the result of past struggles and conflicts and on the basis of past and present power relationships. Power not only is a resource resulting from women's empowerment and mobilization but must also be conceived in relational terms among women, the state, and employers who have power to construct job hierarchies and set wages.

In what follows, I argue that equal-value strategy within the federal government developed out of the historical conjuncture of liberal feminism and liberal democratic capitalism. Linked to this argument is a second. Because the implementation of equal value has, in general, involved the use of job-evaluation procedures, it often results in what seem to be purely technical disputes over evaluation plans, processes, and implementation. Underlying these disputes, however, is usually profound conflict over the right and the power to define the value or worth of jobs, how job hierarchies should be structured, and, as a consequence, how much women should be paid.

The above arguments are made in the context of historical examination of equal value in the federal sector, both as a set of practices and meanings and in the context of the relationship between the federal government and its own women workers. The first section examines the renewed demand by women in the 1970s for equal pay, followed by a historical overview of the National Action Committee's (NAC) contestation of the federal government's policy towards women's unequal pay and the legislative outcome in the form of the Canadian Human Rights Act (CHRA). The next section analyses how the equal-value provisions of the legislation were given structure and meaning as a result of the conflict between Treasury Board as employer of women workers in the federal sector and the Public Service Alliance of Canada (PSAC) as the union representing their interests. In the final section, I draw some conclusions about unequal pay, political power, and technical disputes. With regards to methodology, it should be noted that the essay combines both secondary and primary research. The first section on the women's movement and NAC draws on interpretations made by a number of researchers, whereas the section on the relations between the PSAC and the federal government is based on my own analysis of primary research material.

The Construction and Contestation of Women's Unequal Pay (1966–78)

In an analysis that is historical and relational, it is always difficult to pinpoint exactly where to begin in history. The beginning is always preceded by other important contestations of structures and meanings, so much so that any starting-point is never a real beginning. It is always to some extent artificially imposed. That being said, the point of beginning is never arbitrarily chosen by the researcher. Implicit in the decision is an assessment of historical events and an analysis of significant turning-points that impact on and contribute to future structures and meanings.

My point of beginning, for the purposes of this essay, involves the judgment that 1966 was a significant moment for Canadian women and for the attempt to change their unequal status. This case-study, therefore, begins with the moment in history when 'several hundred of Canada's well-educated and publicly minded women gathered in the Railway Room in the Houses of Parliament to demand government action to improve the status of women' (Findlay 1987, 34). It was this meeting and confrontation with the male-dominated Liberal party and government that provided the impetus for the establishment of the Royal Commission on the Status of Women and its subsequent report to the government in 1970. The terms of reference of the commission were framed in the language of liberalism, instructing the commission to 'inquire into ... the status of women in Canada ... to ensure for women equal opportunities with men in all aspects of Canadian Society' (Report of Royal Commission of the Status of Women 1970, vii). Over the next twenty years, Canadian feminist consciousness and practice developed, was moulded and formed in the context of the discourse outlined in the commission's report (Findlay 1987, 34–5), which reflected the material realities of Canada as a liberal capitalist society.

The report was the end result of a three-year inquiry involving submissions from groups and individuals across the country. Significantly for women's struggle for equality, the report gave substantial recognition to their contribution to the economy. For the first time in the history of the Canadian state, women were conceived as producers in terms of both their paid and unpaid work. In section two, on the economy, the commissioners stated unequivocally that women 'produce goods and services but often receive no pay in dollars and cents' and that 'women often produce the same goods and services as men for lower pay' (1970, 17). With regard to women's unequal pay, the commissioners went on to document that the problem extended far beyond the fact that women do not receive either equal pay for equal work or recognition for their unpaid work. Women in the main, they pointed out, are engaged in different kinds of work from men, so much so that 'the present use in legislation in Canada of such terms as "same" and "identical" are much too restrictive. The term "equal" is more within the intent of the international Labour Organization Convention (ILO) 100, which speaks of "work of equal value"' (1970, 76).

Paving the way for the federal government's endorsement of the ILO's

Convention 100 in 1972, the commission's report served as an important confirmation of women's own experience and provided an important focus for consciousness raising and mobilization in communities across the country (Lewis 1988, 42–3). The movement for women's liberation, which was reactivated in the 1960s, was mainly confined to the universities and to professional, middle-class women. It was mainly these women who came together in April 1972 to examine the prospects for implementing the recommendations from the royal commission.[3] 'From it emerged, in addition to a set of resolutions and recommendations, formal recognition for the newly formed National Action Committee on the Status of Women' (NAC) (Marsden 1980, 244–5). It should be noted, however, that even at the inception of NAC there were women present who represented working-class and marginalized groups of women. For example, Madeline Parent, a long-time union activist in Quebec and Ontario, and Mary Two Axe Early, a Mohawk woman from the Kahnawake reserve in Quebec, both were active in NAC at the early stages (Parent 1989, 30), as was Grace Hartman, who later became president of the Canadian Union of Public Employees and was president of NAC in 1974–5. It was also apparent that it was not only middle-class women who were touched by the commission's report.

By the mid-1970s the growth of a distinctive working-class feminism was apparent (Maroney 1988, 87). Although limited at first to workplace issues, it involved the conscious attempt to make sense of the changes in women's participation in the labour force over the preceding twenty years and women's unequal position in the workplace.[4] At first, this newly developing brand of feminism adopted the equal opportunity language of the royal commission (Canadian Labour Congress 1976), but over the next fifteen years women undertook action within their unions over a wide range of issues, including sexual harassment, child care, and dominance of male leaders, issues that inevitably involved the attempt to change the language of equal opportunity to that of special measures in order to achieve equal results (Canadian Labour Congress 1990). Processes and forums where union women learned and strategized together gradually developed. These include women's committees and caucuses at the level of the Canadian Labour Congress (CLC) and federations of labour as well as locals, together with educational courses and conferences in which union women share their experiences of subordination in the workplace and in their unions and communities (Briskin and Yanz 1983).

The issue of women's low pay became a central issue for women in unions in the 1970s. Instead of relying on the state to enact legislation with respect to women's unequal pay, women in unions focused on traditional union methods of collective bargaining as the principal means for improving their wages. During the 1970s and early 1980s, there was a series of important strikes that demonstrated women's determination to undertake militant action in support of the right and need to earn a working woman's wage. These included strikes at Fleck, Blue Cross, and Radio Shack, the clerks' strike in the federal government and that of Lower Mainland municipal workers in British Columbia (Maroney 1987; Canadian Employment and Immigration Union [CEIU] 1982; White 1980; Cuthbertson 1978). In the process, women, both in unions and in feminist organizations such as NAC, learned that unionism and collectivity can be important weapons for fighting subordination.

By 1975, NAC had solidified its position on women's unequal pay. It was essentially the same position as that outlined in the royal commission's report, which called for the federal government to adopt ILO Convention 100, embodying equal pay for work of equal value (Marsden 1980, 250; Morris 1982, 87–108). Support for this position was outlined by Lynn McDonald in *Canadian Forum*, where she documented the wage gap between the average wages of men and women workers and called for people to 'be paid according to the skill, effort, responsibility and working conditions associated with the job they do, whether it is a job done by men, women or both' (McDonald 1975, 6). The article was also a response to the federal government's introduction of Bill C-72, the proposed Canadian Human Rights Act (CHRA), that included the principle of equal pay for similar work but made no reference to equal value. Early in 1975, material about the wage gap and equal value, taken from McDonald's article, was circulated as a factsheet to meetings of women in Ontario and elsewhere (Marsden 1980, 259–60). It was at these meetings that NAC began to put in place a campaign with its main goal of changing the provision in the bill from similar work to work of equal value.

It was a campaign conceived mainly in terms of changing the mind of the Liberal government legislators and did not attempt to mobilize women in general or embark on a widespread debate about the type of legislation that would exist or what was meant by value either in the context of ILO Convention 100 or in the minds of the members of NAC. 'Of value to whom?' was a question that seemingly was not posed. The campaign involved mainly professional women, for the most part lobbying Liberal politicians. In this sense, it reflected the side of the debate within NAC that argues that the resources of the organization should mainly be devoted to political lobbying rather than directed towards organizing and mobilizing 'grass roots' women,[5] as is evident from Lorna Marsden's statement: 'Like-minded, hard-working, for the most part highly educated, and solution-oriented, these women understood the issue and pressed hard wherever possible. There was no attempt to build mass support for the concept, to sell it to the private sector or even unions. All the focus was on changing the law' (1980, 257). As a result of their influence, the law was changed! The Liberal party affiliation of women like Lorna Marsden was important when lobbying ministers of the federal government, while feminists within the federal bureaucracy played an important role (Marsden 1980, 257; Morris 1982). In November 1976, the federal government reintroduced the proposed Canadian Human Rights Act (CHRA) as a new bill (C-25) including the principle of equal value. Section 11(2) of the CHRA stated that, 'in assessing the value of work performed by employees employed in the same establishment, the criteria to be applied are the skill, effort and responsibility required in the performance of the work and the conditions under which the work is performed.' The bill received assent on 14 July 1977 and came into force on 1 March 1978.

In stating that women in NAC understood the issue, Marsden seems to mean that they assumed that different jobs with very different content and tasks could be compared. This is apparent in McDonald's paper. She states that 'comparisons of jobs would be made on the basis of *objective* criteria – difficulty of task, job training required, responsibility for other workers, equipment and so forth.' Then she adds 'This is not an argument for job evaluation as *such*, but for machinery to challenge unfair evaluation schemes in use' (McDonald 1975, 6). It is apparent that there was some inquietude regarding job evaluation and what that procedure might involve, but, in 1975, little research was available on how gender bias formed part of traditional job-evaluation plans and processes. There seemed to be little realization by feminists at that time that the move to equal value might involve an entirely different approach to the problem of women's unequal pay, resulting in an entirely new set of problems and conflicts.

NAC's lobbying in favour of 'machinery to challenge unfair evaluation' of the work women do resulted in a compromise. The equal value provisions of the CHRA provide for implementation through a complaint process. Thus the CHRC has responsibility to respond to complaints filed by individuals or third parties. The commission also has power to initiate its own complaints, although it has never made use of this power. The implicit assumption of a complaint-orientated mechanism is that the system basically works and is free from discrimination and bias. In other words, it is assumed that systemic discrimination does not exist, but in those few individual cases where it does occur, it can be corrected through the complaint procedures (Armstrong and Armstrong 1990). This approach contrasts with a proactive one that places an obligation upon the employer to determine whether systemic gendered wage discrimination exists in the workplace and, if so, to remedy the situation following a predetermined time frame.

The principle of equal value is enshrined in a restricted manner in a number of different legal jurisdictions in Canada in one of three ways: 1 / through a complaint-driven process; 2 / through a proactive requirement on the employer to initiate plans; or 3 / a combination of complaint and proactive methods. Pay equity laws existing in Manitoba, Ontario, Nova Scotia, and Prince Edward Island require the employer to initiate plans in accordance with a set timetable, which to this date are one-time provisions. At a certain date, pay equity will be assumed to be implemented and the proactive requirements on employers will die. In some jurisdictions, a complaint process will remain in effect. Such is the case with the provisions of the Canadian Human Rights Act (CHRA).

When the principle for equal value was enshrined in the CHRA and given assent on 14 July 1977, the provisions for equal pay for the same or similar work, which were previously found in Part 1 of the Canada Labour Code, were repealed and replaced by a new clause (Niemann 1984, 58). Section 38.1, Part 3, of the code 'empowers Labour Canada Officers to inspect the compensation records of federal jurisdiction employers to ascertain the existence of sex discrimination in pay and, if found, require an employer to refrain from such practice' (Cornish 1986, 12). This means that Labour Canada has the responsibility to enforce the new labour standard of equal value. On occasions, this responsibility is referred to as the 'proactivity' of the federal sector equal-value provisions. It was not until 1984, however, that Labour Canada established its Equal Pay Division, with a program of education and promotion. It took several more years to put in place a policy designed to monitor and encourage compliance and response to non-compliance by firms in the federal sector. But, despite these programs, there is little change in the wage gap in the federal sector, and no complaints have been filed with the CHRC by the Equal Pay Division of Labour Canada.

NAC's original position in their 1975 lobbying campaign was that the equal-value principle should be enshrined in the Canada Labour Code 'since the Department of Labour already had the machinery for implementation and the necessary initiatory and monitoring powers' (Marsden 1980, 253). Although they did not call for proactivity, it is clear that they were sceptical of the CHRA complaint process and how effective it would be. Their suspicions about the CHRA proved to have grounds. Not only has the complaint process been very slow and cumbersome but the relatively few successful complaints were almost entirely initiated by unions in the public sector (Durber 1990, 3), leaving unorganized and organized women in the private sector effectively outside the provisions of section 11.

With the insertion of equal value into the CHRA, the attempt by women in the federal sector to readdress their unequal pay moved to a new terrain and a new type of relationship between the federal state and women. Quickly it became clear that certain women in unions perceived the provisions for equal value not only as a process for remedying individual cases of discrimination, but as a means of dealing with the systematic undervaluation of women as a whole. They set out to use the machinery of the act for the goal of raising women's significantly lower pay and narrowing the wage gap. In the next section, I consider how the equal-value provisions were used towards this end by women and their union operating within the federal government.

Political Power and Technical Disputes: Treasury Board versus Women in the Public Service Alliance of Canada

Once the equal-value provisions came into effect on 1 March 1978, the stage was set for the creation of new structures and meanings regarding equal pay for women. It was not clear at that point which groups and individuals would be able and prepared to make use of the complaint provisions.

Although the federal sector covers only approximately 10 per cent of all workers in Canada, the federal government is one of the largest employers of women in the country. The majority of these women are represented by the union called the Public Service Alliance of Canada (PSAC), which currently has a total membership of 175,000, of which nearly 47 per cent are women (PSAC 1990). Although up to that point, the PSAC had taken very little action regarding the subordinate position of its women members, both in the workplace and in the union, it did respond to the equal-value provisions of the CHRA. At its 1979 triennial convention, the union delegates were presented with a policy paper on equal value. In the paper, the problem of women's low pay was conceived as systemic, requiring a collective response rather than merely the filing of individual complaints. It recommended the pursuit of equal value for the female membership through formal complaints to the CHRC and through the collective-bargaining process (PSAC 1979). Adoption of the paper was unanimous. One of the first collective complaints to the CHRC was filed by the PSAC in February 1979, on behalf of predominantly female librarians, many of whom worked at the National Library in Ottawa. The endorsement by the alliance (PSAC) convention of the equal-value policy paper, therefore, was in support of this action. The complaint charged that librarians earned an average 20 per cent less than historical researchers (predominantly male) for performing work of equal value.

In 1976 the librarians left the Professional Institute of the Public Service (PIPS) because they perceived that their interests were not well served by the predominantly male professional union/association. By joining the PSAC, which overwhelmingly represented non-professional and lower-paid workers, they had 'thrown in their lot' with a relatively more proletarian and militant union. Librarians had joined the PSAC because they wanted a more aggressive stance adopted at the bargaining table with Treasury Board (the employer for all workers in the federal government system).[6]

Leaders among the librarians were aware of the equal-value provisions before the CHRA was promulgated and approached the PSAC negotiators concerning the possibility of making equal value a bargaining demand (Cornish 1986). Even before section 11 of the CHRA came into force, the PSAC made it clear to Treasury Board that they intended to try negotiating equal value at the bargaining table. Also, the librarians took a majority decision to change the method of settlement from binding arbitration to conciliation/strike in the event that a dispute might arise between themselves and the employer. This decision was important in that it changed the power relations between the women librarians and senior management in Treasury Board. With the change in the dispute-settlement route, the possibility of strike action was a threat the librarians held over negotiations. And although a librarians' strike would not cause any great inconvenience to the operation of the public service, the possibility of librarians striking and picketing in support of including equal value in their collective agreement when it was already a provision of the CHRA was a potential embarrassment to the government.

In the course of the negotiations, the PSAC negotiators, the librarians, and the leadership of the union discovered for the first time that the Treasury Board negotiators adamantly opposed the inclusion of equal value in the collective agreement and were unsympathetic to the demand for a pay adjustment based on the comparison with the Historical Researchers group. As the president of Treasury Board was part of the cabinet of the ruling party that had recently supported enshrining equal value in the CHRA, it was assumed incorrectly by some women in the PSAC that senior managers in the administration would be supportive of equal value. Treasury Board officials were opposed not only to a measure that had the possibility of substantially increasing the wage bill, but also to any measure that might undermine their control of the entire system of classifying categories and occupational groups.

Faced with Treasury Board's intransigence regarding the equal-value principle, the PSAC decided to take the case as a collective complaint to the Canadian Human Rights Commission (CHRC). Both the leaders of the librarians and the PSAC leadership were keen to avoid taking the group out on strike if at all possible, although this possibility remained a threat hanging over the process. The outcome of such a strike, however, was not at all certain, especially given the relatively low impact it was likely to have. Both the librarians and the leadership, therefore, decided to explore the possibilities of the CHRC's complaint process rather than risk a raw confrontation of power.

In consultation with officials of the CHRC, a sample of jobs was drawn from both the librarian (LS) and Historical Researcher (HR) groups. Responsibilities of these jobs were then evaluated using the same plan. Finally, two years after the equal-value bargaining demand had been delivered, a settlement was reached in conciliation with the assistance of the commission. It provided the 470 librarians with a total of $2.3 million back-dated to 1 March 1978, the point that the original bargaining demand was delivered to Treasury Board. Librarians individually received wage adjustments varying from $500 to $6,000, together with annual adjustments to ensure that 'equality' is maintained as new contracts are negotiated (PSAC 1988, 4; Labour Canada 1986, 18–19).

Although the librarians and their union, the PSAC, were seen to have successfully used section 11 of the CHRC in a case of systemic discrimination, it was assumed by all parties that the principle of equal value meant value as measured by a job-evaluation plan. That they should do so is not surprising. The practice of job evaluation is long-standing within the federal government and was set in place long before its workers unionized. Immediately following the First World War, a group of consultants from the United States were hired to examine the federal public service. Their recommendations led to the beginnings of the present complex and elaborate system of job classification and hierarchies (Hodgetts and Corbett 1960, 250–64). Given the well-established classification system, from its inception the PSAC employed its own job-evaluation experts in order to criticize and contest certain group and individual evaluations. It was these experts who now took up the responsibility for the union's initiating equal-pay complaints. Since evaluation was well established within the federal public service, it seemed 'natural' to the union that it would provide the basis for assessing equal value. As an inherited structure and set of practices, job classification and evaluation now act as determinants of what constitutes equal value in the attempt to achieve equal pay (Harrison and Mort 1978, 81).

Although some unions operate on the basis of trying to reduce differentials between higher and lower 'skilled' workers,[7] the PSAC had, on the whole, accepted the classification hierarchy devised by the employer, right up to the point of filing the complaint on behalf of the LS group. Furthermore, it has and continues to be Treasury Board's position that, under the Public Service Staff Relations Act (PSSRA), the union is denied the legal right to bargain classification and job-evaluation plans. Attempts by the union to do so were always rejected by Treasury Board negotiators. Given this situation, the PSAC operated within the confines of management's value system with respect to the ranking of job groups. In general, wages are negotiated as percentage increases, resulting in the higher-ranked groups receiving more pay over time, in absolute terms. With the filing of the librarian (LS) complaint, the PSAC, in effect, made a demand for a different value system to be applied to the work of these women. Equal value as a strategy for dealing with women's demand for equal pay was, therefore, grafted onto the job-classification and -evaluation system, so becoming a technical problem that apparently could be solved through the expertise of classification and job-evaluation consultants.

The success of the librarians in achieving a comparison with the Historical Researchers encouraged the filing of other group complaints. By December 1984, the PSAC had filed complaints on behalf of approximately 65,000 members (the majority were women, but this number includes men who were also members of the complainant groups), more than a third of the membership and covering approximately two-thirds of its women members. The largest group was the 50,000-strong clerical (CR) group, of which 80 per cent were women.

Up to the filing of the clerical workers' (CR) complaint, Treasury Board had taken a similar approach with all groups; it consisted of a refusal to insert clauses concerning equal value into the collective agreement and the argument that it was a classification matter and was not negotiable under the Public Service Staff Relations Act (PSSRA). In the face of this refusal to negotiate, the PSAC continues to take group complaints to the CHRC. During the federal election campaign in fall 1984, all three main political parties made pronouncements on women's low pay and supported the principle of equal pay for work of equal value. There was some hope among women in the PSAC that, once the Conservatives were elected, they would carry through on their leader's promises and agree to the insertion of the principle in collective agreements. Such was not to be the case, and the union received the same response from Treasury Board officials as earlier, when the Liberals were in power (PSAC 1990, 6).

The filing of the clerical workers' complaint in December 1984, however, brought a different response. It was clear that the number of workers implicated in the complaints was now large. Up to that point, the PSAC had some success with a few settlements involving small numbers of workers and similar if not identical work.[8] With large numbers of workers now involved, Treasury Board moved to take control of the process. Instead of playing a seemingly subordinate role to the rulings of the CHRC, Treasury Board officials acted in a way that visibly revealed their power in the federal departmental system.[9] As one of the most powerful departments in the system, Treasury Board moved to assert its dominance (Mahon 1977).

On 8 March 1985, International Women's Day, Treasury Board announced that all thirteen unions within the public service had 'agreed to work together on achieving equal pay' (PSAC 1990, 6). The vehicle for this was a joint union-management committee that would undertake a government-wide study. Immediately upon the making of this announcement, the PSAC found itself in a less powerful position than it had had through the complaint procedures of the CHRC. Even though the union represented most of the women who would be affected by the study results, they were allocated only one seat on the committee, despite the fact that the PSAC has twice as many women members as all the other unions put together. This action substantially reduced their power as the largest union within the federal government. There was reluctance by some of the PSAC leaders and staff to place the equal-value complaints in abeyance, but the union was not in a position to refuse to participate in a seemingly genuine attempt by the employer to resolve the equal-pay issue. Agreeing to participate in the study, the PSAC retained the right to pursue the equal-value complaints if not satisfied with the outcome.

Technical disputes and delays were the order of the day throughout the nearly five years it took to complete the study process. It took two years just for the terms of reference and a plan of action to be settled. Agreement was reached finally to sample 4,300 employee positions from 9 female-dominated groups and 53 dominated classifications. Information regarding the job content was collected by questionnaire, and responses were rated by rank-and-file union members and management representatives. Once again the PSAC was allocated only one position on the master evaluation committee (interview with PSAC evaluator, 6 March 1989). Bench-marks were set by this committee and provided the basis for evaluations made by a further ten subevaluation committees, which also included representatives from the unions and management. Disputes continually took place between the PSAC rank and file and management representatives regarding how fair their respective evaluations were. Allegations of bias were made on both sides (interviews).

As the study progressed it became clear to the PSAC that Treasury Board found the results of the Master Evaluation Committee unacceptable. As the PSAC evaluator on the Master Evaluation Committee remarked concerning Treasury Board officials: 'They may be willing to increase women's salaries 3 or 4% but in many cases we are looking at increases of 15%. The union recognises there are some inconsistencies in the Master Evaluation Committee results, plus we were unable to move the others about the secretaries comparison with trade workers, but over all we think the results of the Master Evaluation Committee are not too bad' (interview, 6 March 1989). The evaluator went on to say that she thought the evaluation plan used in the study worked much better for professional women than for secretaries. In her view, the results of the study may result in a widened gap between women in support positions and professional women. For example, the results were positive for nurses and librarians but she was unable to get the rest of the committee to accept the secretary-tradesperson comparison. She stated that, while the consultants were astonished by the comparison, 'it really frightened' Treasury Board officials.

Despite the limited results of the equal-pay study for women lower down in the hierarchy, the overall results were considered by the PSAC to be step forward in the process of closing the wage gap. Estimations made by the union, based on the study's evaluations, indicated that women in the public service are owed over a billion dollars in retroactive equal pay adjustments, together with 250 million dollars per year for future pay adjustments (an average of approximately 15 per cent increase).

The study was finally completed by September 1989. For approximately four months after its end, Treasury Board remained silent about the results and would make no commitment towards their implementation. Given the lack of response from the employer and deciding that the study had revealed sufficient data to make a good case for an average 15 per cent increase for women, the PSAC decided to withdraw from the process and reactivate its complaints with the CHRC (interviews).

Shortly after this decision, Treasury Board made its own move, unilaterally announcing the results of the study and the payments that would be made imminently. These results were, however, very different from those arrived at by the evaluation committees. The retroactive payments are about one-quarter of those shown by the study results and only one-third of those for correcting pay inequities in the future (PSAC 1990a). Max Yalden, chairman of the CHRC, when asked by the media if Treasury Board's proposed payments represented true pay equity, gave two answers. He replied: 'I think the answer to that is that it has not. I mean it's a step in the right direction.'

Faced with the real possibility that Treasury Board would gain consent from women in the public service to implement its version of the study results, the PSAC immediately geared up for a campaign to spread information about the study and to encourage members of the female-dominated groups to file grievances. The success of this campaign is not apparent at the moment but it faces a number of difficulties. Because of the complication of job evaluation, it is not easy to explain why the union has 'right' on its side. It is difficult to raise consciousness and mobilize women on the basis of graph's and pay lines. Furthermore, there was a fear that Treasury Board might refuse to pay their estimate of pay equity to those who file grievances. Added to these problems, and probably the most serious stumbling-block, is the union's low visibility and allegiance among many of its members. Within many workplaces, the PSAC does not have well-developed and organized union locals in action, so there is a real possibility that the information and grievance forms may never reach many of the affected members.

On the positive side, the experience of participating in the equal-value study helped to raise the consciousness and awareness of the rank-and-file evaluators with respect to the meaning of value and job worth. The secretaries/trades comparison that they supported and attempted to achieve revealed for many of them the ideological basis of the employer's evaluation of women's work and of how job-evaluation operates. This experience, together with Treasury Board's unilateral announcement of management's version of the study, made visible the power relations underlying the technic of job evaluation. Many of the rank-and-file evaluators, together with other women's activists who were kept informed of the study process, played an important role in the grievance campaign and in spreading knowledge and information regarding the process. Women's committees in the PSAC have taken up the campaign and issue of equal pay as the main focus of their activity, which may result in their further growth and extension, together with greater empowerment of women within the PSAC. Whether this will lead to the issue's becoming a focus of collective bargaining next time round is an open question. What is certain is that the union leadership is pursuing the issue through the complaint mechanism of the CHRC. Redress through this process alone promises to take a very long time, given the large number of occupational groups and technical questions involved.

Conclusion: Learning from a Federal Case

In the mid-1970s, the National Action Committee on the Status of Women addressed itself to the federal government and demanded that women be allowed to participate in liberal democratic society on the same terms that men participate – as individuals who compete on the basis of merit for a place in the market hierarchy. In demanding that women should have the same equality of opportunity in the market for jobs and positions, the leaders of NAC did not differentiate between women in terms of the unequal effects of class and race. Their liberal equality discourse demanded that women be given the opportunity to take their place in the workplace hierarchy on the same meritocratic basis as men. In the process they were successful in pressuring the federal government to legislate equal pay for work of equal value, albeit through the restrictive complaint process provided by the Canadian Human Rights Act.

The concept of equal value appeared to women in NAC to be a logical extension of the principle of equal pay for equal work – since women do not do the same work as men the pursuit of equal pay for work of equal value seemed to be a logical next step in remunerating women fairly (McDonald 1975, 5). Yet, to be an employee means not only to sell one's labour power but also to enter a system of management control. Job-evaluation systems with Canadian society and liberal-democratic capitalist societies in general highly value managerial control and professional skills, reflecting the class and gender hierarchy that exists, both in the workplace and in society in general (Warskett 1990). Job-evaluation reinforces the hierarchical structuring of status and pay within the workplace because it assumes the existence of fine gradations of skill and responsibility and is part of the ideology and practice of perpetuating hierarchies of control and knowledge rather than the attempt to reduce differentials between workers (Hyman 1974).

Pay equality has come to mean, for the most part, value as measured by job-evaluation systems. Equating equal pay with job evaluation tends to mask the inequality inherent in a structure where management control is assigned the highest weighting and value. The concepts of 'equality' and 'fairness' serve to legitimize the existing hierarchy and structured inequality, which is based only on gender discrimination but also on class divisions emanating from the market economy.

To advocate that women's pay should be based on this logic is to affirm a certain faith in the operation of market pricing and the class hierarchy it supports. Underlying the strategy of equal value is the assumption that gender bias and discrimination have prevented women from being valued on the basis of merit and achievement, so denying them their proper place in the hierarchy. The hierarchy itself is not questioned despite the fact that large numbers of women, aboriginal peoples, people of colour, and new Canadians are found at its lower end. As Ackelsberg points out, 'the liberal paradigm denies people their roots in communities (a fact that particularly denies the social reality of many Black and White working class women's lives)' (1988, 302). From the standpoint of liberal feminism, all women are perceived to experience discrimination equally, and no account is taken of the differential experiences of race, class, or other kinds of social and community conditions.

Once the principle of equal value was inscribed within the state structure, it became the focus of union women who, up to that point, primarily had sought traditional collective-bargaining means of addressing their economic subordination. Treating section 11 of the CHRC as a means of addressing the systemic defects in the government's classification system, the PSAC filed group complaints and participated in the evaluation of women's jobs as they compared to men's. In this way, the meaning of equal value was grafted on to the process of job evaluation, with all its appearance as an essentially technical procedure. The success of their efforts in bringing into question the traditional classification system of the federal public service, however, necessitated that Treasury Board assert its power and control over the technical process. Initially it attempted to do this by establishing the equal-pay study, effectively placing the PSAC's equal-pay complaints in abeyance. The Canadian Human Rights Commission, as a subordinate site within the federal government system, has limited power to represent women, and, in the contest between Treasury Board and the PSAC over women's unequal pay, is currently marginalized. Given the power of Treasury Board, the commission seems incapable of acting independently.

Despite the problems with the equal-pay study from the standpoint of the PSAC, the results of the evaluation committees did point to the systemic undervaluation of many women's jobs compared to men's although it did not produce exceptional results for certain groups, especially secretaries. The results, however, seemed to touch the core interests of Treasury Board. In its role as employer, it acted unilaterally to keep wage costs to a minimum and maintain the hierarchy of the public service's classification system. It remains to be seen if the union can organize the power of its membership to contest the employer's unilateral decision through the grievance and collective-bargaining process and also to what extent women will gain effective representation from the CHRC.

The disagreement between Treasury Board and the PSAC was not fundamentally technical in nature but derived from different conceptions of what value should be placed on the work women do. It is a matter of political power rather than technical rationality whose view will prevail and be implemented. Attempting to use the technical processes of the CHRC's complaint mechanism and job-evaluation procedures in order to rectify what is essentially a question of political power, women in the federal government came up against or rather met 'head on' with the political power of Treasury Board. It is a matter of future history how effective this power will be in convincing the CHRC and any tribunals that may be established regarding their interpretation of the study results.

Exercising power in an authoritarian manner is never without contradictions and costs. The unilateral actions of Treasury Board had the effect for some of uncloaking the political power that stands behind the definition of what is job value and of worth to whom. By participating in and contesting the structures and conditions that are given from history women inevitably participate in constructing new structures and meanings. As a consequence they have the potential to learn about the limitations and possibilities of these very structures and the meanings defining them – and, more important, to develop consciousness regarding who has power, who needs to become empowered, and what strategies need to be developed to end discriminatory pay.

NOTES

1 I would like to thank Wallace Clement, Sue Findlay, Judy Fudge, and Pat McDermott and two anonymous reviewers for their comments. The research for this and other papers on Pay Equity was funded by a SSHRC strategic research grant.

2 Interview with Elizabeth Millar, Head of Classification Division, Public Service Alliance of Canada, April 1989

3 This was at the Strategy for Change Conference in Toronto. Women came from across the country, although the 500-strong meeting was dominated by women from Toronto (Marsden 1980, 244).

4 The labour-force participation rate for women is now approximately 55 per cent as compared to 27 per cent in 1961, and women now represent nearly 40 per cent of all unionized workers as compared to 16.6 per cent in 1965. These significant material changes underlie the push by the women's movement and unions for strategies designed to raise women's pay.

5 Personal communication with Sue Findlay, January 1991

6 The data for the cases cited in this paper come from my own notes, papers, personal recollection, and interviews conducted with members and officials from 1975 to 1988 while I was a union representative for the PSAC.

7 For example, see Julie White (1990). Her study of the Canadian Union of Postal Workers (CUPW) reveals that the union developed a perspective that valued solidarity and equality and hence generated the demand to decrease pay differentials between different kinds of workers, including those occupying predominantly male and female positions (1990, 209–10).

8 This had been case with the librarians' complaint. Their work in the National Library was very similar to that of the Historical Researchers, who worked mainly in the National Archives. See also Lewis (1988, 46). In the case of the General Services group, the complaint was settled in March

1982, and involved female-dominated food, laundry, and miscellaneous service groups in comparison with male-dominated stores, message, cleaner groups. Although workers engaged in different work, the current evaluation plan revealed them to be of equal value even under the employer's present classification plan. See PSAC (1988).

9 See Mahon (1977, 1984) for an analysis of Treasury Board's powerful position in the 'unequal structure of representation' of the departmental system.

10 Job Evaluation and Managerial Control: The Politics of Technique and the Techniques of Politics

Ronnie J. Steinberg

Pay equity policy has two faces. Proponents have succeeded in constructing a theory of wage discrimination on the foundations of systemic discrimination that acknowledges the link between occupational segregation and the devaluation of women's work. The movement for pay equity has also broadened public thinking on what discrimination is and redefined standards of fairness. In contrast, actual pay equity adjustments fall far short of the estimates of wage discrimination that have been generated in those few pay equity studies that are carried out in accordance with state-of-the-art knowledge of gender bias in job evaluation.

In attempting to explain initiative outcomes, most studies focus on the effectiveness of proponents' tactics and resources, while paying insufficient attention to the tactics and resources of opponents.[1]

This focus needs to be balanced by an understanding of the strategies, tactics, and resources that undercut the full realization of reform efforts. Further, proponents' strategies are often shaped in reaction to opposition campaigns. Even in so-called easily implemented pay equity initiatives, wage adjustments to historically female jobs fall far short of eliminating discrimination. Why has this been the case?

The struggle around pay equity has not been the war between advocates and opponents characteristic of ERA or reproductive-rights policies, but has rather been one of jockeying to expand or contain the meaning and outcomes of the reform. In other words, rather than being openly opposed, pay equity has been effectively contained. With few exceptions, even when it has been defeated, pay equity has rarely evoked strong, visible, openly political opposition.[2] And, as will be described at greater length below, few of its strongest proponents have seen the process through implementation. The issue of how reforms like comparable worth are contained at the same time as they are implemented has received little scholarly attention. Eisenstein (1981) has argued that in theory radical feminist demands are filtered through the liberal state, resulting in policies that undercut the radical features of the original proposals. But what does it mean, concretely, to 'filter' a reform through the state? Writing more broadly about Canada, Barnsley (1988, 18) holds that, as women's issues are institutionalized, they are redefined and compromised, 'often beyond recognition.' Through the appearance of neutrality and the mediation of competing interests, the state, in fact, contains the reform, serving some interests better than others. The outcome of such efforts is to absorb the reform into 'traditional frameworks and dominant ideology' and to render the critique of social institutions invisible (see also Mitchell 1988, 64). But how is this achieved?

I, too, have argued that feminist advocates have had to abandon their feminist critiques of existing institutional arrangements in exchange for practical political gains (Steinberg 1987c, 1987d, 1990). They are forced to choose between defeat and accommodation. In the case of pay equity, proponents have had to publicly support proposals for wage adjustments based on compensation policies they were aware maintained significant gender bias. It has also meant that they justified their demands in terms that maintained the ideologies of job hierarchies and the market (Steinberg 1987a). How do advocates come to find themselves in this position?

Only Acker (1989), in her detailed study of the Oregon pay equity initiative, offers a sustained discussion of this issue, although it is not the primary theoretical focus of her book. She documents a number of features of initiatives that are important in understanding how advocates come to support the outcomes of initiatives, even when such outcomes bear little resemblance to their original objectives. These factors include the composition of the legislative task force, the relationship between the job-evaluation consultant and the task force, the tactics used by the personnel department to undercut task force control, the dynamics of job-evaluation committees, tension among unions, and dilemmas surrounding collective bargaining.

This essay builds on the insights of Acker by using information gathered from several pay equity initiatives to trace the tactics used for containing the reform by seemingly neutral administrators and policy makers. Within individual initiatives, most strategies of containment involve manipulation of the process and results of job-evaluation studies that are used as the basis for determining pay equity adjustments. The message of this essay is simple: since job evaluation involves hundreds of detailed decisions, each of which has implications for the final estimates of wage discrimination, those who control job evaluation control the outcome. Thus, the tactics for containment generally involve specific ways of maintaining the appearance of full participation of advocates, while minimizing proponent input into the decisions surrounding job evaluation.

In pay equity, managerial control of job evaluation has been directed towards two ends: 1 / achieving the lowest pay equity estimates that can be obtained without noticeable opposition from proponents, and 2 / increasing managerial control over classification and compensation practices. The case materials illustrating the general patterns have been drawn from U.S. experience between 1972 and 1989 in an effort to facilitate dialogue on developing strategies for overcoming containment tactics. While comparisons across countries are necessarily limited by their differing political structures and cultures, an analysis of containment tactics may offer some useful lessons as implementation in Canada unfolds.

Background Conditions

Administrative containment of pay equity has been facilitated by four background conditions that set the parameters within which most of the specific battles were fought and immediate strategies developed. First, because pay equity is a controversial reform, it is quite easy to mobilize opposition from among the business community and among male employees, two relatively powerful political constituencies. Pay equity is inconsistent with dominant legal, ideological, and cultural norms. It collides with laisser-faire legal doctrines that have been gaining ascendancy since 1980 and with the widely held concept of the market. It seeks to attach higher value to activities performed by women, something that inevitably threatens male dominance (Steinberg 1986). Both administrators and advocates are aware of these potential sources of opposition and negotiate with them in the back of their minds. Progressive politicians who rely on feminist support do not want to activate the opposition and then have to make a choice among constituencies. Far better is a course of implementation that allows the reform but contains it. The ease with which opposition can be mobilized has often been used to secure concessions from advocates.

Furthermore, there is no consensus over pay equity as the appropriate strategy for correcting the low wages of women workers. Nor is there a consensus that the skills differentially found in historically female work should be positively valued. As a result, proponents fear that, if they make the reform effort go public and mobilize women, they will trigger a backlash. A general debate may turn into a struggle among competing interests in which women will lose even more than they do when concessions are made (Evans and Nelson 1989). These fears have led proponents in the United States to shy away from grass-roots mobilization and from private-sector employers.[3] Administrators are aware that feminist advocates fear going too public, for fear of discrediting themselves with administrators and politicians with whom they must continue to work on any political issues. Administrators also fear losing whatever control of the reform they are able to command to a mobilized opposition.

Second, the general structure of the discourse and debates surrounding the early years of the reform quickly put proponents on the defensive in reaction to strong and vocal general opposition from organizations representing business interests such as the Business Roundtable, chambers of commerce, and personnel management associations. These interests cornered many of the symbols consistent with sound business practice, consequently painting pay equity advocates as unreasonable middle-class feminist radicals out to destroy the free-enterprise system. Proponents, in turn, were unable to define the reform proactively. Instead, they were beset with criticisms that they were forced to respond to – criticisms designed to undercut the reasonableness of the reform and the reformers. Pay equity was criticized in terms of four somewhat inconsistent arguments – that there is no problem; that the wage gap doesn't measure discrimination; that you can't measure the problem; and that solving the problem would create new, and even worse problems (Steinberg 1986). The opposition resorted to a defence of the free market, to the ideology of free choice, and to the need for a stable economy.

In answering these criticisms, proponents found themselves defending social institutions that were, in fact, detrimental to the achievement of pay equity and contrary to their political philosophies. Proponents defended the use of job evaluation, even though they were highly critical of the practical application of the technique. They argued that pay equity was not inconsistent with the market, that job evaluation could be used to disentangle legitimate wage differences from those that reflected discriminatory practices, and that pay equity adjustments would not 'break the bank.' The necessity of responding to these criticisms drained proponents of time and resources that could have been better spent achieving pay equity. This framework had the consequence of committing proponents both to job evaluation and to realistic cost figures.

Third, precedents set in the states that first implemented pay equity restricted how advocates elsewhere could proceed and what they could get. Washington State, Connecticut, San Jose, and Minnesota used unmodified job-evaluation systems to estimate the extent of wage discrimination.

In Washington State, a pay equity study was funded on the heels of a job-evaluation study of management jobs. State managerial jobs had been found to be undervalued relative to comparable private-sector jobs. Proponents were able to get the same procedures applied to a comparison of male and female jobs within the state (Remick 1980; Hutner 1986). Sixteen years, one major court case, and four studies later, the state agreed to a modest implementation plan that would adjust female wages over a five-year period.

In San Jose, proponents also piggybacked their study onto a study of management salaries. The management study was implemented without controversy. The pay equity study was not. After lengthy attempts to negotiate, the union went out on strike, which facilitated a settlement with the female-headed City Council (Flammang 1986, 1987).

In Minnesota, a study of state jobs had already been conducted, using a conventional job-evaluation system, but it had not been implemented. The state's Commission on the Economic Status of Women reanalysed the data to determine the pay gap for male and female jobs of equivalent complexity. The gap in pay averaged between 5 and 20 per cent. The commission drafted legislation proposing that inequities be eliminated. The legislation passed. The relative success of this initiative rests on a unique conjunction of factors: a completed job-evaluation study that had not been undertaken by feminists; a Commission on Women with close ties to the governor and to the legislature; a little-known reform that engendered little opposition; reasonable wage adjustments. In addition, the legislature was operating at a budget surplus, and the unions were supportive. To implement this and several other reforms for state employees, the governor appointed the executive director of the commission to be the head of the personnel department responsible for implementing the adjustments (Evans and Nelson 1989, ch. 12).

These cases are important for the limits they set on future initiatives. In each of them, unmodified systems of job evaluation perpetuated gender bias and the invisibility of skills and responsibilities found in women's jobs. Indeed, in two of the three early studies, the specific job-evaluation system used to estimate wage discrimination was the one that had been most visibly criticized by technical proponents – the Hay system. By the time of implementation, the Minnesota commission leadership were aware that its recommended wage adjustments were based on a system that perpetuated the undervaluation of women's work, but they believed that conducting a study that would modify this system would be too costly in terms of money, time, and political success. They didn't risk it.

Only Connecticut set out to conduct a job evaluation from scratch. The first study led to a second, general classification study of all state jobs, partially as a result of the final report of the compensation consultant who conducted the first study. Over a decade later, the study is still under way, having experienced labour-management battles every step of the way.

These early precedents resulted in modest pay equity adjustments. Not surprisingly, the implementation plans that grew out of further political negotiations watered down even more the already limited technical results. Wage adjustments that result from pay equity studies using unmodified job-evaluation systems usually are based on the consistent application of these systems to female and male jobs. In other words, all jobs are described and evaluated, using the same set of factors and factor weights, and salaries are set according to one pay line. Even if the factors and weights are biased to favour characteristics differentially found in male jobs, correcting the inconsistencies of past evaluation procedures usually uncovers some wage discrimination.

Early outcomes affected later initiatives in two opposing ways. On the one hand, a political demand had become a policy outcome, making it easier for proponents elsewhere to argue that pay equity was a feasible political objective. On the other hand, it set the narrow precedent of using job evaluation and using it in certain ways.[4] By 1983, the use of job evaluation was firmly established through the release of the final report of the National Academy of Sciences, *Women, Work and Wages,* which cautiously endorsed the use of job evaluation as a method for determining wage discrimination (Treiman and Hartmann 1981). It came to appear that, in the United States, in conducting a job-evaluation study, all that was necessary was consistency in the application of the system, even if the system that was being applied consistently was male-biased. Any attempt to modify existing systems of job evaluation was now made more difficult because policy makers and administrators faced with demands for comparable pay could point to Washington, Minnesota, San Jose, and a few other early efforts as evidence that using an unmodified system was good enough to achieve pay equity (Haignere, this volume, ch. 8). Advocates might provide lengthy critiques of the sources of sex bias in job-evaluation systems, but, in all but a few initiatives, they proved unable to translate these critiques into studies using modified systems.

These early outcomes limited the success of later initiatives in at least one other important respect. For the first decade of the reform's implementation, there were no consulting firms able or willing to cleanse their systems of sex bias in a manner consistent with proponents' criticisms. The first Washington State study was completed in 1972. San Jose, Minnesota, and Connecticut followed in the late 1970s. The first published critiques of job-evaluation systems did not appear until the late 1970s (Thomson 1978; Remick 1979). The growth in recognition of the need to modify job-evaluation systems got under way in the late 1970s and early 1980s.[5] The New York State Comparable Pay Study, begun in 1983, was the first to be carried out by proponents. A second study group was founded several years later and has conducted studies in a number of jurisdictions in which advocates have been powerful enough to oppose hiring a mainstream compensation firm. However, even with the emergence of technical consultants sympathetic to pay equity and with an understanding of the scope of gender bias in systems of job evaluation, it has been difficult to put their knowledge into practice. In the New York State study, proponents were constrained politically from modifying their job-evaluation system to cleanse it of gender bias, as they understood it. Not surprisingly, the study yielded relatively low estimates of wage discrimination, providing a powerful source of legitimation for the even smaller adjustment recommendations offered by the state to union leadership.

More commonly, it has been difficult to get firms with modified systems hired. Precedent studies have provided relatively low estimates of wage discrimination – certainly lower than those that would result from studies using modified systems. Administrators are loath to hire such firms, viewing them as threats to their jurisdiction's budget, especially when they don't have to in order to be perceived as achieving pay equity. In addition, administrators fear firms with modified systems, because they view them as 'uncontrollable.' In other words, they see the firms as driven more by their commitment to pay equity than by their commitment to meeting the needs of their client which is to contain pay equity while giving the appearance of realizing it. Thus, administrators in most jurisdictions have found it easier to hire consultants with unmodified systems (Haignere, this volume, ch. 8). At best, these consultants are willing to make minor modifications, as long as the essential integrity of their system is preserved.

Strategies for Containing Pay Equity

A second phase of pay equity initiatives emerged in the early 1980s. Spurred by the first round of successes, by the impact of the gender gap on the 1982 U.S. elections, by positive court cases, and by a favourable report on the feasibility of pay equity released by the National Research Council, proponents in many states and municipalities fought for pay equity studies. Many hoped that these studies would be based on the use of modified systems of job evaluation.

Containment tactics used to control implementation of job-evaluation studies – while not new – came more clearly into focus in this second phase. By this time, many proponents were aware of the technical difficulties involved in job evaluation. They were also aware of how sensitive the results of job-evaluation exercises were to the detailed design of factor definitions and factor weights (Treiman 1984). At this point, job evaluation was used strategically and cautiously. None the less, proponents underestimated the strength and tactics of administrators in shifting the locus of control away from them. The loss of control by proponents has had serious consequences for the resulting pay equity adjustments. Job-evaluation systems have emerged largely intact and relegitimated. Adjustments for wage discrimination turn out to be less costly than annual cost-of-living adjustments. Illustrations of five different containment strategies reveal how this is accomplished.

Control of Technical Decisions

A first strategy involves turning political decisions into technical decisions. These decisions are consequently removed from the realm of negotiation. For example, the definition of a female-dominated job has far-reaching implications for the number of job classes and the eventual cost of pay equity wage adjustments. It is a highly political decision that more often than not is made by the compensation consultant. The design of the job-evaluation system and the construction of factors and factor weights also give the appearance of a set of objective decisions made on technical grounds. That is why the choice of the job-evaluation consultant is such a critical one. Most systems of job evaluation have been designed to reproduce the wage hierarchy, including wage discrimination (Treiman 1984).

It is not surprising, then, how, in many initiatives, control of the job-evaluation study has been placed in the hands of personnel administrators, including control over the choice of the consultant. Personnel administrators have defended their expertise, their neutrality, and their jurisdiction over this matter before legislatures with great success. Often a condition of getting a study through collective bargaining has been to allow management unilateral control of the study, ostensibly because the relative wage structure (as opposed to the general level of compensation) has not been a bargainable issue. Unions are extended only 'meet and confer' rights.

Even in instances where the compensation consultant has agreed to modify the system, it is quite easy to do so in appearance only. Acker (1987, 189) reports on this tactic as it was used in Oregon. The task force in that state debated with the job-evaluation consultant about gender bias in several factor definitions. With great resistance, the consulting firm agreed to modify its system. It did so by adding factor levels and redefining factors so that no job classes would be rated within the additional levels. Specifically, it added a first level to a factor measuring human relations for jobs that involve 'no courtesy' and a fifth level for jobs that require an extraordinary amount of skill, 'stretching a three-level factor into five factors.' Ironically, the consultant admitted that 'a job with that high a level of skill probably did not exist in the State of Oregon.' By the time the advocates understood what the consultant had done, most jobs had been evaluated, and the task force, in order to correct the new problem, would have had to appropriate additional monies, delay the findings, and explain to their constituencies how they had allowed this to happen.

In Massachusetts, the compensation consultant redesigned its own system in line with administrators' concern with maintaining the relative wage structure so as to protect managerial interests. One major concern about pay equity is that it will lower the wages of managerial relative to non-managerial jobs. In the modification of its job-evaluation system, factor definitions were refined to lower the value of complexity of male non-managerial positions, increase the value of non-supervisory professional functions common to personnel administrators and labour-relations lawyers, and maintain the relative positions between female-dominated and male managerial job classes.

Another example is drawn from the modification of a working conditions factor of a standard evaluation system, resulting from labour-management negotiations. Additional job-complexity points were added to this factor, providing for a total of 50 points instead of 40. All the additional points were distributed to the top three levels of a six-level factor. Unfortunately, the union negotiating the modification was not made aware that *none* of the job classes being evaluated scored above the fourth level.

Perhaps the most egregious way in which political decisions are obscured as technical involves the manipulation of the final estimates of undervaluation. Typically, pay equity studies involve comparing, for each historically female job class, the actual wage to a predicted wage in the absence of discrimination. The predicted wage is derived by using a pay line that represents a standard of non-discrimination. There are several standards, including the use of a male pay line or the use of an average pay line that has been adjusted to remove the impact of 'femaleness' on pay. Wage discrimination is defined to be the difference between the actual pay and the wage predicted based on the salary line.[6]

What compensation consultants have done is to create a 'zone of error' around the pay line, usually as wide as plus or minus 15 per cent. In San Jose, California, for example, the management consulting firm proposed a

band form by the area within 15 percent of either side of the trend line ... [It was] referred to as the 'error factor' zone and represent[ed] the margin of error expected from the rating process. Jobs outside the band were earmarked as needing special pay adjustments if achieving internal equity was to be realized. Those classes within the band were considered to be paid sufficiently close to their organizational value. (Farnquist et al. 1983, 362)

Pay equity adjustments in Washington State were based on bringing undervalued job classes up to 5 per cent below the average line (which includes unadjusted wages paid for historically female classes). To understand how effective this decision is in lowering costs, consider the results of one pay equity study of a large city. This study recommended bringing undervalued female classes up to 10 per cent below the average line. Consider further that using an average line already lowers the estimates and incorporates the undervaluation found in women's classes into all classes (Treiman et al. 1984; Steinberg and Haignere 1987). The additional decision to bring classes to only 10 per cent below the line further reduced the cost of pay equity in this city from $33.5 million to $13.7 million.

Compensation consultants cannot justify their use of an 'error zone' on technical grounds. Confidence intervals around estimates are typically used when statisticians are deriving conclusions about a population based on a sample. Comparable-pay studies involve the entire population of job titles. Other procedures are used in the evaluation process to smooth out inconsistencies in evaluation across jobs. No technical error is corrected through this procedure. In fact, in Connecticut, a union that saw through this tactic brought the issue to arbitration. The 'zone of error' proposal was dropped by management during the arbitration hearings. By obscuring political issues, administrators and policy-makers are able to provide legitimacy for study results.

Because reform efforts hinge on such technical details, the fact that most of the technical decisions are inaccessible and incomprehensible to advocates and employees means that they are powerless to protect their own interests.

Control of Information

A second strategy for containing reform outcomes involves withholding information, making it impossible for advocates to develop a counter-proposal in a timely fashion. In New York State, for example, a staff of seventeen state employees spent almost two years developing a pay policy after the completion of a pay equity study by an outside consultant. Although the technical unit was funded by joint labour-management monies, and the two major labour unions were periodically updated on progress, management refused to share either the data or the details of its model, hiding behind both technical and collective-bargaining considerations. It argued that the union was entitled only to 'meet and confer' status on issues of classification. The state also reasoned that to inform the union of the details of the model would enable it to educate employees to distort information about their jobs to maximize their salaries. The reasons why the unions involved accepted these arguments are complex and beyond the scope of this paper (see Steinberg, forthcoming).

Neither union felt troubled by receiving only progress reports, which they believed provided them with sufficient knowledge of the activities of the technical unit. No advocate monitored the activities of the technical unit. Nor did either union involved have a member of the staff or a consultant available to decipher the technical results. The pay equity adjustments recommended by the state were a shock to the leadership of the two unions, especially to the union representing entry-level professional employees. With no warning, the state recommended significant wage downgrades for almost one-half of all the job classes in the professional-bargaining unit. The leadership of this unit, caught off guard and without information, with its membership having waited more than five years for the study results, ended up trading off the downgrades for most of the pay equity adjustments it expected to get. Since the state recommendations were timed to dovetail with union elections, leadership of that union spent most of its energies trying to get re-elected in the face of these outrageous choices. In this example, the state also played off long-standing hostilities between the unions, a containment strategy that will be discussed below.

Cost Ceilings

After participating in a number of initiatives, I have come to learn that administrators often go into pay equity studies with a cost ceiling for pay adjustments. They share this information with the compensation consultant, who is asked to develop a model that will yield estimates of wage discrimination that do not exceed the arbitrarily imposed cost ceiling.

Haignere (see ch. 8) and Evans and Nelson (1989) point out that many jurisdictions are quite open about cost-containment mechanisms. Manitoba, for example, specified that pay equity adjustments would come to 1 per cent of payroll for four years, following the path of Minnesota (Haignere, ch. 8). In New York, as already mentioned, 1 per cent of payroll was set aside for three years for pay equity adjustments. Announcing the plans for implementation in an Office of Employee Relations newsletter, the state's then director of that office, Tom Hartnett, said: 'We had a bottom line on dollar resources and pay equity was part of the wage equation. Both labor and management recognized the need to establish pay equity. Both knew the bottom line of the resources available ... The resolve of the state and its public employee unions to address pay equity together, without outside interference, has established a national model for labor/management cooperation.'

In this example, both labour and management agreed to treat wage adjustments under a more general clause in the collective-bargaining agreement concerning reclassification. The New York State system of classification is divided into 38 salary grades. Within each salary grade, there are pay steps for seniority. The classification provision creates ceilings on wage increases that can occur as a result of reclassification. Each salary grade represents approximately a 5 per cent wage increase. Yet, based on this provision, incumbents of classes found to be undervalued by one salary grade received up to 2.5 per cent wage increases, depending on seniority. Incumbents of classes found to be undervalued by two salary grades received up to 4 per cent increases. Incumbents of job classes found to be undervalued by three salary grades received up to 6 per cent wage increases. Thus, the more undervalued, the greater the difference between step-to-step adjustments and clause-constrained adjustments. Ironically, it also turned out that the longer the tenure of the job incumbent in the undervalued title, the lower the wage increase.

Perhaps no single decision saved New York State government more money. Without being consulted, incumbents traded off seniority for salary-grade increases. Both unions were male-dominated. Neither union had been a significant force initiating the pay equity effort, although they became key players once the study got off the ground. Thus, these unions didn't want pay equity adjustments that would create problems with their male membership. With this approach, the unions were simultaneously able to provide adjustments and to minimize them, holding off potential backlash from incumbents of white- and male-dominated jobs. The need, especially of many unions, to accommodate multiple constituencies has been used magnificently by management to contain the reform. It is a variant of the third strategy of containment, involving efforts at dividing and conquering natural allies.

Creating Divisions

This third, and perhaps the most common, tactic involved placing proponents in a minority position on a task force or advisory committee, dividing them, or pushing them out entirely after they have succeeded in gaining monies to undertake a study. In Hawaii, New Hampshire, North Carolina, and Vermont, advocates were excluded from all decisions surrounding the job-evaluation study. None of these studies has been completed.

Dividing unions among themselves and unions and feminist advocates is another frequently used approach. In New York State and in Massachusetts, the adjustments recommended for each of the major unions representing state employees were designed to further fuel an already hostile and competitive relationship among unions. In New York, as mentioned above, one union was offered downgrades. The other was offered face-saving adjustments, especially to job classes with few incumbents. Since the latter union's leadership did not have a deep commitment to the reform, it found the state's recommendation 'good enough' to offer to its membership. In Massachusetts, the Department of Labor Relations bargained over the results of the job evaluation separately with each union. There are eight unions representing public employees, and bargaining units are highly sex-segregated. Preliminary estimates suggest that the raises for male jobs were as high as the wage adjustments to female jobs, cancelling out any shift in the relative position of female jobs in the wage structure. Historical antipathy precluded unions from sharing information and working together to bring about pay equity.

One group is often offered special privileges or fuller information as a tactic to divide a potential coalition before it gets entrenched. Unions are often privileged when women's advocates outside the union movement are marginalized, on the argument that unions formally represent the incumbents of historically female jobs. Thus, it would be illegitimate to remove decisions from the bargaining parties. In dividing union and feminist groups, management often plays on historical antipathies among these constituencies as well. While these are legitimate claims, there are problems with leaving the implementation of pay equity solely in the hands of labour and management. In some instances, where the membership is overwhelmingly female or where those directly representing the union in day-to-day decisions over pay equity are female, this may not materialize into a problem.[7] Yet, In many other instances, administrators extend special rights to certain unions because these unions have developed comfortable and reasonable relationships with managements. This tactic has hurt unions because, at the point at which administrators lower the boom on unions, they have undercut their ability to quickly mobilize a coalition of support.[8]

The fact that all unions do not support pay equity has been used to great advantage by administrators. Acker (1989) shows how, in Oregon, unions representing male employees actively opposed the reform in the legislature, thereby facilitating managerial objectives. In Connecticut, a state in which proponents have been unusually successful against containment tactics, proponents have worked against considerable odds to create a coalition among unions at critical junctures of the job-evaluation process. They have not always been successful, however, which has undercut their efforts to maximize wage adjustments. For example, as an interim strategy, the union representing health-care workers – the lowest-paid state job family – negotiated an adjustment model that would bring all undervalued job classes in its unit to a pay line based on male jobs in the unit. This tactic provided very high wage adjustments to the job classes represented by the union. But their tactic was subverted by administrators who subsequently used it to undercut adjustments to other classes in other unions. The state decided to use this male pay line from the lowest-paid bargaining unit as the state's pay equity line to be applied to all historically female classes in all bargaining units. The next union representing female classes accepted the state's proposal, although it lowered the pay adjustments of the female members considerably. Because female jobs represented by this union were so undervalued, this artificially low pay line could allow for pay equity adjustments and still leave the state with monies left over for additional raises for male classes in the bargaining unit. This expedient outcome was accepted even though the pay line used was significantly lower than a male line for all state jobs would have been. A third union bargaining with the state strongly rejected the state's proposal and ended up in arbitration. It won, but it took almost two years from start to finish for the progressive unions in that state to overturn the administrators' proposal.

The most common variant of this tactic is to place proponents in a minority position on a decision-making or advisory body. Because there is no consensus on pay equity, what typically happens is that, at some point in the study, proponents are defeated or compromised in a series of technical decisions. These controversial decisions are usually made near the end of the study. Having participated in and publicly supported the study, proponents find themselves cornered: they can compromise their goals and achieve something or lose face among their constituents and lose pay adjustments. Too much has been invested in the process to abandon it at that point. In Oregon, Acker tells of a lengthy and fragile study process, which shattered at the end, as proponents had to jockey with others on the task force, with the personnel department, with the major labour unions (one of which represented only male-dominated job classes), and with the management consultants. With this many gatekeepers it is remarkable than any wage adjustments were made!

An ironic twist involves hiring proponents to carry out the pay equity study and then constraining them from estimating undervaluation based on their understanding of it. Unlike Oregon, New York State hired the Center for Women in Government to conduct a study of wage discrimination. Two years into the study and six months before its completion, through a series of manoeuvres that cornered the advocacy organization, the state modified the contract for the study to prohibit the centre from performing certain, technical analyses. Specifically, the centre was prohibited from developing a policy-capturing wage model that would modify the weights to positively valued job characteristics differentially found in historically female jobs. The models presented in the final report either did not contain those characteristics or actually weighted the characteristics negatively, net of the impact of other job characteristics. Since the contract modifications were piggybacked onto additional monies to complete the study, the Center's choice was to accept the contract modifications or fail to complete the study. Based on subsequent analysis of the data this constraint probably lowered the estimates of undervaluation by two to four salary grades, which represented 10 to 20 per cent in lost salary adjustments (Jacobs and Steinberg, forthcoming).

Following the completion of this study, the state moved into what it called 'an interim phase' in which it spent two years designing a wage model that would serve as the basis of implementation. It carried out yet another analysis of wage discrimination, using the data collected by the Center for Women in Government. Although the wage model formulated by the state was even more watered down than the one in the Center's final report, in announcing its recommendations, the state implied that the model was the outcome of this data set. Many state employees disappointed at the results held the Center responsible. Here management used an advocacy organization as a front to legitimize what were perhaps the lowest pay equity adjustments that had been announced to date. As this New York State example vividly demonstrates, even in situations where job-evaluation consultants are committed to pay equity and have modified their job-evaluation systems, such consultants are frequently stymied in their abilities to freely estimate the extent of wage discrimination.[9] Their reputation, however, acts as an endorsement of the results.

Modifying the Issue

A fourth tactic that is frequently used to contain pay equity involves piggybacking other political agendas onto the effort to achieve pay equity and then minimizing pay equity while realizing the other agendas. The most common example of this involves redesigning the entire compensation system as a route to pay equity. In Massachusetts, for example, the Department of Personnel had conducted a lengthy job-evaluation exercise of all state jobs in the late 1970s. They had been unsuccessful in getting the state legislature to implement the new system. When the Special Committee on Comparable Worth of the state legislature began its activities, it met with personnel administrators, who suggested that implementing its new classification system would be consistent with pay equity. The committee hired two pay equity consultants to review the proposed system. The consultants endorsed certain features of the system, but concluded that there were several major aspects of the system that would sustain gender bias.

One major problem for the consultants was that each (sex-segregated) bargaining unit had to establish its own pay line. The consultants were asked to drop this concern from their report and they refused. The release of the report was held up for one year, at which time the special committee stated: 'Since compensation for state employees in Massachusetts is subject to collective bargaining and there are numerous bargaining units, the complex statistical effort required to prepare a single "pay policy line" is of little value and might even be considered to compromise the right of employees to bargain over wages' (1986, 4). At approximately the same time, the Department of Personnel received funding to implement the new classification and compensation system unmodified, and argued that it was a first step in achieving pay equity. It appears that this first step has turned into the last step, as the system remains intact some four years later. Similarly, the Connecticut initiative discussed above began as a pay equity study but turned into a classification study.

A more common pattern involves the conversion of a pay equity study into a classification study at an early point in the reform's history. What typically happens is that proponents push through a piece of legislation that calls for a pay equity study and appropriates funds for hiring a consultant. Either through explicit legislative directive or through informal negotiations, the personnel department takes unilateral control of the study. They pick the consultant. They decide on the job-evaluation system, including factors, factor weights, pay lines. They withhold information throughout as confidential.

Not surprisingly, such studies result in very conservative estimates of wage discrimination. Perhaps the worst set of recommendations was offered to a task force in a mid-Atlantic state. The consulting firm recommended that all jobs be downgraded because it held that wage inflation had put the state's wage structure out of alignment with private-sector pay scales.[10] At the same time, it argued that pay equity would be accomplished because the downgrades recommended for female jobs were lower than the downgrades recommended for male jobs.

Some initiatives have used pay equity to introduce red-circling of jobs for which the wage bill has grown too steep. Red-circling involves lowering the entry-level wages for all new employees in a job class while preserving the wages of current incumbents. It is received hostilely by current employees, however, because it represents a loss in status and relative position, if not in economic terms. Red-circling was threatened in New York State and in many initiatives on the West Coast. Few of these threats have been implemented, but they are effective in gaining other concessions. Finally, management has proposed to contract out certain job functions to avoid pay equity adjustments. Like red-circling, these have emerged thus far as threats used to modify pay equity adjustments.

Timing Strategies

A fifth and final tactic used by management to contain pay equity involves control of the timing of the study. Many of the initiatives I have observed have timed the completion of the study to occur before union elections or after general elections. In Massachusetts, for example, collective bargaining over the first set of pay adjustments was timed to coincide with Governor Dukakis announcing his candidacy for president. He was extremely interested in gaining union endorsement. His ability to raise everyone's wages in the name of pay equity contributed to his being viewed favourably by unions.

In Boston, a pay equity initiative currently under way has been delayed for more than five months for no apparent reason. Some suggest that the delay is linked to the mayor's plan to run for governor. Since the mayor is pro-life, it appears that he hopes to time the study to allow him to announce some positive move right before the elections. While timing was not necessarily a containment tactic in these illustrations, it allowed for announcements to be made at high-visibility moments, with follow-through at lower visibility.

Haignere (this volume, ch. 8) points to a second way in which timing affects results, which she calls 'the ravages of time.' Under severe deadlines, short-cuts work in favour of maintaining the status quo. She suggests that meeting the deadline can replace achieving pay equity, once again demonstrating that a decision can be reached for symbolic purposes, but remain unimplemented, saving management millions of dollars in pay adjustments.

Delays can be functional for management because they also contribute to a loss of reform momentum. In Oregon, for example, the legislative task force chose Hay Associates over a competing consulting firm who would have designed a customized job-evaluation system, doing so, in part, because Hay appeared to be able to complete the study in a timely fashion. In this initiative, however, they neither completed the study to meet the deadlines nor modified their system to cleanse it of gender bias. In the case of Ann Arbor, the job-evaluation study was extended over several years, during which time the city manager committed to the study retired, the budget situation deteriorated, and the major proponents gradually lost the momentum they had started out with. While this pay equity study utilizes state-of-the-art knowledge in constructing a customized system for the city, it does city employees no good as it sits on the desk of the city manager unimplemented.

Putting the Lessons to Use

Pay equity has resulted in wage adjustments for millions of employees working in historically female jobs. But it has not yet resulted in a social reconstruction of the value of women's work. In taking the very systems of job evaluation they have criticized and utilized them to estimate the extent of wage discrimination, proponents have failed to appreciate the extent to which these systems, in the hands of others, could be used to legitimate the existing wage hierarchy and even strengthen managerial control in the name of revaluing women's work. In the early initiatives the use of job evaluation as a political resource which would lend an aura of objectivity to proponents' claims reflected as well their limited understanding of gender bias.[11] Proponents in later initiatives, while aware of the general critiques of the undervaluation of women's work, were, in general, unable politically and technically to translate these criticisms into new definitions of skills and responsibilities.

Proponents have underestimated how those less wedded to comparable worth could use these studies to contain the reform. Reliance on job evaluation made the process and results of estimating wage discrimination inaccessible to the job incumbents who would benefit from the results of the study. Administrative control of the implementation of pay equity is not a neutral process of managing competing interests. Rather, administrators enter the process with interests of their own, one of which is to maintain the control of compensation. Good administrators also protect the interests of those that hire them and public personnel officers are no exception. Even if they don't oppose pay equity ideologically and believe that there is wage discrimination, their position requires that they protect the interests of their employers, which, in this case, means cutting costs and maximizing control.

Proponents have gained sufficient power to expose the relationship among skill, labour-market value, and gender. They have also proved to have sufficient power to get the reform on the political agenda. However, they have not yet eliminated major sources of gender bias from skill definitions, which means that pay equity adjustments are significantly lower than they would be were it possible to reconstruct systems of job evaluation. The construction of new job-evaluation systems ultimately rests on either shifts in power (i.e., sufficient political muscle to force implementation of a job-evaluation system consistent with pay equity or to control the implementation process) or shifts in labour market and political culture (i.e., a new consensus among bargaining partners that accepts as legitimate new conceptions of skill complexity). These two are not necessarily independent of each other. Since cultural values serve as power resources, wage adjustments that flow from the revaluation of women's work ultimately reflect the interaction of power and culture operating in a context of economic constraints.

Pay equity outcomes do vary among initiatives and the sources of variation are not difficult to predict. In initiatives in which labour and feminist proponents have been able to control or even to share decision making around job-evaluation studies, the consulting firm is likely to be one utilizing a modified job-evaluation system. Adjustments in these cases are higher than average. By contrast, in initiatives in which labour and feminist proponents have been pushed out or kept in the minority – which are, in fact, the majority of initiatives – pay equity adjustments are likely to be minimal as job-evaluation systems perpetuate the sex bias that studies were intended to eliminate.

Building on these insights, some efforts to achieve comparable worth have moved into a third phase. Utilizing technical knowledge of gender bias and political understanding of the politics of containment, proponents are conducting unilateral pay equity studies. The Pay Equity Program of the National Education Association has designed a job-evaluation system customized to value positively the distinctive characteristics of non-teacher school staff, including food-service workers, librarians, secretaries, and teaching assistants. The Collective Bargaining Committee of Local 34, Federation of University Employees, at Yale University realigned the jobs in its bargaining unit without recourse to a job-evaluation study. It placed its new wage structure on the bargaining table. Yale University accepted the union's proposed reorganization. Wage adjustments amounted to an average of 28 per cent. The union and the university are jointly supervising a job-evaluation study to create a new evaluation system that will legitimate this new ordering of jobs.

Proponents are also maintaining greater control of every step of the job-evaluation process. In Philadelphia, a proponent consulting firm was hired to feminize the standard job-evaluation system operating in the jurisdiction. In Ann Arbor, the same consulting firm designed a customized system based on achieving gender neutrality, given state-of-the-art technical knowledge. Among other actions to protect their interests, proponents in both cities hired a technical monitor to review the work of the consultant at every decision juncture of the study. In Boston, a coalition of unions and women's organizations has turned an advisory committee into an advocate-controlled decision-making body that reviews all the details of the job-evaluation process. This group stopped the initiative when the city excluded it from choosing the job-evaluation consultant and went public with their complaints. The consulting firm chosen was one of the two proponent firms that had submitted proposals. While none of these initiatives has been implemented, they already have gone farther than any undertaken in phases one or two.

Finally, path-breaking legislation in Ontario explicitly prohibits gender bias in systems of job evaluation as well as extending pay equity to the private sector. Unfortunately, the government has thus far only issued guidelines about gender neutrality, preferring instead to allow its scope to be determined through labour-management negotiations. The law establishes a pay equity tribunal to consider unresolved issues. Among others, the Ontario Nurses' Association has taken cases concerning gender bias before the tribunal. If the tribunal sustains these claims, it will be the first explicit legal decision sustaining proponent claims. The spillover within the United States and throughout Canada would be enormous. Compensation consulting firms would no longer be able to exert the kind of monopolistic control over the definition of skill and gender bias that has been observed over the last decade.

Conclusion

This exercise in dissecting administrative strategies for containing comparable worth also reveals dilemmas that underlie the possibility of acting on the lessons that have been drawn. The first concerns the conditions under which job evaluation can most effectively lead to minimizing wage discrimination in the labour market. For job evaluation to truly cleanse compensation practices of gender bias, it is necessary either for proponents to conduct the job-evaluation exercise unilaterally, thereby maintaining complete control, or for all interests to share a common conception of the value of women's work. Unfortunately, neither seems possible. If feminist advocates commanded the power to control job evaluation, they wouldn't need to conduct such studies in the first place. And one of the purposes of conducting a job-evaluation study is to develop the very consensus that is a prerequisite for its success.

The second concerns the dualistic role of job evaluation in the process of implementation. Ironically, job evaluation initially became associated with comparable worth out of expediency in the early initiatives, although evaluation language found its way into early drafts of the U.S. Equal Pay Act. None the less, as this essay has demonstrated in some detail, and as others have argued, job evaluation has contributed to the narrowing and redefinition of the reform. It has been manipulated by administrators to yield minimal outcomes to a greater extent than by advocates seeking to achieve large adjustments.

At the same time, given the power position of women, without job-evaluation studies, pay equity might not have taken off. While there is widespread consensus that women's wages are not fair, there is no political consensus that policy to correct this injustice is necessary. Identifying the problem was not enough. Feminist advocates had to create the idea of wage discrimination and offer a method for measuring it. The method they developed had to be one that would be acceptable in a male-defined political context. Job evaluation offered them the legitimacy and they understandably used the techniques, although without thinking through the consequences of early strategic decisions.

The third dilemma concerns the dualistic role of unions. Here again, unions have simultaneously been responsible for moving the reform forward at an unprecedented pace and for limiting its impact on the relative wages of women workers. Many of the examples offered in this essay have pointed to cases in which union leadership has been less than fully committed to this reform. In some instances, unions representing male employees actively opposed wage adjustments. In other, more frequent, instances, unions represented both male and female employees – and leadership balanced interests in a way that enabled them to remain in leadership positions. Often this meant containing the reform as well, especially if their actions were not being monitored by other proponent groups. And yet, few initiatives get very far without strong union support. Of course, the answer to this is to unionize and to bring rank-and-file women members into leadership positions. The literature addressing these goals is rich in its delineation of difficulties in bringing about these changes.

At the same time, many of the feminist advocates referred to throughout this essay were also union activists who used their privileged position to further the gains of women workers. Many women leaders have worked tirelessly to achieve pay equity with and for their membership. Unions have also invested enormous resources in educating workers about this issue, in lobbying legislatures, and in filing court cases. Without their involvement, non-union women advocates would not have gone very far.

The very same factors that have been distinctively responsible for the minimalist character of pay equity have also been responsible for its having spread so quickly, compared with other reforms that violate laisser-faire doctrines (Steinberg 1982). This raises important questions as we move forward to create new, potentially more effective strategies.

Pay equity advocates must enter the policy arena assuming that administrators are there to contain and control. With increasing sophistication and awareness of the importance of breaking the stranglehold of managerial control, more advocates will be able to transcend these dilemmas by participating fully in the reform's implementation. They must gain greater control of the debate, greater access to information, and greater control over policy decisions. Policy agendas are not implemented because the intrinsic validity of advocate arguments is compelling – although that is a useful power resource – but because the costs of not implementing the reform are greater than the costs of implementing it. Those are the techniques of politics underlying the politics of technique.

NOTES

1 Mansbridge (1986), for example, points to the tactical mistakes of the women's movement, blaming its inflexible, purist posture throughout the campaign for the defeat of the ERA. Gelb and Palley (1982) list six conditions that facilitate successful policy outcomes in four issue areas, each of which focuses on the characteristics of proponents. On comparable worth, Blum, for example, mentions only in passing that the outcome in Contra Costa County differed from the outcome in San Jose largely because of effective managerial resistance.

2 The events surrounding initiatives in Wisconsin and in Ontario are exceptions to this general pattern. In both these initiatives, business opposition was strong and highly visible.

3 According to Evans and Nelson (1989, 218–19), 'AFSCME, the union representing two-thirds of Minnesota State employees, felt that 'too much publicity would have raised concerns not applicable to the implementation of pay equity for state employees, concerns focusing on whether the raises of women workers came from what might have been a larger general salary settlement ... The paradox of AFSCME's strategy is that in order to dampen opposition the union implicitly chose to dampen support.' See Evans and Nelson (ch. 12) for a fuller discussion of how and why AFSCME controlled the dissemination of information to its members.

4 An alternative approach was used in the State of New Mexico but not until 1983. In this state, $3.2 million was appropriated to 'upgrade the wages of approximately 2,000 workers, 86 percent of them female,' without recourse to a comparable-pay study (Young 1985, 135). This received little attention. Local 34, Federation of University Employees, bargained pay equity adjustments with Yale University without recourse to a formal job-evaluation study. In San Francisco, monies were appropriated for salary adjustments, also prior to a formal study. However, in the last two cases, studies were conducted after these agreements to realign jobs according to a legitimized and articulated compensation rationale.

5 See Remick (1980, 1981, 1984a, 1984b), Steinberg and Haignere (1986), Steinberg (1984, 1985), and Treiman and Hartman (1981).

6 The Ontario Pay Equity Act defines the standard of non-discrimination in a way that contains the cost of the reform to employers. Rather than using a pay-line method, it calls for raising female wages up to the lowest male comparator within the bargaining unit where there are several unions or in a firm. This approach has the effect of allowing for several pay lines by job family within a workplace and then of further reducing wage adjustments by bringing female jobs up only to a male job that is below the average line for sex-segregated job families. Unfortunately, male jobs within female job families are usually paid lower points to pay than male jobs in historically male job families. The impact of this seemingly technical decision of wage adjustments is substantial.

7 In highlighting the major contribution to pay equity of female-dominated unions and female union leadership and staff, I in no way want to exclude the role played by many male union leaders, staff, and membership. Yet, this essay is an attempt to articulate dominant patterns in pay equity implementation. In general, female unions have been more consistently energetic and less likely to compromise than mixed-gender unions. Female leaders and staff within unions have, on average, fought harder for larger pay equity adjustments than male leaders and staff of unions.

8 It is beyond the scope of this essay to analyse why women's groups allow themselves to be marginalized, especially after they have invested so much time and energy in seeing the reform through to the point of appropriating monies for a study. In some instances, commissions on the status of women have been the instrumental advocacy group. They bow out because there is another government agency responsible for compensation matters. Cook (forthcoming), for example, notes without explaining that women's organizations in Hawaii were instrumental in passing legislation on pay equity, but allowed themselves to be marginalized throughout the study process. The unions representing public employees demonstrated very little commitment to pay equity, which accounts largely for the defeat of the initiative in that state.

9 In addition, consulting firms are profit-making organizations. The next contract is often a function of how satisfied current clients are, so that even the most well-intentioned and committed consulting firms find themselves trading off commitment to pay equity with staying in business.

10 See Haignere (this volume, ch. 8). She also points to an example in which managers realign the internal wage structure to reflect external market pay scales.

11 One problem that proponents had was providing a rationale for reconstructing factors and factor weights that had an aura of objectivity. Conventional job-evaluation systems are constructed by relating skill-complexity levels to existing wage rates. These jobs-complexity definitions are then used in other work settings, reproducing the wage structure. Because jobs are aligned in a way that reproduces the wage hierarchy in general, the procedure for accomplishing this remains unexamined. This larger consensual foundation masks the subjective underpinnings of the scores. By reproducing the wage structure, they appear non-arbitrary. By contrast, proponents' efforts to reconstruct systems cannot be obscured as easily. They cannot derive the factors and factor weights from existing wages, because they assume that these wages are artificially depressed by wage discrimination. They also cannot build a consensual understanding of the revaluation of women's work, because that is to be the outcome of the reform. They do not have the luxury of either precedents or consensus, making it difficult to hide the subjective basis of system reconstruction.

PART FOUR

The Potential and Limitations of the Pay Equity Strategy

11 Pay Equity and the State's Agenda

Debra J. Lewis

At the beginning of the 1980s, the term 'pay equity' did not exist in any meaningful way. By the end of the decade, pay equity was being called 'the working women's issue of the 1980s.' This reputation persists into the 1990s. But the phrase is problematic in that it illustrates how pay equity has come to be seen. To put it simply, *pay equity is not an issue.* Pay equity as it has come to be defined – wage adjustments based on comparison of job content or job evaluation – is just one possible solution to the real issue of wage discrimination: that women systematically get less money than men for the work that we do.

The distinction is not just a semantic one. The term 'pay equity' has evolved to describe a very specific model of reform. In the process, it has virtually swept alternative possibilities off the feminist agenda. This has serious implications for the future of feminist work on the issue. A couple of examples confirm the fears suggested in the book *Just Give Us the Money* (Lewis 1988).

The first occurred in Vancouver in July 1990, when the Committee on Affirmative Action for Women in the Civic Workforce made a proposal to City Council on remedies for the underpayment of women working for the city. The committee, composed primarily of representatives of city unions, recommended a series of steps (including the equalization of base rates between inside and outside workers and elimination of increments) to be taken immediately in order to make a substantial difference in clerical wages. Surprisingly, the proposal had passed the city's finance committee – surprisingly, because Vancouver's City Council is dominated by the political right.

However, in the month between the finance committee and council meetings, the bureaucracy and the politicians went into overtime to defeat the proposal. They made sure that the Conservative majority on council was back on side. And the argument they used was that because the proposal did not do job comparison or job evaluation, it had absolutely nothing to do with pay equity. Apparently, direct action on women's wages did not count. This opposition to the committee was supported by the city's Equal Employment Opportunities officer, who said that, despite the committee's recommendation, she personally favoured job evaluation as a requirement for a pay equity plan.

So, in place of the committee's recommendation, City Council passed 15 or 20 motions, doing, in the words of one union representative, 'just about everything but giv[ing] women money' (Lewis and Barnsley 1990). Score one for the status quo.

Another example occurred at the National Committee on Pay Equity conference in Washington, DC, last fall. In the panel on job evaluation, the four panelists gave increasingly forceful critiques of job-evaluation systems. The final panelist recommended that it is essential to decide first what one wants to accomplish for women and then to shop around for the system that will do the job. That may be a rather polite way of saying that job evaluation is a complete sham, although if one was stuck with job evaluation, that would be the only way to go.

The question period further emphasized the single-minded acceptance of job evaluation. There were several questions on the details of job evaluation and the importance of good technical advice – not irrelevant questions, to be sure. But when one woman finally bit the bullet and asked if job evaluation does not really work; if it, in fact, misrepresents what it does; and if it has been very difficult to implement in Ontario, shouldn't we question whether we want it at all, the response was simply, 'That's a very good question', but it was not answered. During the remaining time the discussion returned to details, and the larger picture was again lost.

At the same conference, a penal on 'Building Community Coalitions' had three panelists. Two of the three worked within the bureaucracy in their respective states. It seems somewhat questionable to identify the bureaucracy with community coalition, but no one raised this issue.

These examples, and others like them, raise serious questions for the issue of wage discrimination and pay equity as a reform:

1 Why have we ended up with a model of pay equity that is not only limited, but also being used actively against women developing alternative strategies?

2 Why has the pay equity model so completely dominated debate on remedies for wage discrimination that it seems unthinkable even to question whether perhaps the model is flawed?

3 Why has the women's movement been willing to abandon the terrain of wage discrimination and pay equity to the 'experts' – albeit experts who may come out of feminist organizations or unions? Or perhaps a better question is: Have women as a group been excluded from the terrain by the very nature of pay equity as a reform?

The answers to these questions become clear is we understand why the state has been willing to act on pay equity. The pressure that feminists brought to bear is surely a major reason, but as much work has been done on other issues with far less apparent success. The state's willingness to accept such a reform is based, at least in part, in its interest in taking control of the feminist agenda and in demobilizing those who understand all too clearly that women need and deserve more money. It has been remarkably successful in doing just that.

Pay equity is an appealing reform for the state for many reasons. First, it is a *procedural reform*, which promises no result. Once a job comparison is done, pay equity can be said to be done – regardless of whether the results are good, bad, or marginal. To criticize the results of procedural reform in retrospect is rather difficult – like trying to nail Jell-o to the wall. If nothing is promised, it becomes very difficult or even impossible to criticize when little is delivered.

A second reason for pay equity's appeal is *the definition of the reform and its basis in the comparison of job content*. Compelling women to be compared to the male standard means that questioning that standard becomes impossible – it's simply outside the parameters of the reform. And pay equity is not the only reform that has led the women's movement into this trap. Increasingly, some feminists are realizing that basing our demands on the concept of equality – where men define the norm and women are expected to fit in – does not reflect women's experience of the world. It means that some gains will be made primarily for those women who can most closely emulate men. When women differ – through the work we do in the paid labour force, through domestic labour, or through our responsibility for children – the gains are marginal or non-existent.

A third reason for pay equity's appeal is that *it divides women workers*. We often hear of how pay equity divides women and men, but that is a secondary concern. Far more insidious is the way it divides women.

Pay equity programs offer some limited gains to groups of women workers who have some degree of relative power – large groups of organized women. It provides a way of buying them off. There is some debate about how many women are left out – either because they are directly excluded or because they cannot use the reform effectively. But there is no doubt of who most of these marginalized women are – women in small workplaces, the lowest-paid women, the most oppressed part of the workforce.

In *Just Give Us the Money*, the wisdom of promoting a reform that excludes the women who need it most was questioned. This issue is magnified by the fact that the structure of the labour force is itself shifting. The greatest growth in women's work is in precisely the part of the labour force that is untouched by pay equity. For example, between 1978 and 1985, 92 per cent of new jobs were in firms with fewer than twenty employees (Thompson 1987). Most of these jobs are women's jobs. To look at pay equity in isolation from these trends is a mistake.

The fourth reason why pay equity has gained as much acceptance is that it is a reform that is *completely reliant on bureaucrats and technocrats for its implementation.* Evans and Nelson (1989b) point out that a major cost of comparable worth (or pay equity) programs is the erosion of an ideal of democratic and participatory decision making and the empowerment of the individual. They point out that, while organizing to get pay equity can be democratic, the very nature of the model stops further democratic development in its tracks. Women are expected to give over control to the experts, and the very best advice they are given is essentially, 'Get the best technical experts you can and rely on them to get the best deal you can.' The women that pay equity is supposed to serve become virtually invisible, and certainly demobilized.

There is a cost to the women's movement, too, as many women are integrated into the roles of bureaucrat and technocrat. Raising this subject is, of course, a very touchy proposition. No one wants to be seen as attacking the motivations and work of women who have chosen this route. And, indeed, some positive results have come about as a result of their work within the confines of their roles. But that last phrase – 'within the confines of their roles' – is critical. Once inside the system, women cease to become advocates and become, in the words of one woman describing her experience, 'managers of change' (Todres 1987). The state limits the scope of the debate by the reform it chooses, and then puts feminists in the role of selling that limitation. And while their personal allegiances may not change, the allegiance expected of the role

– allegiance to the specific reform and to the structures that implement it – is another thing altogether.

This might not be such a problem if pay equity were not a reform that compels everybody else to rely on the experts. But it does. For example, conferences on pay equity are not accidentally top-heavy with academics, bureaucrats, and consultants – not only the resource people but the participants as well. Similar patterns can be seen everywhere. Women – and women's experience – are getting lost.

One additional cost of pay equity as a bureaucratic and technocratic reform is the obvious one – the enormous expenditure of time and money trying to play the pay equity game. It's costing literally millions of dollars and thousands of hours – time and money not available for other strategies. For the state – and for employers – that's the final beauty of pay equity as a reform: it simply consumes so many resources that there's little left for anything else. And there's really very little choice. Once women have agreed to play the game, we must play by the rules. And the rules are very expensive ones.

The future action on wage discrimination may, then, elicit despair. Despite some discussion of the need for a model that is defined by the results, not the procedure, little progress has been made. We seem trapped within a frame work that compels women to compare job content and hence accept the male standard as the norm. Pay equity has eclipsed other strategies that could deliver much greater gains for the women who need them desperately – for example, a campaign for a real minimum wage. And, as others have noted, there is currently no non-technocratic method for implementing pay equity.

There are two possible responses to all of this. The most predominant response is that, since pay equity is the only game in town, we have to play it. And that's true to the extent that the game is being played, with or without our participation, and we have to make the best of it.

But, it will be a huge loss for women if we allow pay equity to remain the only game in town; if we let it consume all the resources we have at our disposal; if we accept that pay equity is the issue and not just one possible solution – and a limited, even dangerous, solution at that.

The alternative is to reseize the issue, not of pay equity, but of wage discrimination. We need to get out of the box that says comparing job content is the only legitimate way of addressing the issue. We need solutions that don't abandon those women who need them most. And we need strategies that mobilize women, rather than tell them to put their trust in someone else.

As Evans and Nelson (1989d) point out the practice of pay equity shows that, as a reform, it is less radical than proponents had hoped and less radical than opponents had feared. Women's economic situation in general, and women's wages in particular, need a radical response. It will be an enormous task to reradicalize this issue. But a radical perspective is essential to re-establish ownership of the agenda and to mobilize women around it.

12 Translating Wage Gains into Social Change: International Lessons from Implementing Pay Equity in Minnesota

Sara M. Evans and Barbara J. Nelson[1]

Over the last century, the development of social and economic policies in North America, Western Europe, Australia, and New Zealand has depended on international sharing and mutual learning across borders. Mother and child allowances, old age pensions, minimum wage laws, protective legislation and the subsequent retreat from sex-based work limitations, and now pay equity – all have developed in both a national and an international context. Unions, business associations, women's organizations, political parties, and scholars have contributed to these exchanges. The traditional public-policy literature characterizes this process as a rather mechanical diffusion of innovation from a few central points to peripheral areas (Walker 1969). That approach underestimates the cooperation, conflict, and change involved in sharing information and initiating policies (Eyestone 1977; Gray 1973; Nelson 1984a).

From an international perspective, two important lessons can be drawn from the Minnesota experience in implementing pay equity for public employees. The first lesson concerns women's experiences[2] in the workplace and is easy to summarize: with vigilance and support from labour and feminist groups, pay equity can improve the wages of people working in female-dominated jobs. Without vigilance and support, job evaluation – the mechanism that determines whose wages will change and how much – remains a technocratic tool justifying patriarchal, racial, and class assumptions about the value of workers and the kinds of jobs they typically hold. We believe that the paradoxes of using job evaluation and other technocratic methods to promote wage justice in the workplace will be similar in large public jurisdictions or private firms in most industrialized democracies. From the perspective of the workplace, unionists and feminists need to ascertain whether engaging in difficult pay equity campaigns and employing imperfect job-evaluation technologies are justified by the wage and solidarity gains they win.

The second, more complicated, finding concerns connecting workplace gains with changes in the operation of the market economy, the nature of the political system, and the organization of domestic life. Supporters and critics of pay equity have hopes and fears about the linkages between workplace improvements for women and changes in other arenas. At a minimum, some proponents hope that pay equity will help transform the market into a set of less confiscatory arrangements for low-wage workers, will encourage greater political participation by women, and will contribute to domestic life based on equal power and respect. As we shall see, in Minnesota (and most likely across the United States), the initial effects of pay equity in these other arenas are indirect, slow, and small. We believe that these linkages do not always have to be slow and small, although they are likely to remain indirect because these arenas encompass different types of activities. There may be significant variation in the possibility of linkages between workplace and market, politics, and home through pay equity depending on the scale of pay equity coverage, and the political and economic conditions of each country. Or said another way, wage-setting processes in workplaces may be more similar cross-nationally than the linkages between systems that shape the wages and the economy, politics, and home.

The international lessons of the Minnesota case derive from making these workplace, market, and home linkages more clear. This chapter recounts the Minnesota experience in implementing pay equity, discusses how pay equity policies affect workers and workplaces, and analyses the immediate prospects for pay equity to transform market, political, and domestic relations in the United States. In this last section, we offer a template against which other scholars and activists may initially assess the short-run transformational value of pay equity from an international perspective.

Minnesota's Experience in Implementing Pay Equity

Understanding the international lessons of Minnesota's experience with pay equity rests on knowing the history of this policy.[3] Minnesota has the distinction of being first in two areas of pay equity policy in the United States. Minnesota was the first state to initiate and fully fund pay equity for state-level employees. The Minnesota legislature was also the first, and is still the only, legislature to have passed a law requiring all local governments – the 1,600 cities, counties, school-boards, transit authorities, and the like – to use pay equity in setting the wages for local-level public employees. Thus, Minnesota is the state most like its international counterparts, requiring pay equity for an entire sector of the economy, in this case the public sector. No other state in the United States has the same sectoral coverage.

Minnesota's activities were unusual in other ways, as well. Minnesota's action came early in policy efforts, before the anti–pay equity groups such as the National Association of Manufacturers and the U.S. Chamber of Commerce were well organized. But, Minnesota was also very typical of early-action states. States that took early action on pay equity tended to meet three political criteria: collecting bargaining for public employees, control by the Democratic party of state government, and a strong commission on the status of women. Minnesota, along with twelve other of the twenty early-action states, met all of these political conditions for policy leadership.

In 1982, the Minnesota legislature passed the State Employees Pay Equity Act. This law makes pay equity 'the primary' principle of payment for Minnesota state employees. The purpose of the law is to 'establish equitable compensation relationships between female-dominated, male-dominated, and balanced classes of employees in the executive branch.'[4] The state used an existing Hay analysis of jobs, without any modifications to remove the well-known gender bias, in determining which job classifications were similar. The pairs of equivalently evaluated male- and female-dominated jobs did not surprise anyone with experience with pay equity policy. In the Hay job evaluation, a general repair worker and a clerk typist received the same points, but, in 1981, before pay equity, the general repair worker made about $350 more per month than the typist. Similarly, pharmacists and registered nurses received the same points, but pharmacists earned almost $400 more per month than nurses. Perhaps the most poignant and politically volatile comparison was between zoo-keepers and 'human services technicians,' the people – mostly women – who take care of profoundly impaired adults and children in state institutions. Before pay equity, animal caretakers received $184 more per month than human caretakers.

The state's decision to use an existing job-evaluation system deserves special attention. The implementation of pay equity at the state level was an extraordinary example of how well the process can go when all parties agree that pay equity is a remedy for the historic and structural underevaluation of women's work. In this case the parties were the

Minnesota Department of Employee Relations, headed by Nina Roth-child, who had led the drive for pay equity legislation when she was the director of the Commission on the Economic Status of Women, and the American Federation of State, County, and Municipal Employees (AFSCME) Council 6, which represented two-thirds of state employees, headed by Peter Benner. Both Rothchild and Benner understood that structural problems require structural solutions. Because these participants believed that the market is a social rather than a mechanical process, and because they also believed that the process was not necessarily fair, they were willing to use a flawed mechanism to begin what they knew would be a long-term process. Rothchild and Benner solidified their commitment to pay equity by raising the wages of women's jobs to the wages of men's jobs at each point level, rather than averaging men's and women's wages and incorporating women's low wages into the remedy for those low wages. The quality of the job-evaluation system was less important to them because adequate political will and organizational capacities existed. In contrast, at the local level, choosing the right technology (solely a management prerogative) was very important to managers because the choice of job evaluation offered another domain in which to fight the ideological and policy battles about equity supposedly settled by the law (Mazmanian and Sabatier 1983).

State legislators were disturbed by the injustice shown in job evaluations where animal technicians and human caretakers have equally valued jobs but zoo-keepers make more money than those who work with the disabled. The legislators passed not only the State Employees Pay Equity Act, but also a special appropriation that would fund the pay equity increases. This appropriation was separate from the regular salary appropriation, giving the appearance at least that pay equity raises did not come out of the general salary settlement. Unions negotiated the timing and amount of the pay equity raises within the general amounts appropriated for each job class that was to be given a pay equity raise.

The total average wage increase over the four years of implementation (1983–7) was $2,200. Approximately 8,500 employees in 200 female-dominated job classifications received pay equity raises. Most of the people receiving pay equity raises worked at clerical or health-care jobs; about 10 per cent of the recipients were men. The total cost for pay equity raises was $21.7 million, or 3.7 per cent of the base payroll. Over the period between 1981 and 1986 the ratio of female to male wages for full-time, full-year employees of the State of Minnesota went from 74 to 82 per cent. Most of this change is the result of pay equity, although part of it is a function of the changing composition of the jobs, in state employment.[5]

No notification of eligibility for pay equity raises was sent to employees. Nor did employees ever learn what their total raise was to be. This was because the unions, primarily AFSCME, which represented 85 per cent of those receiving pay equity raises, did not want management to take credit for the raises the union had won in the legislature and implemented through collective bargaining. Also, AFSCME did not want those of its members who were *not* getting raises to be reminded of the situation.

The only notification, so to speak, employees received was through their paycheques, and that was probably not very evident. Pay equity raises were distributed unequally over four years of implementation. Thus, the 'average' employee who received the 'average' $2,200 raise over four years received the highest pay equity increase in years one and two. Both years saw $800 added to this average worker's wages. The raise came in $33 increments every two weeks and could not be distinguished from an employee's general raise. It is no surprise, then, that when we surveyed State of Minnesota employees, we found that 43 per cent of those who received a pay equity raise *did not know that they had received this wage increment*. This suggests that the transformational potential of pay equity is more complicated than had been originally imagined. Are increased wages, without knowledge of increased resources or the source of the increase, sufficient to lead to economic, political, and familial changes?

There are no easy answers to this question about the relationship between material resources, consciousness, and change. One perspective on the raises can be seen by comparing salaries available to entry-level clerks, the lowest-paid position in state employment, to the poverty line for a family of four. In 1983, the poverty line for a family of four was $10,178 and the base salary for an entry-level clerk was $11,922, or 117 per cent of the poverty line for a family of four. If over the next four years, this position had received only the pay raises negotiated between the union and the state, the base salary would have risen to 122 per cent of the poverty line. The salary at the end of the pay equity implementation was 142 per cent of the poverty line. In dollars, this meant that, with pay equity, the salary for this position was $15,931 rather than $13,675. Of course, not every entry-level clerk supported a family of four, but the salary change indicated the change in the capacity of people working as clerks to support themselves and their families.

In addition to raising salaries, pay equity also promoted job satisfaction. As in most public employment, job satisfaction was generally high for Minnesota state employees. Overall, almost 58 per cent of state employees reported that they were 'very satisfied' with their jobs. But the most satisfied state employees were those who knew about the pay equity raises they had received: 68 per cent were very satisfied with their jobs. The least-satisfied workers were those who had received pay equity raises but did not know about them. Only 39 per cent of these state employees were very satisfied with their jobs (Evans and Nelson 1989a, 122–4).

Both the wage improvements and the job satisfaction derived from implementing pay equity in state employment were purchased by the strategic management of information, and thus conflict, on the part of AFSCME. The union emphasized pay equity in its communications with the mostly female health-care and clerical bargaining units, while remaining silent on the issue when communicating with the mostly male blue-collar bargaining units. In this way AFSCME's leadership managed the recurring conflict in pay equity policy between traditional, patriarchal calls for working-class solidarity, which do little to address the wage needs of women, and strategies for women's solidarity, which reach across class, increasing wages for female-dominated occupations, regardless of social position. AFSCME was able to dampen this conflict because it was the largest and most powerful union of state employees, representing 62 per cent of state employees and 85 per cent of those receiving pay equity raises. This situation was never repeated in the 1,600 local jurisdictions in Minnesota, where with the exception of school-boards and very large cities and counties, few localities were highly unionized and none had a single, dominant union.

Where local-level collective bargaining existed, separate unions representing male- and female-dominated occupations often fought between themselves, in traditional public union style (Cassell and Baron 1975). The conflict was not merely between blue-collar men and white-collar women, as right-wing opponents of pay equity often assert. Rather cross- and intraclass gender conflict existed. Indeed, traditional definitions of class are inadequate to capture the class and gender relations in pay equity. 'Class,' as it is conventionally used, is a patriarchal concept as well as a patriarchal experience in which women's interests are seen as subordinate to the paid work and reproductive interests of the men in each class.

Pay equity reveals these complexities at every turn. For example, police officers in many local jurisdictions saw themselves as the victims of pay equity, as blue-collar men doing manly work that was socially devalued by the mere fact that wages in women's occupations would rise. But, in fact, police officers are among the highest-paid local employees, often making managerial-level wages although not experiencing a managerial-style organization of their work. Thus it is hard to interpret the objections of police officers to pay equity. Was it, as is commonly described, a blue-collar objection to an attack on the family (really manly) wage, or was it a middle-class or managerial objection to giving higher wages to less 'skilled,' less 'important,' and less 'dangerous' work, mixed with the thought that there would be less left in the wage pie for themselves? Clearly, the organization of interests in pay equity does not fall into neat categories.

In addition, implementation on the local level was much more complex because of the variety and number of units adopting this wage change. In 1984, the Minnesota legislature passed the Local Government Pay Equity Act.[6] This act was never as strong as the State Employees' legislation. In the local law, pay equity was demoted from 'the' principle of payment to 'a' principle of payment. The act prescribed a process by which local governments could determine if gender-based pay inequities exist. In each jurisdiction, all jobs had to be evaluated, and a plan for remedying inequities devised. The act also provided immunity from prosecution in state courts for a specified period of time.

Most localities did not have an existing job-evaluation system they could plug into a pay equity analysis, and most large and medium-sized jurisdictions did not use the state's job-evaluation system as state officials had hoped. Instead, local jurisdictions wanted job-evaluation methods that would capture the unique characteristics of their workforces and respond to the specific political interests of their managers, who alone (without union participation) controlled the selection of methodology. To reduce the burden of developing or choosing job-evaluation systems, the professional organizations of school-boards, counties, and medium-sized cities created their own job-evaluation systems or modified existing methods for adoption by their members.

With the exception of county officials, who were led by their professional association to be more suspicious of gender issues, the dominant reaction of local officials was 'How can we do this right so that we won't get sued and it won't cost us a fortune?' One leader in the school-board association put this technocratic imperative in perspective when he said, 'School boards always want to get an "A."' Ideological issues were rarely discussed, and only where there were significant numbers of women public officials did pay equity retain its equity flavour. In most localities pay equity did not remain a remedy for the historic undervaluation of women's wages, becoming instead one more standard, statistical personnel technique.

The difference in problem definition led to different technological decisions. Localities often chose to bring female-dominated salaries up to the all-job pay-practices line, while holding male-dominated wages steady. Localities also used 'equity corridors,' often 7 to 15 per cent above and below the all-jobs pay-practices lines, as a zone of non-discrimination. The legality of equity corridors has not been tested yet. Supporters of pay equity argue that these zones establish gender-unequal pay policies and are therefore unlawfully discriminatory.

Local officials often complained about the disruption implementing pay equity entailed. They used apocalyptic language like 'agony and pain' and the 'biggest upheaval an employer will see.' It is unquestionable that some conflict accompanied reclassification, job evaluation, and changes in pay. Yet, when we asked local public officials and managers how these conflicts and administrative efforts compared with other problems, most readily agreed that implementing pay equity was not unusually conflictual or difficult. Public officials and managers were used to conflicts and problems, and pay equity was not first on their list of headaches.

Indeed, pay equity gave managers an unexpected treasure-trove of information about what public employees did. Management's penetration into the work process gave it a great deal of power over fragmented unions and unorganized workers. One of the best examples of this comes from the study of what police officers do. Most job evaluations require information about what incumbents do over a year or what they must be trained to do. Police officers always argue that they deliver babies, certainly a highly skilled job requirement, and that skill had to be factored into their wage rates. But the job analysis done in several local jurisdictions showed that only three babies had been delivered by police officers in the seven-county Minneapolis–St Paul metropolitan area in the previous ten years. While some public managers had more information than they knew what to do with, others felt extraordinarily empowered by the kinds of information they acquired about employees. Privately, many were willing to say that the information they developed about employees was worth the cost of the raises.

Local public wages in female-dominated jobs also increased as a result of pay equity although not as dramatically or evenly as did state wages. One suburban school district employed health associates at an entering salary of $6.81 per hour. If the associate worked full-time (40 hours a week for 39 weeks), which many did not, her earnings were $9,688 for the year, or 86 per cent of the poverty line for a family of four. After pay equity, the salary would be $12,090, or 108 per cent of the poverty line for a family of four. Currently the most serious problem facing local implementation is that the manipulation of job evaluation is permitting large raises for male-dominated managerial jobs in some localities. This is possible because pay equity is considered a method of determining pay for points.

When Is Money Valuable?

The mixed experience implementing pay equity leaves us with many questions, first among them being: When is money valuable? It is not easy to ask this question because money has a contentious place in the ideologies of social stability and change. On the right, neoclassical economics offers money, and implicitly unfettered choices, as a solution to many policy problems while paying scant attention to the social-structural implications of these solutions. Housing or educational vouchers are examples of the flawed assumptions of this approach. Theoretically and strategically, feminists and unionists shrink from policies that reduce citizens to consumers and leave the structures of production and distribution unquestioned. On the left, money, especially higher wages, is the traditional demand made by male workers, a demand that alone falls short of helping working women who must also manage the double day. Women's labour demands are frequently more inclusive, joining demands for money with demands for a more manageable workday and work week, as well as benefits related to child-caring responsibilities.

Thus the money solution seems tainted from the beginning. But, if the question of the value of money is asked as part of a socially grounded concern for the relationship between individual agency and systemic processes, then feminists and unionists have a better opportunity to decide how much and what kind of energy to give to the monetary goals of social movements. The general question elaborates into a series of questions. When is money valuable to individual employees? When is it valuable as a workplace gain? When and how does money translate into institutions of greater economic justice, fuller political participation, and equal domestic power and respect?

Workers and the Workplace

Money can be very valuable to employees. It is clear from the Minnesota experience in implementing pay equity that this reform put money in the paycheques of public employees working in female-dominated jobs, improving the standard of living of all employees receiving them, and moving the most poorly paid employees away from poverty-level wages. Wage gains were especially large in jurisdictions where there was ideological commitment to the anti-discriminatory intent of the policy on the part of participants.

The pay equity policies implemented in Minnesota will also have a profound effect on lifetime wages and retirement benefits. Imagine Jane Brown taking a job as an entry-level clerk in state employment in 1987, one of the examples of pay equity wage changes used above. Because of pay equity her yearly wages were approximately $2,300 higher than they would have been without the policy. If she remains in that position for thirty years, her lifetime wages will be $150,000 higher because of pay equity.[7] In addition, her retirement benefits will be 17 per cent higher than if pay equity had not been implemented. Certainly these are significant improvements for Brown and the other workers who hold this job, 98 per cent of whom are women.

The meaning of pay equity in the workplace is more complicated. Getting money to employees is neither easy nor unambiguous. While the broader notion of pay equity does not necessarily imply the use of job evaluation, most workplaces that implement pay equity policies use job evaluation as the tool for determining equivalently valued jobs and new wage rates. Job evaluation is a very complicated example of the dilemma of using the 'master's tools to dismantle the master's house' (Lorde 1981). Job evaluation can, although it does not have to, revalue women's work, making visible previously unrecognized skills, effort, responsibilities, and working conditions, and remunerating them. For example, job evaluation can reveal that working with 'indoor dirt' (i.e., nurses' responsibilities to handle bodily excretions) is as much a negative working condition as is 'outdoor dirt' (i.e., street cleaners' responsibilities to handle refuse). Both deserve recognition and remuneration.[8]

There is a better chance for both to be recognized and remunerated when feminists and unionists have some control over job evaluation or its application to wage setting. Where they have little control, or where their interests are organized to enhance the differences between gender- and class-based claims on wages, management will use job evaluation for the purpose for which it was invented more than seventy years ago: to rationalize wage rates to conform with the production needs of owners, managers, and the state, in part by reproducing the culturally assigned value of workers in their wage rates.

Pay equity makes clear the necessity of thinking hard about the meaning and processes of solidarity in the workplace. This, too, has been a difficult conversation to initiate. Feminists, and to a lesser degree unionists, generally support pay equity, but some have wondered whether pay equity undermines working-class solidarity with the infusion of gender claims on wages, claims that cross class lines and permit managers to divide workers (Acker 1989). Most of the attention to this concern has focused on working-class interests. Whether working-class men and women have unity of interests is a hotly debated topic in labour history. Jane Humphreys (1977) argues that it was a conscious choice and a strategic necessity for working-class women in nineteenth-century England to demand a family wage and remove themselves from the labour force, thus reducing the surplus of labour, increasing male wages, and permitting the completion of vital domestic tasks. Heidi Hartmann and Anne R. Markusen (1980) counter that the exclusion of most women from paid labour in the nineteenth century was also an important and valued way in which working-class men could extend their patriarchal control over women in the new economic conditions. Much less acknowledged in this debate is the fact that English male working-class solidarity had the support of the male bourgeoisie and industrial interests. This support is the silent partner in the discussion about the challenge pay equity poses to traditional concepts of solidarity. Working-class men have had cross-class support in establishing male control of the workplace (Simm 1980; Nelson 1984b).

A similar gender division of labour developed in the United States is made more intricate by the effects of race. Black women were more likely to work for pay than white women throughout the late nineteenth and early twentieth centuries, and were less likely to be able to use the ideology of separate spheres to the benefit of their families (Jones 1985). White society devalued the position of black women within their families, a comment on the white view of black womanhood as well as the nature of productive relations in the United States. As more women of all colours entered the labour force in the twentieth century, the gender division of labour was maintained with remarkable consistency. The development of an industrialized and bureaucratic economy fully incorporated a set of gender, class, and race assumptions about work and workers. A job is not merely a bureaucratic description, as Joan Acker recognized when she defined the term in the context of the drive to incorporate sex-based pay equity in Oregon: 'A job is implicitly a gendered concept, even though organizational logic presents it as gender neutral. "A job" already contains the sex-based division of labour and the separation between the public and private domains and assumes a particular organization of domestic life and social production' (Acker 1989).

In this situation, the hardest pay equity questions to pose concern the relationship between male and female wages. Does pay equity mean the redistribution of wages from men to women, in terms either of a fixed wage bill or of claims on wage growth? In practice will working-class men pay this price but not managerial men? Or, is it possible to increase the overall wage bill? What does a larger wage bill mean in the public sector when increased wages are themselves a public policy, competing with other public purposes?

Merely asking these questions makes pay equity look to some like a policy that reduces the possibility of alliance politics. Johanna Brenner, for one, fears that 'comparable worth seems to offer an immediate remedy to a pressing problem, but it may institutionalize divisions among women and between women and men that will make future collective campaigns difficult'[9] (1987). These concerns are important because they urge us to pay attention to strategies, contexts, and the larger scope of social movements. Pay equity does demonstrate that class and gender can act as cross-cutting social cleavages. Pay equity also demonstrates that new forms of solidarity need to be developed, forms that recognize male privilege as well as female claims within and across class. For pay equity, the political necessity of this approach is rooted in the reality of public-sector organizing. The existence of broad-based feminist movements within the political arena and in some unions means that the historic male, working-class view of worker solidarity is only possible through the active suppression of women's voices and interests. This suppression can arise from unionists or management.[10]

Perhaps the greatest value of pay equity in the workplace is that it initiates the discussion on how gender and class conflicts can be mediated. The variety of experiences implementing pay equity in Minnesota provide examples of more and less successful approaches to acknowledging and accommodating these divisions. In practice, and probably not consciously, three approaches to responding to competing wage claims developed: a workplace élite approach, a political élite approach, and a managerial élite approach. Each represented a different constellation of experiences with job evaluation, unionization, and leadership. Each suggests a different workplace meaning for pay equity.

But it is also important to recognize that the workplace consequences of pay equity depend on the range of efforts that are made for a more just and participatory workplace. Pay equity is part of a repertoire that includes workplace organizing, collective bargaining, affirmative action, and occupational health and safety laws. Pay equity cannot bear the full brunt of our hopes for workplace change. Neither can pay equity be expected to be the major vehicle for resolving the subordination and exploitation of women in the workforce, or generally. Rather, pay equity shows in great detail how the gender and class stratification of the labour force actually works, provides a technocratic wage solution, and helps to reveal the conflicts that must be attended to in order to develop a more inclusive worker solidarity.

The state of Minnesota is a good example of a workplace élite approach to resolving the tensions between gender and class claims on wages. The setting was different in state employment than in all other jurisdictions. Eighty-six per cent of the workforce was unionized, with AFSCME representing almost two-thirds of unionized employees. AFSCME also bargained for 85 per cent of the employees who would receive pay equity raises because it represented the female-dominated health and clerical workers destined to get these raises. But importantly, AFSCME bargained for virtually all the workers employed in the skilled trades; hence the union itself provided an arena in which decisions about the relationship between men's and women's wages in the same 'class' could be made prior to engaging in negotiations with management.

The importance of places and procedures that permit discussion and negotiation before facing management cannot be overemphasized. Gender and class claims on wages are part of complex gender and class systems permeating every facet of life. It is not reasonable to expect that experiments in new types of gender and class solidarity, difficult to fashion in general, will be forged in the actual negotiations. At the bargaining table the resolution of gender and class claims on wages works like a classic prisoner's dilemma. To get cooperation, the difficult but more desirable solution to a prisoner's dilemma, requires shared ideology, prior planning, or a long-term commitment between the parties. These conditions are not facilitated when managers and representatives from several antagonistic unions are sitting across the table from one another.

In this situation there are many ways in which to deal with class and gender demands, including universal or selective member education, explicit negotiations among unions or bargaining units, policy voting by all members, or élite decision making. The leadership of AFSCME chose a selective education strategy designed to dampen gender and class conflicts by disbursing more information on pay equity to employees in female-dominated jobs than in male-dominated jobs. The success of this strategy in turn depended on two considerations. The state was going to use its existing job evaluation. In almost all instances job evaluation causes conflicts because it makes evident the cultural biases in what are portrayed as the neutral bureaucratic functions of establishing job classifications and determining their pay rates. The union knew it would not have to deal with male bargaining units on the findings of a job evaluation. The state was also extremely supportive of pay equity. Leaders in the Department of Employee Relations could be counted on to support rather than sabotage union efforts to achieve pay equity. Thus union élites, supported by management, in a context of a clear legislative mandate for pay equity, suppressed most gender and class conflicts.

AFSCME's leadership wanted to develop women's consciousness and allegiance to the union through pay equity, for the sake of the women and for the long-term effect that allegiance would have on the strength of the union. 'We're in it for the long haul,' remarked Peter Benner, meaning that pay equity would rise and fall on the union and political agenda, but what mattered was the overall capacity of the union and its members to have continuous leverage for all its workers.[11] And while AFSCME is a democratic union, pay equity was managed by male union élites who were more sympathetic to women's demands than they believed their male members would be.

The AFSCME strategy for state employees is consistent with the implementation of other equity policies in the United States. A review of programs employing busing to establish racial balance in the public schools shows that the most effective programs were those designed by élites and quickly implemented (Hochschild 1984). The busing example reveals a classic democratic dilemma. Choosing popular participation may result in anti-democratic outcomes. Pay equity in Minnesota extends our understanding of this dilemma. Once out of the bottle, the genie of technocratic analysis may have the same anti-egalitarian consequences as some forms of popular participation, extending the time frame in which decisions are made, delaying action, and changing the criteria for evaluating policy success.

Outside state employment, different workplace consequences flowed from pay equity. No single powerful union covering both male- and female-dominated jobs existed, even in highly unionized localities. Nina Rothchild and her associates at the Department of Employee Relations were more ideologically committed to pay equity than any other group of managers. Where political support was strong, especially where women were well represented and integrated into political leadership, political solutions to gender and class conflicts often prevailed (Browning et al. 1984). In Minneapolis and St Paul untested job-evaluation systems caused no end of technical and political problems. Both cities had to retreat from their initial job evaluations and both eventually used a mixed technical and political solution, where political leaders supported a new technocratically derived wage base for women while also greasing some squeaky wheels in male-dominated occupations. Strong political support for the ideology of increased wages for women's work on the part of political élites permitted this mixed solution, where most women played by the rules but some men did not.

In the vast majority of local jurisdictions, managerial solutions predominated. Weak political élites (especially in manager- rather than mayor-controlled cities), the absence of women in powerful positions, and limited ideological support by political élites, managers, or unions (only male-dominated jobs tended to be unionized) meant that managerial-controlled technocratic solutions won. The negotiations for pay equity did not occur on a level playing field. Women were rarely unionized, meaning that their interests were neither well articulated nor well transmitted. In many places the job-evaluation committees, established by well-paid consultants hired in part to legitimate management-controlled job-evaluation and wage changes, became the vehicle for women's education about the existing ad hoc job-classification and pay schemes and the proposed alterations. By and large women workers were angry and dissatisfied with their wages and their treatment in public bureaucracies and often also their treatment in pay equity proceedings. For those who participated in pay equity discussions or job-evaluation procedures, the ability to focus and name this anger was one of the consequences of the implementation. In these jurisdictions, female-dominated positions received raises smaller than similar jobs in larger, more unionized workplaces, although workers rarely knew much about other raises.[12] The most interesting aspect of the workplace changes in local jurisdictions is that worker changes occurred at the individual level, but management changes occurred at the institutional level. Women got angry and got money, while managers got increased information about the functioning of the labour force.

Considering the range of experiences in Minnesota, it is evident that the workplace value of pay equity depends on the context of its implementation. Pay equity can strengthen unions, strengthen management, frustrate unorganized women workers, give them their first opportunity to understand their status, increase women's salaries and job satisfaction in some instances while increasing their anger in other instances, increase men's anger, and promote the recognition and practical difficulties of gender and class claims for wages. The value of pay equity in the workplace needs to be assessed in terms of all of these dimensions.

Market, Politics, and Home

If the workplace effects of pay equity are highly contextual, the market, political, and domestic effects are even more contingent. One of the most important lessons from analysing the pay equity movement in Minnesota and across the United States is that social-movement theories need to pay more attention to *translation processes*, the activities that transfer gains in one arena to gains in another. For reforms like pay equity, which are valuable to employees but difficult to control in the workplace, the possibility of social gains in other arenas is important in creating support for the policy.

Currently there are very limited data suggesting how pay equity affects these three other arenas. The design for studies that examine the economic, political, and domestic changes arising from pay equity would need to be individual as well as structural in focus, longitudinal as well as cross-sectional, and attuned to the place of pay equity in a shifting political, economic, and cultural milieu. So too, such research designs would not want to make pay equity bear the entire burden of social change, but instead see this policy as part of a constellation of labour and feminist polices.

In the absence of this kind of research there are indicators of the magnitude of changes that might flow from pay equity. If we determine where pay equity policies are located in the economy, in the political system, in women's and labour movements, we can begin to think about both the processes of translation and the content of changes. The extensiveness of coverage of pay equity policies and the political strength of the supporters of the reform suggest the magnitude of the social change that could come from initiating pay equity policies. These determinations will vary markedly from nation to nation, or setting to setting. The Minnesota experience, nested in the larger context of pay equity reform in the United States, provides one example of how the transformational capacity of pay equity can be assessed.

In Minnesota, pay equity covered the entire public sector, 14.3 per cent of the labour force of almost two million workers. Comprehensive figures do not exist, but the focus of pay equity advocates on the public sector and the concentration of the policy in unionized state governments and a few large cities lead us to estimate that less than 1 per cent of U.S. employees are covered by pay equity wage policies. If pay equity were extended to the entire public sector – unionized or not – 17.6 per cent of the labour force would be covered. Pay equity for the full public sector would be especially valuable for minority women, who are concentrated in public employment (Malveaux 1985a, 1985b). If the unionized private sector adopted pay equity through collective bargaining, another 18.1 per cent of the labour force would be covered. From a comparative perspective, the economic effects of pay equity are likely to be greater where the coverage is greater, and the coverage is likely to be greater where the public sector is larger, unions represent a greater proportion of the labour force, and central or regional governments can legislate the policy for the private sector.

Coverage limited to some parts of the public sector reduces the structural economic consequences of pay equity in the United States at the present time. Any pressure that pay equity exerts on wages in the private sector is only felt in local labour markets. Pay equity tends to magnify the effects of the public-employee wage curve, i.e., the distribution of wages across public-sector jobs. Public-sector non-managerial jobs tend to be better paid than their private-sector counterparts, while the opposite is true for managerial jobs. With pay equity, non-managerial female-dominated jobs benefit more equally from the flattening of the wage curve, one of the few ways pay equity contributes to vertical as well as horizontal equity.

With limited coverage, pay equity in the United States ought to be thought of as a successful demonstration project that gives supporters the experience necessary to fine-tune the policy as opportunities for greater coverage occur. Indeed, pay equity has done extraordinarily well as a reform policy, despite its very limited coverage, considering that it has been implemented during the greatest movement to the right that has occurred in the United States in fifty years. Moreover, should the

Democrats, who are on record supporting pay equity, control the presidency and both houses of Congress, the scope of pay equity coverage, especially in the public sector, could increase dramatically. One of the economic and political consequences of pay equity policies so far is that they provide a crucial staging ground for future efforts.

The federal system in the United States, with its decentralized policy making, both creates the opportunities and exposes the limits of translating workplace gains into political changes. The current movements for pay equity, locally directed but connected to national feminist and labour resources, offer avenues of participation and changed consciousness beyond the workplace, even when élite-controlled and technocratically determined pay equity raises encourage workers to consume rather than produce pay equity in the workplace. The monetary and organizational costs of sustaining pay equity organizing in many communities and states are enormous, however. The success of decentralized activism depends on keeping pay equity alive on the agendas of popular movements while also promoting the issue on feminist and union institutional agendas. Movement activism on pay equity has levelled off, with feminist energy currently more focused on retaining safe and legal abortion. Because unions, where they exist, will monitor job evaluation, it is especially important to note the position of pay equity on labour's agenda. Not surprisingly, in the United States public-sector unions with high percentages of female members – notably AFSCME and the Service Employees International Union (SEIU) – continue their pay equity efforts in an otherwise ambivalent union climate. Similarly, unions and feminist organizations in the United States need to keep the issue alive on the agendas of their allies, especially the Democratic party. In the short run, the transformational potential of pay equity depends on institutionalizing the demand for a gender-fair wage system in organizations that regular participate in politics.

At the individual level, there is every reason to believe that U.S. women's participation in electoral and community activities is enhanced by increased material resources. Survey data from 1980 suggest that poor women talk about politics as frequently as more well-to-do women, but poor women participate actively much less often (Nelson, 1984b, 214–76). Everything that money buys, from peace of mind to an evening of child care, makes it likely that women will participate more politically as their incomes increase – if they want to. The uncertainty in this scenario is whether politics is welcoming to women, and whether it is important enough to women to use their extra resources to participate more.

The most contingent of the changes that might arise from pay equity are those in the domestic sphere. It is arguable that increasing wages for working women decreases their economic dependence on men, increases mutual interdependence among two-earner households, and enhances economic sufficiency in one-earner households. Again, the exact and certainly varied translation mechanism has not been very well imagined.[13] One thing is certain: domestic life is more than the location of the negotiations over domestic, reproductive, and paid labour. For many people domestic life is the place of deepest emotional ties, of love, friendship, power, and sexuality, as well as economic relations, and the domestic consequences of pay equity need to be evaluated within this entire matrix.

NOTES

1 We would like to thank Johanna Brenner and Barbara Laslett for sharing their thoughts on these issues with us.

2 In Minnesota, pay equity focused only on comparisons between female- and male-dominated occupations. Similar methods have been used to demonstrate discrepancies in the wages of jobs in which radical and ethnic minorities are concentrated. Such an analysis was not possible in Minnesota, where less than 4 per cent of the population is made up of minorities of colour.

3 For a detailed account of the Minnesota pay equity experience as seen from the perspective of national pay equity efforts in the United States, see Evans and Nelson (1989a).

4 Minnesota Statutes Annotated, Section 43a.01– 43a.47 (West 1988).

5 Commission on the Economic Status of Women, *Pay Equity: The Minnesota Experience,* rev. ed. (St Paul: Commission on the Economic Status of Women, 1988)

6 Minnesota Statues Annotated 471.991–471.999 (West 1988)

7 In this example we have assumed that Jane Brown does not move up to another position, that she receives a 4 per cent pay raise every year, and that there is no cap on the highest possible wage of the Typist I position. Over the last twenty years, inflation has run higher than 4 per cent on an annual basis, but wages in the public sector, especially in Minnesota, are not pegged to the cost of living. Thus, a 4 per cent wage increase is a generous policy assumption even if it means less than adequate response to the expenses of many employees. The example does not discount the future value of wages.

8 Both are unlikely to be positively remunerated, however. See Jacobs and Steinberg (forthcoming).

9 For a different view with an emphasis on the politics of reform, see Steinberg (1987).

10 A language of women's claims to higher wages that values male blue-collar work would go a long way to creating the atmosphere necessary for developing new visions of solidarity. Many of the arguments for pay equity have implicitly been based on encouraging shock and horror that blue-collar work is better paid than pink-collar work. In a culture that devalues all the work done by the traditional working class, this reaction diminishes the respect given to labour in general. Similarly, and more difficult, the development of a language and politics of the value of women's work in traditional blue-collar unions would go a long way to reducing the women-bashing that occurs privately in male unions when pay equity is argued.

11 Interview with Peter Benner, Executive Director, AFSCME Council 6, St Paul, MN, 4 June 1987

12 In the United States, pay equity policies, like traditional equal pay policies, are implemented in each workplace without regard to the wages paid in other workplaces. Pay equity was not designed to create similar wage scales for similar jobs in different workplaces, but to compare male- and female-dominated jobs of similar skills, effort, responsibilities, and working conditions in the same workplace.

13 Johanna Brenner is concerned that pay equity overemphasizes independence in a world where dependence is the norm. She asks whether an emphasis on economic independence and sufficiency clouds our understanding of the pervasiveness of domestic dependence on men's income and the dependence of the young, the old, and the ill on others, mostly women, for their care.

13 Pay Equity in Sweden and Other Nordic Countries

Joan Acker

The comparable-worth approach to pay equity, or the idea that women-predominant jobs have been historically undervalued in comparison with male-predominant jobs, has only recently been seriously taken up in Norway, Sweden, and Finland,[1] although some women activists in these countries became interested in pay equity as early as the late 1970s. Since 1987, however, discussions about comparable worth have become more widespread among women trade unionists, women politicians, feminist academics, and, in Finland, within the government office charged with the responsibility of overseeing enforcement of the sex equality law. In this essay, I will discuss the reasons that comparable-worth efforts have developed so much later in the Nordic countries than in many other northern industrial-capitalist societies, why the debate is emerging now, concretely what is happening in 1990, and some possible lines of further development.

One reason for the late interest in comparable worth is that the wage gap between women and men is comparatively small in the Nordic countries. However, it still exists. In Sweden, for example, full-time year-round women workers earned 78 per cent of the earnings of men in 1985. Women production workers in private manufacturing earned almost 90 per cent of the earnings of their male counterparts, but these women comprise only about 15 per cent of women workers. For the largest categories of women workers – clerical employees in the private sector and care workers in the public sector – earnings were about 73 per cent of those of men in 1988. In other Nordic countries the gender-based wage gap is somewhat larger: Finnish women earned 71 per cent of what men earned in 1988, but the patterns are similar in Norway and Finland.

Countries with the most active comparable-worth movements are ones in which the wage gap is relatively high – the United States, where full-time year-round women workers earned only 64 per cent of what men earned in 1988, and Canada where the gap is about the same. It is not only the size of the gap, but the existence of institutional action other than that which is specifically addressed to the gendered wage gap, which has had some success in raising women's wages, that helps to explain the late entry of Nordic countries into the pay equity arena. The three countries are similar, but I focus again on Sweden, which has had the most successful process. In Sweden, almost all wages are set by collective bargaining; thus, the wage policies of the trade unions, successful pursued, have been the institutional mechanisms that have raised women's wages.

In the early 1950s, the Swedish blue-collar trade-union confederation (LO) established a wages policy of solidarity as a means of increasing wage equality and contributing to the economic stability of the country (Meidner 1974). Wage equality was pursued through disproportionate raises to low-wage workers achieved by coordinated bargaining. Since women were disproportionately low-wage workers, they benefited greatly from this policy. In addition, LO gave attention to the special wage problems of women. Until 1965 separate wage scales for women and men existed in Swedish industry, and until 1965 women received larger percentage increases than men in almost every bargaining round (Meidner 1974, 44). After 1965, when the separate wage scales were abandoned, women still continued to be awarded higher increases as a consequence of the continuing wage-solidarity policy in bargaining. These wage policies were reflected in other sectors of the economy, and the wage gap declined everywhere, although not so precipitously as in the manufacturing sector. The annual earnings of full-time year-round employed Swedish women were 71.5 per cent of those of men in 1973, and 81.5 per cent in 1985, the high point for women's relative wages (Gustafsson 1988).

The relative wage gains for women resulted from the strength of the trade unions that made possible the implementation of their policy of equality and wage improvement. The strength of the trade unions was greatly enhanced by the close ties between the LO and the Social Democratic party, which together constitute the labour movement.[2] As the welfare state expanded to become the employer of the majority of women, under the almost continuous fifty-year-long rule of the Social Democrats, state policy on wages for public-sector workers was consistent with that of the LO. Although the wage gap persisted, it was declining almost everywhere, and until the mid-1980s there seemed to be little need for other efforts to achieve pay equity.

Things begin to change in 1983 as the wage gap began to increase overall and in most sectors. By 1985, full-time year-round women employees were earning 78 per cent of what men earned, down from 81.5 per cent in 1983. Several reasons for this trend reversal have been suggested, including the weakening of coordinated bargaining and the virtual abandonment of the wage-solidarity policy, all complex results of economic restructuring and the growing influence of neo-liberal ideology. Market arguments have gained influence as solidarity arguments have weakened. In the public sector, for example, employers argue that higher-level managers and technical experts often go to better-paying jobs in the private sector. The state established a special wage-addition fund to attempt to retain such workers (Gustafsson 1988), who were overwhelmingly men, contributing to the erosion of wage equality. Although the market wage-addition was abandoned by 1990, its efforts will continue to be felt for some time. In the banking sector, my recent study (Acker 1990; Acker and Ask 1989) suggests that, as soon as measures pressing for equalization are no longer in active use, the underlying processes creating the wage gap reassert their effect and the wage gap increases.

These are the new conditions that encourage Swedish and other Nordic women to think about new strategies, including pay equity. The strategies they are choosing differ from those in the United States and Canada, where legislation, and not collective bargaining, has been the motor behind comparable-worth efforts, because the trade-union movement in both Canada and the United States is relatively weak.[3] The strength of the Nordic labour movements means that effective action probably has to be through those movements. However, tradition and the structure of power within labour unions limit the possible strategies for the pursuit of women's interests (Ruggie 1984, 169–73). Attention to women's wages has always been viewed as part of the more general socialist effort to achieve equality of distribution, but never as a separate issue having to do with gender. Trade unions are dominated by men with whom still lingers the old ideology that women's issues are bourgeois and potentially destructive of working-class unity. Thus, women's caucuses within the unions are unwelcome – this is much more true in Sweden than in Finland and Norway – and autonomous women's groups pressuring from outside are suspect. As in other non-Nordic countries, women's issues are sometimes bargaining cards that can be given up to achieve other goals. In addition, women are rarely present at the top levels where critical policy decisions are made.

Other new developments are weakening these barriers. Most important, women are becoming an ever-increasing part of the Nordic trade-union membership. The largest LO unions in all three countries are now women-predominant unions, organizing public-sector workers, and their leadership is also becoming more female. Particularly in women-dominant sectors, union leadership recognizes the importance of female membership and the need to act on the wage gap. In addition, some union women are taking action outside the formal organization boundaries.

For example, in Sweden, an informal committee of women from several different trade unions representing both white- and blue-collar employees began meeting in the mid-1980s to talk about pay equity. The committee developed a plan for a national education campaign about pay equity and received one year of financial support for concrete planning in 1989 from a government-mandated 60 million kronor fund to be used for action projects to increase gender equality in the labour force. They were initially refused continuing support after 1989, but are now (spring 1990) preparing a new proposal. At the same time, the educational material they have already prepared will be used in 1990 as the basis for study circles organized by the educational organizations affiliated with both the blue-collar and white-collar union confederations. Study circles are a widespread form of adult education in Sweden, and their entry into the question of pay equity may substantially increase the membership support for pay equity initiatives. In a parallel development, the union-management contract for the state sector in 1990 includes a provision of 60 million kronor for equity raises. Negotiations about how to distribute these funds were under way in spring 1990. Union staff saw this amount as only a beginning that would allow them to explore and experiment with different ways of determining undervaluation and inequity.

Another example of pay equity action in Sweden is from the banking sector. Here the wage gap between women and men is higher and has been growing since 1983, after ten years of improvement. The bank employees' union had tried several measures to improve women's wages, without success (Acker 1990; Acker and Ask 1989), and women activists began to explore the possibilities of a comparable-worth attempt. Instead, the union decided to attack the problem directly in negotiations.

In January 1990, after the employers refused to present an acceptable offer, the union took 1,500 key employees out on strike. Management responded with a lock-out of all bank employees in the country. Three weeks later, after an outpouring of public support for the workers and the union, the lock-out was settled with a 15 per cent increase disproportionately going to lower-level workers, of whom 72 per cent are women. The union had made it clear in the media that the primary issue in dispute was the low pay of the majority of women bank workers. Thus, bank employees have gone back to the old solidarity policy, but with a new twist that emphasizes the relative disadvantage of women. However, union leaders were still of the opinion in spring 1990 that they had only begun to deal with the problem, and they were still interested in exploring a pay equity–job-evaluation approach in the future.

In Finland, at the initiative of union and academic women and with the support of the gender-equality commission of the national government, a general campaign for pay equity was developing in spring 1990. Workshops, seminars, and meetings have been going on since 1988. At the last central negotiation between unions and employers in the winter of 1989–90, an agreement was reached to appoint a working group on job evaluation. Collective bargaining is still very centralized in Finland, with frame agreements concluded among three parties – employers, workers, and the government. These agreements cover both the public and the private sectors. Therefore, the decision to establish a commission on job evaluation with a pay equity intent could lead to wage improvement throughout the entire labour market. Members of the working group were appointed in spring 1990 and included feminists representing organized labour as well as representatives of political parties and employers. The working group will make recommendations on a job-evaluation system for the country and on the development of statistics that will enable a better tracking of changes in women's pay problems.

Still another tactic is being tried in Norway where a broad discussion of skill and the competence of workers is part of the debate about how to meet the economic crisis. The communal workers' union is arguing that public-sector care work is skilled work and is seeking to secure recognition of that claim through the use of the Apprenticeship and Training Act (Rode Fane 1989). The intent is to establish formal apprenticeship programs for day-care assistants, home-help workers, and other jobs that provide the front-line care services in the welfare state.

These workers receive on-the-job training now, but an apprenticeship program would systemize such training and ensure common content and standards, as well as certification at the end of the training period. The pay equity result would come later, once the basis for claims to skill and undervaluation of that skill had been laid.

These country-specific initiatives are supported by the new Nordic Project on Pay Equity, an activity of the Nordic Council of Ministers. This project is also concerned with developing both comparable-worth technical tools and new statistics that will better reflect the economic problems of women. Each country has representation on the project, and the measures developed will be country-specific.

These are only a few of the paths to wage equity between women and men that are being tried in the Nordic countries. Trade unions dominated by men failed to put the gender-based wage gap at the top of the their priority lists, but women's relative wages did improve as long as unions had a wage-solidarity policy. Job evaluation was opposed by many trade unionists because, as a management-controlled tool, it could be used as an argument for wage differentiation, thus undermining worker solidarity. New conditions of international competition have, particularly in Sweden, led to the weakening of wage solidarity and a push for more wage differentiation between individuals, groups, and sectors. The public sector, where large proportions of women work, has been under particular pressure to move to individualized wage-setting, a change that will not benefit most women, as increases in the wage gap indicate. At the same time, in all these countries, a majority of women work for pay, and women are expected, and expect themselves, to be self-supporting. Under these conditions, job evaluation in a pay equity strategy may now be a tool unions can use to counter the wage erosion for large women-predominant job categories.

The campaign for pay equity is analogous to the nineteenth- and early twentieth-century drive by male workers for a living wage. Women workers also demand a living wage. Their claims have, however, a different rationale, which reflects the changing gender arrangements of the late twentieth century in northern industrial countries. The male wage as a family wage had disappeared for all except the most affluent professionals and managers. Consequently, women do not argue for a family wage, because today most households must have more than one wage earner to survive at a conventional standard of living. They do argue for a fair wage that recognizes as valuable the caring, supporting, and nurturing aspects of many women-predominant jobs. This is a challenge to the privileged place given to production of things in social and economic policy and theory, a challenge rooted in the emergence of welfare states that have transformed some of women's caring work from the confines of unpaid family work to public waged work. Assigning a value to such work now becomes a political and budgetary problem for governments, private employers, and families (see Waring 1987), and, perhaps, signals the beginning of opposition to a neo-liberal world in which only efficiency, productivity growth, competition, and profit count.

NOTES

1 I do not discuss Denmark primarily because I have scant knowledge about Danish developments.
2 Explanations for Sweden's exceptional history of a powerful labour movement and a Social Democratic party that has remained in power for many years have been offered by many social scientists, including Korpi (1979) and Esping-Andersen (1984).
3 In 1987, 97 per cent of Swedish workers were union members, whereas in Canada and the United States only 35 and 17 per cent, respectively, of the workforce belonged to trade unions (Coates et al. 1989, 21).

14 Pay Equity and Economic Restructuring: The Polarization of Policy?

Isabella Bakker

The idea of restructuring the world economy offers a rubric to examine both the objective restructuring of the political economy, as the systemic and structural features interact, and the subjective restructuring strategies of capital and the state in response to their perceptions of crisis. Every government and many important industries now speak of restructuring to adjust to the realities of an 'interdependent' world economy in order to resolve the persistent crisis. These plans, reflecting interests and ideologies, interact, in unintended ways, with the objective features of the economy.

Joyce Kolko, *Restructuring the World Economy*

This essay argues that key aspects of economic restructuring, along with deregulation of labour markets, heightened international competition, and technological change, may undermine the goals of current pay equity policies or, at the very least, dramatically challenge their effectiveness. Pay equity emerged in an economic environment in which a number of fundamental structural changes had not yet come to the fore. The question for policy makers now is how pay equity can be adapted to take into account these new trends. Without such re-evaluation, pay equity legislation may run the risk of addressing a smaller and smaller segment of the workforce. Such concerns also raise questions about the substantial public and union resources going into this policy initiative. A serious assessment of changing labour markets and economic conditions and their effect on the principles surrounding pay equity is required. This essay only begins the process by offering some observations based on the findings of several recent labour-market studies.

The current 'restructuring' of the transitional features of capitalism in the past decade and a half has manifested itself in a number of dramatic changes in the structure of production and employment, technology, and the greater economic integration of the global economy. These changes signal a break in the structural and institutional arrangements that characterized the post-war period (Lipietz 1989).[1] At the same time, they continue to be driven by the same forces of accumulation, competition, and profit that marked earlier phases of capitalism. Technological innovation, ranging from information technologies such as semiconductors to fibre optics and new biotechnologies, has contributed to a radical reordering of the basis of production across a wide range of industries and sectors. For example, the application of new microelectronic-based process technologies in the goods-producing sector of the economy has led to a relatively limited increase in employment ('jobless growth') and a steady increase in productive capacity (Wolfe 1990).

The relative decline in manufacturing and the growth of services in terms of employment is a related change that characterizes the restructuring of production. The growing interdependence and convergence of goods and services is part of this structural trend.

The structure and conditions of employment are also changing. For instance, there are significant shifts in the occupational composition of employment across all sectors of the economy, especially increases in professional, technical, clerical, and other specialized occupations. In addition, the conditions of employment are changing with the trend towards greater reliance on part-time as opposed to full-time employment, the move towards the contingent workforce, and non-unionized labour.

We will examine the Canadian labour market in light of these changing structural conditions, and their implications for women workers in particular. The workings of pay equity will be examined from the vantage point of several key trends, particularly the significant structural changes in employment as a result of:

- trade harmonization (free trade) and the continued attempt to reduce and remove the public sector from all aspects of 'civil society' in order supposedly to enhance competitiveness. This harmonization will not only have direct adjustment consequences in terms of location and nature of employment but will also affect the policy environment vis-à-vis labour-market deregulation and programs like pay equity and

employment equity, which employers perceive as an extra cost that limits their competitiveness.
- the growth of the contingent workforce. This trend, along with contracting out, privatization, and other moves towards smaller establishments, will have a significant impact on coverage of pay equity and comparisons of all-female establishments or female-dominated establishments.
- the incompatibility of part-time employment and current labour legislation in attempts to redress pay disparities that might arise under collective bargaining.
- the convergence of goods and services and the emerging good jobs/ bad jobs scenario. The trend towards wage and skill polarization, with the majority of women stuck in 'bad jobs,' may limit comparability and increase the economic and political gap among women in 'good jobs' versus 'bad jobs.'
- the call for skill diversification, which may have implications for pay equity since it will increase the gap between workers' training and the actual job that is defined, evaluated, and rewarded on the basis of narrowly defined job-evaluation methods. Employers' increasing knowledge of job content many facilitate downward re-classification of jobs.
- the changing role of the state and the movement towards labour-market deregulation.

Structural Changes in Canadian Employment

International Competition
Increased international competition, free trade, technological and demographic changes, as well as the 'convergence' of goods and services, are major structural forces influencing the nature of Canadian employment. These changing economic conditions are not unique to Canada but part of the global spread of flexible labour practices (labour deregulation) and changes to the supply-side of the economy. In examining the global picture, Standing (1989) suggests that 'there has been *explicit* deregulation, whereby formal regulations have been eroded or abandoned by legislative means, and *implicit* deregulation, whereby remaining regulations have been made less effective through inadequate implementation or systematic bypassing.'

Other aspects of this strategy include export-led industrialization; the shift, especially in the industrialized countries from direct to indirect forms of employment, such as subcontracting from larger to smaller units; changing skill and job structures, including the trend towards skill polarization and greater reliance on external as opposed to internal labour markets.

In a new study prepared for the Canadian Advisory Council on the Status of Women (CACASW) entitled *Women and Labour Market Poverty*, Gunderson, Muszynski, and Keck (1990, 118) highlight the effects of increased international competition on women: 'Whatever the pros and cons of the Canada–U.S. free trade agreement, it will undoubtedly have considerable adjustment consequences. Many of these will be in female-dominated industries like textiles, footwear, clothing, food processing, and electrical products. Other female-dominated jobs in the business service sector (e.g., data processing, financial services, telecommunications, transportation, and culture) may also be jeopardized, while some growth may occur in the low-wage personal service sector.'

According to the Economic Council of Canada, nearly 90 per cent of the job growth in Canada since 1967 has taken place in the service sector (see Chart 1 and Table 1). Employment growth has been most pronounced in the business-service industry, with rapid gains in social services, health and finance, insurance, and real estate (see Table 2); these are the industries that employ a majority of the female labour force.

The Economic Council has identified industries in which Canada is at a comparative disadvantage and therefore at risk because of international competition. As can be seen from Table 3, women are overrepresented in the industries that are at risk and underrepresented in the five industry groups in which Canada is at a comparative advantage. It has been noted that within the former category of 'at-risk industries' women are overrepresented in the lower-skill/low-paying jobs, which are most susceptible to competitive pressures (Urban Dimensions Group 1989, 15).

These findings have led to concerns about the disproportionate effects of restructuring and adjustment on many women workers. Marjorie Cohen (1988) has raised questions about the potential implications for women of trade in serves given women's disproportionately high employment in these industries and their greater reliance on social services.

The Economic Council notes that the employment implications of trade in services cannot be measured directly because 'information on the amount of service sector employment that is directly involved in

Chart 1
Contribution of major sectors to employment growth, 1967–88

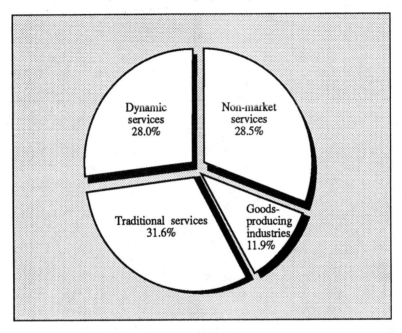

Source: Economic Council of Canada, *Good Jobs, Bad Jobs* (1990), 5. Based on data from Statistics Canada.

trade and simply not available.' A rough estimate based on input-output analysis information from the 1981 Census, however, provides an approximation of the magnitudes involved. The council finds that 9 per cent of all jobs in the dynamic-service subsector (230,000) jobs were directly dependent on service exports. (See the detailed list of dynamic services, traditional services, and non-market services on page 262.) However, the council points out that 'earlier studies have estimated that the magnitude of *indirect* service exports – i.e., of services "bundled" in exported goods – is about 50 per cent greater than that of direct service exports. If the effect of both direct and indirect service exports on employment are considered, then the total employment effect of service trade is more significant as over 20 per cent of the jobs in dynamic services may then be dependent on trade' (Economic Council of Canada 1990).

TABLE 1
Employment shares and employment growth, by industry, 1967–88

	Industry employment		
	As a share of total employment (%)		Annual growth rate, 1967–88 (%)
	1967	1988	
Service sector	59.4	70.9	3.4
Dynamic services	19.7	23.0	3.2
Transportation, communications, and utilities	9.0	7.4	1.5
Wholesale trade	4.5	4.6	2.7
Finance, insurance, and real estate	4.3	5.9	4.1
Business services	1.9	5.1	7.3
Traditional services	21.7	25.7	3.3
Retail trade	12.1	13.1	2.8
Personal services	9.6	12.6	3.8
Non-market services	18.0	22.2	3.5
Health and social services	6.2	8.9	4.3
Education	5.8	6.6	3.2
Public administration	6.0	6.7	3.0
Goods sector	40.6	29.1	0.9
Primary industries	10.3	6.0	−0.1
Manufacturing	23.9	17.2	0.9
Construction	6.5	5.9	2.1
Both sectors	100.0	100.0	2.5

Source: Economic Council of Canada, *Good Jobs, Bad Jobs* (1990, 5)

These jobs may be more vulnerable to competing with deregulated labour markets (Standing 1988). At the same time, employers who face increased competition under free trade may become even more opposed to programs like pay equity and employment equity (which specifically benefit women) because their cost is perceived to be an unfair competitive burden.

This problem is not unique to Canada. As Europe moves towards a single economic market in 1992, there is increasing concern about shifts in production to deregulated labour markets within the European trading bloc. Even firms that are well established and operating in economies that have strong social safety nets and highly regulated labour market

TABLE 2

Percentage distribution of the employed labour force by sex and industry divisions, Canada, 1971, 1981, and 1986

Industry	1971			1981			1986		
	M	F	%F	M	F	%F	M	F	%F
Total	100.0	100.0	34.3	100.0	100.0	40.1	100.0	100.0	42.6
Agriculture	6.8	3.9	23.1	5.3	2.5	23.8	5.2	2.7	27.6
Forestry	1.1	0.1	4.9	1.0	0.2	11.4	1.0	0.2	13.6
Fishing and trapping	0.4	0.0	3.5	0.4	0.1	8.3	0.5	0.1	12.9
Mines (including milling), quarries, and oil wells	2.3	0.3	6.7	2.5	0.6	14.2	2.0	0.5	15.5
Manufacturing industries	23.0	13.2	23.1	22.6	12.4	26.9	21.1	11.2	28.3
Construction industry	8.6	0.9	5.0	9.1	1.4	9.6	8.3	1.3	10.7
Transportation, communication, and other utilities	9.9	3.9	16.8	10.2	4.7	23.4	10.1	4.5	24.9
Trade	14.3	15.5	36.2	15.6	17.5	42.8	16.2	17.0	43.7
Finance, insurance, and real estate	3.2	6.3	50.9	3.5	8.1	60.6	3.8	7.7	60.2
Community, business, and personal service industries	15.4	40.1	57.7	18.8	42.2	60.0	21.1	44.6	61.1
Public administration and defence	8.6	5.6	25.5	8.0	6.8	36.3	8.0	7.0	39.2
Industry unspecified or undefined	6.4	10.1	44.9	2.8	3.4	44.5	2.8	3.1	44.9

Source: Connelly and McDonald (1990, 21)

TABLE 3
Employment by sex in industries in which Canada is at comparative disadvantage, 1986

Industry	M	F	Total	%F
Knitting mills	5,560	11,400	16,960	67.2
Clothing	28,085	94,000	122,085	77.0
Leather	5,230	9,210	14,440	63.8
Textiles	38,805	30,945	69,750	44.4
Printing and publishing	88,280	64,580	152,860	42.2

Employment by sex in industries in which Canada is at a comparative advantage, 1986

Industry	M	F	Total	%F
Wood	122,165	15,450	137,615	11.2
Paper and allied products	111,500	19,885	131,385	15.1
Primary metals	110,310	11,025	121,335	9.1
Petroleum and coal products	19,395	5,385	24,780	21.7
Transportation equipment	184,150	37,185	221,335	16.8

Source: Economic Council of Canada, *Employment Policies for Trade-Sensitive Industries* (Ottawa: Supply and Services Canada), 19. Presented in Urban Dimensions Group, *Growth of Contingent Workforce in Ontario* (1989)

(e.g., Germany) may have their quasi monopoly market situation threatened by this shift in production. An ILO study warns that 'the labour market "deregulation," implicit and explicit, of recent years will be accentuated by the shift to the "international market" in the European Community in 1992. The hype currently attached to this project may herald much less in reality once the various implications are digested by Governments. But if it does occur, almost certainly enterprises will move production and employment to those where deregulation is greater. This will greatly strengthen the bargaining position of employers and probably increase the insecurity of employment and income of many groups of workers' (Standing 1988, 25).

For the United States, for example, Thurow (1985) found that the major effect of foreign competitive pressure has been that of increasing the variation in earnings within each occupation of industry and pushing workers down the earning ladder.

As with others, such a trend may create a negative environment obstructive to the realization of labour-market legislation that addresses itself to the economically disadvantaged position of women workers. Effective consideration of universal, regulated standards of competition

The Structure of the Service Sector*

Dynamic Services

Transportation, communications, and utilities
  Air, rail, and water transport
  Ground transportation
  Pipelines
  Storage and warehousing
  Broadcasting – radio, television, cable
  Telephone systems
  Postal and courier services
  Utilities – electricity, gas, water, and sewage systems
Wholesale trade
Finance, insurance, and real estate
Banks and trust companies
  Credit unions and mortgage companies
  Insurance companies
  Investment dealers
  Real estate operators
Business services
  Employment agencies
  Advertising services
  Architectural, scientific, engineering, and computing services
  Legal services
  Management consulting

Traditional Services

Retail trade
  Food stores
  Drug stores and liquor stores
  Furniture, appliance, furnishings, and stereo stores
  Car dealers, gas stations, and auto repair shops
  Department stores
  Jewellery stores and photographic stores
Personal services
  Hotels
Restaurants and bars
Film, audio, and video production and distribution
Movie houses and theatres
Barber and beauty shops
Laundries and cleaners
Funeral services
Machinery and car rental companies
Photographers
Repair shops (excluding auto)
Building security services
Travel agencies

Non-market Services

Education services
  Schools, colleges, and universities
  Libraries, museums, and archives
Health services
  Hospitals
  Nursing homes
  Doctors and dentists
Medical laboratories
Social services
  Daycare, meal services, and crisis centres
  Psychologists and social workers
  Religious organizations
Public administration

Source: Economic Council of Canada, 1990. *Good Jobs, Bad Jobs*, 3

* For data-related reasons, this classification scheme has been organized within the framework of Statistics Canada's Standard Industrial Classification.

(Ostry 1990) or the social dimensions of economic integration with the United States is unlikely in this type of competitive environment. So far, the ability of the national trade unions to influence decision makers has been very limited (Standing 1988).

Growth of the Contingent Workforce
A recent study prepared for the Ontario Women's Directorate (OWD) entitled *Growth of the Contingent Workforce in Ontario* identifies a series of changes taking place in the Canadian workforce that are funnelling more workers into the contingent, as opposed to the mainstream, workforce. This shift towards contingent forms of labour that are not full-time and regular, but part-time and temporary, represents a dramatic aspect of current labour-market restructuring (Sacouman and Veltmeyer 1990).

These changes, exemplified by such practices as corporate downsizing, contracting out, privatization, increased homework, and self-employment, have a disproportionate impact on women, as this section will illustrate. What is directly significant to this essay is the study's conclusion that women's association with the contingent workforce will have repercussions for labour-market equality legislation: 'It is commonly perceived that economic and employment disadvantages experienced by women are in the process of being resolved by new legislative and regulatory activities such as employment equity and pay equity. These initiatives, and much existing legislation and regulation, are principally targeted on the organized, "mainstream" workforce. Federal employment equity initiatives, for example, deal only with employers having 100 or more employees. Ontario pay equity legislation deals only with employers having ten or more employees. In 1985, nearly 84% of all of Ontario's registered businesses had fewer than 10 employees' (Urban Dimensions Group 1989, 9).

What follows is a brief discussion of structural trends contributing to the greater reliance on the contingent workforce.

Corporate Downsizing, Contracting Out, and Privatization
International competition and technological change are two of the driving forces for corporate downsizing (as measured by number of employees, Sengenberger and Loveman, 1988). Establishment size is key to the nature of coverage and enforcement of anti-discrimination and labour law in Canada.

In Ontario, 87 per cent of all jobs created between 1976 and 1984 were in forms employing fewer than twenty people. The trend towards employment in small firms so far has affected only a minority of employees (Urban Dimensions Group 1989). The OWD reported research by the Ontario Ministry of Industry, Trade and Technology (1988), estimating that 'in 1984, 7.4% of the labour force was employed in the

75% of firms which employed fewer than 5 people; another 11.6% was employed in the 18% of firms which employed between 5 and 19 people; another 16.4% was employed in the 6% of firms which employed between 20 and 99 people; another 16.3% was employed in the 1.5% of firms which employed between 100 and 499 people; and 48.2% was employed in the 0.5% of firms which employed more than 500 people' (Urban Dimensions Group 1989, 29).

The extent to which small-establishment growth will continue is, however, the subject of some debate (Standing 1988). But, if the trend continues over the 1989–2001 period, it could have major implications for the composition of the labour force by size of employer. Table 4 shows the potential importance of small employers to employment growth under the assumption that establishments with fewer than twenty employees continue to account for 87 per cent of employment growth up to the year 2001.

The OWD study goes on to note the possible consequences for women's economic position because of this trend. It suggests that larger establishments may be more beneficial employers as they tend to pay employees more than they would be paid in comparable jobs in smaller establishments. More comprehensive and generous benefits packages characterize larger establishments, along with more extensive internal labour markets, resulting in greater chances for promotion and advancement (Brown and Medoff 1988). Most important to the focus of this essay, 'larger establishments are more likely to be subject to union organizing drives and collective bargaining and in some cases (e.g., pay equity) more likely to be subject to regulation and enforcement by Ontario's anti-discrimination and employment law' (Urban Dimensions Group 1989, 28–9). The study concludes: 'To the extent that this female dominance of employment growth is taking place in the context of a labour market which favours lower wage, lower benefits, lower career advancement and unregulated (or less-regulated) job opportunities, women will continue to be disadvantages in the labour force' (29).

Given the current trend towards small establishments, pay equity and equal employment initiatives may be less and less effective alternatives to promoting economic equity for women compared with, for example, traditional collective-bargaining mechanisms. Of course, women's rates of unionization remain substantially below those of their male counterparts. In 1981, only 24 per cent of women employees in Ontario were union members, compared with 37 per cent of men (Bakker 1988).

Contracting out of goods and services as a means of maintaining flex-

TABLE 4
Projection of employment by establishment size (number of employees): Ontario, 2001*

Number of employees	1986 employment		2001 employment		Per cent growth
	N	%	N	%	
0–19	962,276	19.0	1,604,013	27.6	87.0
20–99	833,186	16.4	847,870	14.6	2.0
100–499	828,105	16.3	571,142	9.8	−35.0
500+	2,448,753	48.2	2,786,476	48.0	46.0
Total	5,075,320	100.0	5,809,500	100.0	14.5

Source: *Growth of the Contingent Workforce in Ontario* (1989)

* This projection is based on the 'most probable' projection of labour force growth presented in Exhibit 4.1b. The 1986 data were obtained from the Ontario Ministry of Industry, Trade and Technology publication, *The State of Small Business* (Toronto: Government of Ontario 1988), 55–72.

ibility and control over fixed labour costs is a practice reinforced by technological change and labour-force and demographic trends. Examples of contracting out are computer services, data processing, and commercial cleaning services. As this practice grows, fewer workers are likely to fall under the existing employment standards and labour law. Unfortunately, direct evidence on corporate contracting-out policies that would support this prediction is not readily available.

Privatization of crown corporations and subcontracting of government services to the private sector will effect women's as well as men's employment. But women will be especially touched by the employment effects of privatization in the service sector, where 83 per cent of them are employed. Traditional targets of privatization are female-dominated occupations such as clerical and cleaning operations, data processing, and child-care services. (Urban Dimensions Group 1989, 34). The OWD points out that most of these initiatives

involve a transfer of employment law jurisdiction, usually from regimes which are more strongly committed to promoting economic equity for women to regimes which are less strongly committed. For example, government contracting-out removes classes of workers from Civil Service designation, protection and collective bargaining; removes these job classes from the contractor's obligation to implement pay equity and replaces this with an obligation on the sub-contractor's part to implement pay equity (often on a weaker basis); ... the selling off of government services and the participation of proprietary firms can also remove job classes from the public sector and place them under weaker private sector jurisdiction. (82–3)

It is also noted that privatization sets an example to private-sector employers that suggests an acceptable 'about face' when it comes to equity policy for women. By taking less responsibility for employment and pay equity, the public sector is sending a signal to the private sector about the priority that this set of policies has on the public agenda. Finally, retrenchment of the public sector or federally regulated sector will probably dampen pay and employment equity initiatives (Gunderson et al. 1990).

Self-employment is part of the tendency towards smaller establishment size that will effect coverage of pay equity legislation. In the past decade, 10 per cent of overall job growth in Canada has been in this category (Economic Council of Canada 1990, 12). Women showed a far greater increase in their move to self-employment over this period, at 136 per cent versus 39 per cent for men (Urban Dimensions Group 1989, 40). This raises questions about the current and future applicability of pay equity for this group of workers. Coverage, of course, is an issue, but a related question is who is responsible for pay equity for the self-employed and what policy tools could be employed to realize pay equity for the self-employed.

Homework is part of this growth in self-employment, although it can be partly classified as a portion of the contingent workforce. Currently, limited data are available on the incidence of this form of work. What is significant for our purposes is the finding that in some cases in Ontario, homeworkers' contracts allow the employer to avoid statutory requirements such as overtime, vacation pay, and benefits (Urban Dimensions Group 1989, 43). In any event, the self-employed are not covered by pay equity legislation, their earnings tend to be lower than those of workers employed by others (Economic of Canada 1990, 12) and as this formerly non-traditional form of employment grows, the need for pay equity legislation will become more urgent.

To sum up, the reduction in establishment size through various mechanisms such as corporate downsizing, privatization, and self-employment appears to present serious challenges to current pay equity legislation. The Ontario model, which is the only provincial legislation covering both the private and the public sector, is regarded as the most

TABLE 5
Part-time and full-time employment growth as a percentage of overall growth, Canada, 1966–87

Category	1966–73	1973–9	1979–83	1983–7
Total employment	100.0	100.0	100.0	100.0
Full-time	74.0	85.6	0.0	86.0
Part-time	26.0	14.4	100.0	14.0
Part-time employment	100.0	100.0	100.0	100.0
Youth (under 25)	55.5	62.6	32.7	43.8
Adult women (over 25)	35.9	43.5	48.9	50.9
Adult men (over 25)	8.6	−6.4	18.4	5.3
Goods industries	10.2	1.0	7.7	−15.0
Service industries	89.9	99.0	92.3	115.0
Full-time employment	100.0	100.0	100.0	100.0
Youth (under 25)	26.2	23.9	–	1.1
Adult women (over 25)	37.1	43.0	–	53.6
Adult men (over 25)	36.7	33.0	–	45.3
Goods industries	10.0	25.1	–	28.1
Service industries	90.0	74.9	–	71.9

Source: Gunderson, Muszynski, and Keck (1990, 126)

promising model. But its reliance on establishment comparisons has limitations that will probably be exacerbated by the trend towards small establishments outlined above. Moreover, 'the law requires that pay comparisons be made with male-dominated groups of the same value as the undervalued female-dominated groups *in the same establishment*. This legislative restriction effectively exempts a large number of all-female establishments or female-dominated establishment where there are no male comparison groups. This is the case, for example, for many establishments in areas such as child care, social services, retail trade, and some manufacturing sectors. The problem is particularly acute for immigrant, racial minority women, who are heavily concentrated in small establishments and all-female job ghettoes' (Gunderson et al. 1990, 163).

Part-Time Employment Growth
The growth in part-time employment is a well-documented and important structural feature of the Organization of Economic Cooperation and Development (OECD) labour markets (Gunderson et al. 1990, 2; Bakker 1988). Table 5 highlights the large gender differences in the incidence of part-time employment.

Continued growth of part-time employment (characterized by few or no fringe benefits, lack of job security, little protection under employment-standards law or collective agreements, and wage discrimination) (Gunderson et al. 1990, 125) could counteract measures such as pay equity that are designed to promote economic equality. This is particularly relevant since it has been found that most of the increase in part-time employment is driven by employers' desire to decrease fixed labour costs and increase labour-market flexibility (Urban Dimensions Group 1990, 49; OECD 1989, ch. 2).

The policy implications of this trend towards more part-time work are highlighted by looking at the Ontario example. From the viewpoint of collective bargaining, the Ontario Labour Relations Act does not deal specifically with part-time employees, although in practice the board generally assumes that part-time and full-time workers have different interests. As the OWD report notes, this difference of interests usually warrants separate bargaining units for full-time and part-time workers 'as a safeguard against the majority group sacrificing the interests of the minority through the collective bargaining process' (Urban Dimensions Group 1989, 86). In this case, separate bargaining units often reinforce pay disparities because the part-time bargaining unit is more likely to be predominantly female and likely has less bargaining power.

From the standpoint of the Pay Equity Act, 'pay comparisons should be made between bargaining units only when there are no comparison groups within bargaining units (sections 6[4], 6[5]). This means that the Pay Equity Act cannot be relied upon to redress pay disparities that might arise under collective bargaining (Urban Dimensions Group 1989, 87). Also, once pay equity is achieved between female and male job classes as between two bargaining units (in those cases where the only male comparator is in another unit), section 8(2) of the act specifically states that pay differences that are attributable to bargaining strength are permitted. Thus, the differing unionization rates of men and women workers and the relative power of male- and female-dominated unions may result in the reintroduction of wage differentials.

Sectoral Change and Income Polarization: The Good Jobs/Bad Jobs Scenario
The Economic Council's study *Good Jobs, Bad Jobs: Employment in the Service Economy* stresses the growing interdependence of goods and services (convergence) in the Canadian economy. The council explains the convergence between goods and services in terms of three develop-

ments: 1 / technological changes are blurring the distinction between goods and services activities; 2 / goods production itself is increasingly taking on service-like features, such as non-storability and direct contact between producer and consumer; and 3 / there is a growing trend towards the 'bundling' of goods and services in an integrated package (Economic Council of Canada 1990, 4).

Indeed, one of the most dramatic structural changes of the last two decades has been the shift from manufacturing employment to service employment.[2] A priori, it might be expected that this shift would exacerbate gender-based job and income segregation, given past employment patterns.

It has been argued that shifts in employment away from manufacturing towards services are contributing to changes in wage-distribution patterns. As a result, wages and earnings are no longer clustered around the middle of the wage distribution, but are moving towards an hourglass configuration, where wages tend to be clustered at the top or the bottom.[3]

Empirical evidence on wage polarization and heightened labour-market segmentation in Canada is so far inconclusive. There is evidence from the Economic Council of a growing earnings polarization but, at this point, researchers are unable to determine whether this is a one-time disturbance attributable to post-recession adjustments or a significant, long-term trend (Economic Council of Canada 1990, 16). In terms of the nature of emerging jobs, the council draws a mixed conclusion: 'Virtually all of the recent employment growth has involved either highly skilled, well-compensated, and secure jobs or unstable and relatively poorly paid jobs' (10).

The growth of services, technological innovation, and changing work organization have transformed both the nature and the level of labour-market skills. The authors of *Good Jobs, Bad Jobs* conclude that 'on balance, the skill distribution in the service sector is more polarized than that in the goods sector, which is characterized by intermediate-level skill requirements. Thus the employment shift to services is contributing to gains in the highly skilled occupations, a decline in the share of middle-level skilled jobs, and a stable proportion of low-skill' (Economic Council of Canada 1990, 14).

Acceleration in the growth of highly skilled jobs has taken place in managerial, administrative, professional, and technical occupations. The study notes that these categories were responsible for a third of all employment from 1971 to 1981 and 77 per cent from 1981 to 1986.

Projections suggest that these occupations will account for more than half of the net job creation in the next decade.

Pat Connelly and Martha MacDonald (1990), in an examination of occupational changes affecting Canadian women workers, note that, in the managerial category, women's share of jobs doubled from 15.4 per cent in 1971 to 31.5 per cent in 1986. However, the male-dominated occupations that had the most dramatic increases in female employees from 1971 to 1986 were also the ones where the initial percentage of women was very low (see Table 6). Moreover, the number of occupations that employ at least 70 per cent women increased from 41 in 1971 to 51 in 1986 (Economic Council of Canada 1990, 22).

Women continue to be employed in traditional services, characterized

TABLE 6
Occupations with the largest increase in numbers of employed women, Canada, 1971–86

Detailed occupations	Growth in female employment, 1971–86		Females: percentage of total	
	No.	%	1971	1986
Total – all occupations	2,141,600	77.0	34.3	42.6
Bookkeepers and accounting clerks	171,640	133.0	67.4	83.7
Secretaries and stenographers	163,665	71.3	97.4	98.8
Tellers and cashiers	134,840	141.5	91.2	90.5
Salespersons, commodities, n.e.c.	129,675	79.8	54.8	56.1
Nurses, graduate, except supervisors	105,905	107.6	95.9	95.2
Waiters, hostesses, and stewards, food and beverage	81,605	87.5	83.1	83.1
Electronic data-processing equipment operators	62,550	331.0	73.4	79.7
Receptionists and information clerks	55,260	140.6	92.7	94.0
Accountants, auditors, and other financial officers	55,100	364.2	15.0	38.5
Supervisors: sales occupations, commodities	49,615	122.0	16.6	31.9
Baby-sitters	46,175	251.1	96.7	97.2
General office clerks	44,275	59.7	62.1	80.4
Chefs and cooks	41,395	114.4	50.9	48.4
Janitors, charworkers, and cleaners	36,095	69.6	32.9	41.7
Barbers, hairdressers, and related occupations	32,615	97.3	62.5	80.4

Source: Connelly and McDonald (1990, 24)

by lower skill levels (Connelly and MacDonald 1990, 4). According to the Economic Council of Canada, there is a gender dimension to skill polarization. The ratio of women in low-skill jobs to men was 1.3:1 in 1986. In other words, 30 per cent more women than men were located in low-skill jobs. This ratio has changed slowly over the past two decades from 1.5:1 in 1971. The proportion of women in high-skill jobs compared with men was 0.73:1 in 1986, showing a slight improvement from 1971, when it was 0.6:1. At both times, female workers were underrepresented in the high-skill jobs in comparison with male workers (Economic Council of Canada 1990).

Have structural changes contributed to greater income disparity? According to the Economic Council, earnings have become more polarized. However, this trend is not attributed to the shift towards services; the study finds that increased income polarization has taken place in all industry groupings within both the goods and the services sector (Economic Council of Canada 1990, 15). A range of explanations has been offered, from economic globalization and technological innovation to the growing reliance upon 'non-standard' workers and the waning influence of unions on the wage-determination process (Economic Council of Canada 1990, 15).

Based on the evidence it has, the Economic Council concludes that, overall, some trends suggest a growing segmentation in the labour market: 'in terms of earnings, skill content, job stability, and the location of employment. Two quite distinct "growth poles" account for virtually all of the employment expansion in the 1980s: one includes highly skilled, well-compensated, stable jobs, while the other consists of nonstandard jobs with relatively low levels of compensation and stability. The implication of our research is that the labour market is offering economic security to fewer Canadians' (Economic Council of Canada 1990, 17).

The CACSW adds that these changes are 'exacerbating the extent of working poverty among women, because the lower-wage service jobs are clearly associated with working poverty and women are segregated in these jobs' (Gunderson et al. 1990, 122).

To what extent will pay equity policy be able to address the dilemmas of increasing income polarization? If the phenomenon of polarization takes a gendered form and women become more highly represented in 'bad jobs' compared with men, and if these jobs are located in small establishments or take non-standard work forms, the current forms of pay equity may be less effective. Conversely, if more men's jobs are now 'bad jobs' as a result of polarization, the remedial impact of pay equity based on job comparisons will not achieve the intended equalization objectives of raising women's wages. Theoretically, if polarization leads to more men in bad jobs, pay equity, the parity of male and female wages, could be realized. However, such equality could be taking place at the poverty level if average wages fall far enough because of sectoral and occupational adjustments.

Another implication of earnings, skill, and job polarization is that, as women continue to be drawn to either pole of employment, the disparity among them will increase. The implications are economic as well as political. Pay equity assumes a commonality of interests among women, but economic restructuring appears to be creating both material differences and skill divisions within their numbers. At the same time, as Steinberg (1987) points out, comparable worth/pay equity legislation legitimates the basis of salary differences among jobs and, we might add, differences among women.

The increasing importance of differences signals, for some authors, a class-based divergence of interests among women in the labour force. Blum (1987) suggests that comparable worth strategy may signal the declining significance of gender and the increasing importance of class for determining life changes.

There is some empirical evidence for the United States to support this view. In the United States, the distribution of women's earnings, traditionally more equal than that of men, is becoming less so. Two factors have contributed to this trend: the percentage of women in high-wage jobs (>$30,000 per year) was far greater in 1986 than in the late 1970s. As for women in low-paying jobs (<$10,000 per year), the period from 1970 to 1978 showed a decline from 21 to 16.5 per cent; however, this trend was reversed between 1978 and 1986 when the percentage increased (a 'U-turn' effect). Wagman and Folbre (1988), the two economists who conducted the study, conclude that this 'feminization of inequality' has important implications for both feminist strategy and economic theory. They argue that the polarization of earnings among women will further weaken 'the fragile bonds of gender solidarity.'

In Canada, over the same period, there has been a steady decline in low-wage–earning women and an increase in high-wage–earning women. For the 1971–88 period, there was an 8.6 per cent drop in the number of women earning less than $10,000 and an 8.2 per cent increase in those earning more than $30,000 per year (Chart 2). Part of this shift may be explained by the employment gains women made in the highly skilled jobs in the managerial occupations and by the employment of women in relatively better-paying state-sector jobs. At this point, it is still difficult to determine the contribution of affirmative-action initiatives and equal-employment-opportunity legislation to earnings since most of these programs have not been in effect for very long and measurement criteria are complex (Gunderson 1989; Jain and Hackett 1989).

The share of low-wage male workers, by contrast, increased until the end of the last recession in the early 1980s and now appears to be dropping off (Chart 3). There was also a drop in the percentage of male high-wage earners that began at the onset of the recession. This drop can, in part, be explained by the loss of manufacturing jobs during the last recession which hit men harder than women. However, explanations relying solely on cyclical factors, such as the rate of unemployment, appear to be insufficient in explaining the historical trend towards greater inequality (Burtless 1990). Preliminary findings from the Economic Council indicate that, while both men's and women's earnings are becoming increasingly unequal (rising Gini coefficients) and more polarized, men's earnings appear to be moving towards greater polarization and inequality, exhibiting the declining-middle syndrome (Economic Council of Canada 1991, ch. 8).

Some Observations on Pay Equity and the Changing Nature and Location of Jobs

Good Jobs/Bad Jobs
As noted in the previous section, women workers are making some advances to the upper pole of jobs in terms of earnings and occupations. However, evidence indicates that women continue to be more likely employed in non-standard forms of employment,[4] and that this type of employment is on the rise. According to data from the Economic Council of Canada (1991), 36 per cent of women (versus 23 per cent of men) were in non-standard forms of employment in 1988. If the majority of workers employed in the 'bad jobs' sector continue to be women, this will no doubt have an impact on the economic security of this group of workers. The additional pressures of free trade, the move towards consumption taxes via the GST, and cutbacks in the public sector will further reinforce such insecurity.

Job Content
There is another aspect of restructuring that we have not yet considered. The increased use and refinement of technology at the work site opens

Chart 2
Women with high and low annual earnings (in 1988$)

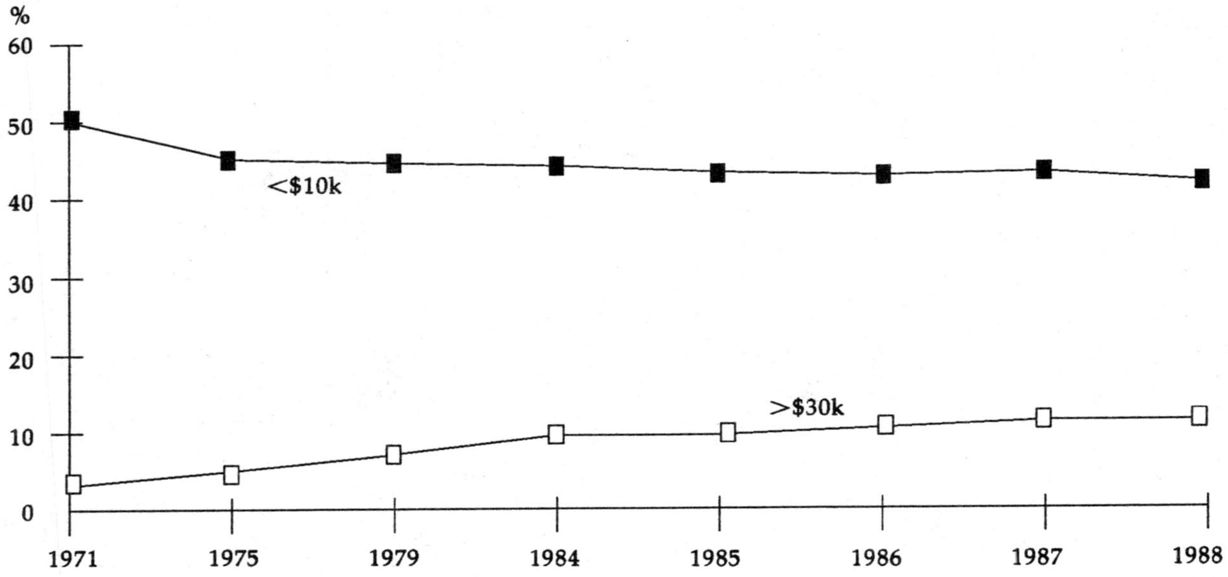

Chart 3
Men with high and low annual earnings (in 1988$)

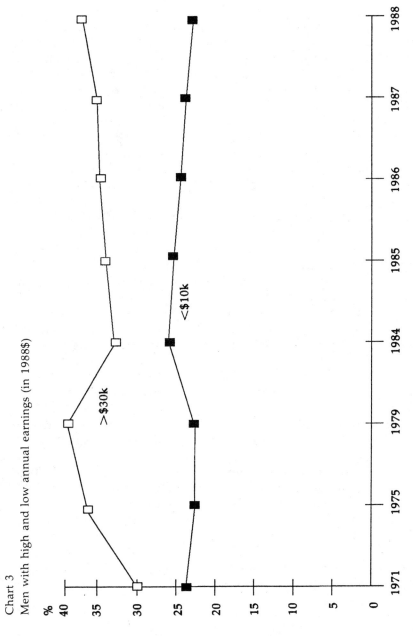

Source: Statistics Canada, *Earnings of Men and Women 1988*, cat. 13–217

the door to greater surveillance, thus, in combination with job evaluation, giving the employer more information with which to control workers. As Braverman (1974) argued, knowledge is the key to control and to maintaining a job hierarchy with differentiated earnings, skills, etc.

For female workers, the implications of office automation for control over the work process are particularly significant. The adoption of new office technologies has been shown to have increased managerial control through 'replacing clerical jobs which required a variety of skills and some discretion over the pace of work (e.g., typing, filing, shorthand) with jobs which break these generic skills down into component parts (e.g., word processor, data entry); and ... by using electronic surveillance features of the new technology to monitor workers' (Urban Dimensions Group 1989, 22).

Several implications flow from these observations. One possibility is that pay equity and job evaluation, especially given the context of technological innovation and increasing managerial control over the work process, may facilitate the reclassification of good jobs into bad jobs.

This reclassification will depend a great deal on the ability of workers to wrest control over the labour process from management. Cuneo (1990, 55) has pointed out that pursuit of pay equity enables unions to play a direct role in determining job evaluation and pay equity plans. Also, there is the potential through this pursuit for individual workers to participate in decisions regarding the relative worth of their jobs through job-evaluation plans (Cuneo 1990, 55). Fudge has noted that employers, under Canadian labour law, nevertheless maintain the right to reclassify jobs as a managerial prerogative. In the absence of a collective agreement, such reclassification constitutes a unilateral change in the conditions of employment, which the employee can, at law, treat as a breach and sue for unreasonable notice in a wrongful-dismissal action. However, because women's jobs are low status, such damages would be negligible. Thus, in practice, the employer can reclassify at will. With a collective agreement, the employer retains the right to reclassify, although unions can challenge particular reclassifications at grievance arbitration. Moreover, the legislation does not prohibit red-circling male jobs classes after a job comparison has been conducted. Thus employers are provided with an opportunity to reclassify the male job classes used for comparisons downwards.[5]

Skill Diversification
It is interesting that much of the literature on labour-market policy is calling for skill diversification and multi-skill training as a response to

the restructuring of the global job market. The limited extent to which a move in this direction is possible, given, for example, the new office technologies and their reliance on breaking skills into component parts, is one aspect of this issue that needs to be considered.

Clearly, the call for skill diversification will also have ramifications for pay equity. There is a contradiction between labour-market training policies that argue for skill diversification (writing, communicating, problem solving) and pay equity, which rests on the notion of jobs being more narrowly defined according to skill, effort, responsibility, and working conditions, for purposes of job evaluation. It has been pointed out that 'one of the principal problems is that it is difficult to equip people with broad skills and then place them in work situations where they have a job that is defined, evaluated and rewarded on a narrow linear base, however objective and laudable that might be' (*Pay Equity Practitioner* 1989).

In order to prevent pay equity from becoming an instrument that narrows the scope and the dimension of work for job-classification purposes, we must try to ensure that pay equity and the job-evaluation process are used to address workplace organization 'to induce organizations to undertake substantive redevelopment in the way jobs and reporting relationships are structured' (*Pay Equity Practitioner* 1989). Current pay equity policies are predicated on a system of job classification that is often modelled on manufacturing skill and work structures and does not capture the current wave of skill and work process changes, particularly in the service sector. Thus, if pay equity policy as currently constituted is locked into classification schemes that will be outmoded, pay equity will, at best, be realized incompletely.

We should not forget that management and labour, women and men, and groups of women themselves all have very different ideas about the skills that are required. According to Rianne Mahon, management, for example, tends to bypass its existing workforce and recruit people directly from the educational system; the emphasis is on short-term skill improvement rather than longer-term skill upgrading (Bakker 1989).

Unions, like the Canadian Auto Workers, tend to argue for skill upgrading so that workers can get the broader theoretical and analytical skills needed for them to make the best use of the new machines and to share in the benefits of economic restructuring (better work conditions, more interesting work, etc.). In order to realize the full benefits of high value-added restructuring and technological change, most literature suggests that work needs to be redesigned and made more interesting. However, as Mahon notes, employers seem to favour Japanese techniques for tapping workers' knowledge and ability that do not involve a shift in the balance of power. Capital and labour also differ when it comes to the ease of access to and quality of training. For unions, the goal is high-quality training as a right given during paid working time.

The legitimate role of unions to represent workers in the redesign of work and work practices needs to be recognized if technological change is to be translated into higher productivity and social prosperity. Yet, women's access, to this representation is substantially less than that of men and will be even less, given their increasing participation in the contingent labour force. This presents a serious problem, since their access to skills training, long-term skill upgrading, and so on will not necessarily be secured through collective-bargaining or cooperative decision-making process. Women's relative lack of access to the collective-bargaining process underscores the role of the state, especially the federal state, in creating the appropriate social and regulatory environment for equitable labour-market policies.

Summary and Conclusions

This essay has pointed to changes at the firm-specific level and to changes at the sectoral and industry levels that will influence occupational structures, income distribution, and the nature of the work process. The potential implications for current pay equity policies of structural trends were identified to be the following:

- increased international competition and free trade will have ramifications for employment adjustments and the policy environment
- the trend towards greater reliance on a contingent workforce because of contracting out and privatization will have a significant impact on coverage of pay equity, comparisons of all-female establishments or female-dominated establishments, and possibly, on future job and occupational structures
- continued movement towards smaller establishment size will affect the nature of employment and coverage of workers
- the polarization of jobs and skills will influence where women work and the skills that they acquire
- women's relative underrepresentation in unions and the collective-bargaining process limits their input into pay equity negotiations and the job-evaluation process. At the same time, pay equity opens up the discussion of how society values work. The process of describing,

evaluating, and comparing jobs may call attention to the problems inherent in job hierarchies for women as well as legitimate them.'[6]

This essay has started an examination of how the effectiveness of efforts by the state to regulate labour markets towards pay equity is influenced by economic restructuring. The limits to state policy in the realm of pay equity arise, in part, from significant and, to a certain extent, unanticipated structural changes to the labour market and economy. The relatively narrow initial focus of pay equity policies is now being diminished even more by shifts in labour-market structure. These trends compound the obstructions already encountered in the private sphere resulting from women's underrepresentation in collective bargaining.

Given these changes and limitations to current efforts to realize pay equity, it may be time to consider more macro-economic approaches. Regulatory policies aimed at micro-economic or firm-level adjustment need to be supplemented by more general policies of social wage solidarity. We have not yet exhausted the range of policies that can help realize greater income equity, but it is perhaps time to turn our attention to forging a social contract that will simultaneously address the need to reduce both earned income inequality generally and women's income inequality specifically. And we must begin to consider how pay equity policies will tie into new economic strategies aimed at addressing the restructuring of our economy.

NOTES

I would like to extend particular thanks to Judy Fudge and Caren Grown (Bureau of Labor Statistics) for the detailed comments they offered me on an early draft of this essay. I am also very grateful to Janine Brodie, Norm Leckie, and Riel Miller for their comments and editorial skills. Of course, all errors remain the responsibility of the author.

1 These conclusions are for the United States but the Ontario Women's Directorate (OWD) study reaches similar conclusions for Canada.
2 Some of this shift is the result of statistical counting. See Gunderson et al. (1990, 122) for a discussion.
3 Myles et al. (1988), Myles (1987). For an excellent discussion of the new-jobs debate and supporting date for OECD countries, see Tilley and Loveman (1988).
4 This refers to part-time, short-term, and own-account self-employment.

5 Judy Fudge, letter to author, 29 April 1989
6 Judy Fudge suggested to me that pay equity may be a useful way for unions that have been involved in the pay equity process to organize women workers. It is likely that establishments with unionized workers are either public-sector or large employers so most unions will have negotiated pay equity plans early on in the process. This offers the unique opportunity for them to use their expertise and pay equity staff to provide workshops and educational materials for non-organized workers. Some could help certain non-organized women workers through the pay equity process. With foresight, unions could use the pay equity process as a way to illustrate to the unorganized why unions are valuable to them.

Conclusion: Pay Equity in a Declining Economy: The Challenge Ahead

Judy Fudge and Patricia McDermott

Does pay equity work? Although it is ostensibly a simple question, feminists have not agreed on how to answer it. In fact, as several of the essays in this collection illustrate the answer to this question has generated a great deal of controversy. But the controversy has not arisen simply because different evaluations of the evidence concerning how pay equity has worked have been offered; rather, the controversy arises because the *question* is complex. What it means to say that pay equity works depends upon how pay equity's goal is characterized and the level at which pay equity is being evaluated. In other words, any evaluation of pay equity's success depends upon how success is defined and measured in the first place.

It is possible to both characterize the goal of pay equity in a number of different ways and evaluate pay equity on a number of different levels. The official public-policy goal of pay equity initiatives is to close that part of the gender-wage gap that results from the systemic undervaluation of women's work. At the level of institutional analysis, then, the important questions include: how the wage gap is defined and whether pay equity has been a successful instrument in raising women's wages, and, if not, why not. At the level of ideology and consciousness-raising, pay equity can be seen as expressing a larger social vision, one that challenges the traditional market-based understandings of the worth of work and conventional gender hierarchies in the workplace. Here the crucial questions are symbolic rather than instrumental: whether pay equity has challenged or simply replicated and reinforced the male norm and hierarchies embedded in the market. An finally, pay equity may be evaluated from a more general perspective that focuses on how the labour market is structured. In this context, the important questions centre around how pay equity fits into the current crisis of distribution and the increasing fragmentation of the labour market on gender, racial, and ethnic lines.

By distinguishing and identifying the different goals of pay equity and the different levels at which it can be evaluated, we hope to illustrate that the controversy over pay equity has arisen because feminists have not been clear about identifying the different, but related, concerns that the broader question of whether pay equity works subsumes. In what follows we will briefly sketch some tentative answers to these questions and identify some additional questions that future research must address.

Closing the Gender Wage Gap

Pay equity is not designed to close the entire wage gap; rather, it is designed to reduce that part of the gender wage gap that is attributable to the systemic undervaluation of women's work. Any difference between men's and women's earning resulting from the fact that women tend to work fewer hours than men, do not receive the same shift premiums and overtime pay as men, and are less likely to be unionized than men is beyond the scope of pay equity. Moreover, most pay equity initiatives seek to redress only that part of the wage gap that is attributable to the undervaluation of women's jobs within an employer's establishment. In other words, that part of the wage gap attributable to the fact that women are employed in establishments or industrial sectors where men are not is beyond the scope of private-sector pay equity initiatives. Because it is extremely difficult to disaggregate the different factors that result in the wage gap, the estimates of what portion of the 40-percentage-point earnings differential will be closed by pay equity initiatives vary widely; Robb (1987) suggests that the gap may be reduced by as much as 10 to 15 points by pay equity initiatives, whereas Weiler (1985) estimates that such policies will reduce the gap by only 2 to 3 percentage points.

In Manitoba, the pay equity process reduced the gender wage gap in the civil service by approximately 5 percentage points. In 1986, women in the government had average hourly wages that were 18 per cent less than men's. With pay equity adjustments, it is projected that the average hourly wages will increase to 87 per cent of the average for men (Manitoba Civil Service Commission 1988, 37). However, it will not be so easy to determine the effect of the Ontario Pay Equity Act on the wage gap. Unlike in Manitoba, where pay equity was limited to the civil service and the results of the process were available to public scrutiny, in Ontario there is simply no way of determining the extent to which the legislation will close the wage gap. The Ontario legislation does not require employers to file pay equity plans – the only documents that set out the pay equity adjustments to which women workers are entitled – with the Pay Equity Commission. Consequently, there is no public record of the results of the pay equity process in the private sector and no data base upon which a systematic analysis of the legislation's effect on closing the wage gap can be performed. Before we can evaluate whether the Ontario Pay Equity Act works to close the wage gap, it will be necessary to obtain this information.

What we have is anecdotal evidence that some women workers in Ontario have received sizeable pay equity adjustments, while others have received nothing. To some extent, the size of pay equity adjustments for female job classes in particular establishments will depend upon the tactics adopted by pay equity advocates, unions, and employers. The selection of a gender-neutral job-comparison system, the definitions of employer and job class will, for example, affect the size of pay equity adjustments for a particular group of women workers. However, for the majority of women workers in Ontario the ability of pay equity to increase their wages is likely to depend upon the sector in which they are employed, whether or not they are unionized, the existence of an appropriate male job class as a comparator, the size of their employer's labour force, and whether or not they are employed on a casual or temporary contract basis. And it is precisely these factors, which strongly correlate with low pay, that are beyond the scope of Ontario Pay Equity Act to remedy. Because women are situated in different positions in the labour market, the range of pay equity adjustments under the Ontario legislation will vary widely across industries and between establishments.

Moreover, there is nothing in the Ontario legislation that would prohibit an employer from characterizing that part of what would otherwise have been the annual pay increase as the pay equity adjustment. The Ontario Pay Equity Act simply requires an employer to divide what it would otherwise set aside for compensation in a way that provides adjustments for the lowest-paid female job classes first; it does not require the employer to allocate additional monies to the wage bill in order to achieve pay equity. The extent to which employers in Ontario may be funding pay equity adjustments by holding back on general wage increases is not known. Although the legislation prohibits the lowering of wages to achieve pay equity, there is nothing that bans the red-circling of male job-class wages after a pay equity exercise has been undertaken (Warskett 1990, 74). Recent research in the United States suggests that, at the same time as male wage rates are in decline, women's wage rates are remaining constant (Tilly 1990, 107). Whether and to what extent this phenomenon is due to pay equity is unknown. As a result, it is impossible to determine whether any reduction in the gender wage gap is due to an overall decline in men's wages or a redistribution from men's wages to women's wages. Detailed and comprehensive research is needed to answer these questions.

Challenging the Market and Revaluing the Worth of Women's Work

While it is possible to see pay equity solely as a technique to rectify sex-based wage differentials, pay equity has been endorsed by feminists because it expresses a larger social vision: one that 'challenges market-based definitions of and cultural assumptions about the value of women's labour' (Kahn 1990, 22). By challenging the power relations that define women's work, pay equity articulates women workers' refusal to accept less pay than men because they do women's work.

But existing pay equity initiatives do not challenge the legitimacy of the practice of ranking jobs and compensating them on the basis of that rank. In fact, they reinforce the notion that some jobs are less valuable to employers and, as a consequence, that employers can legitimately pay people who work in these jobs less. Pay equity prohibits sex discrimination in the evaluation of the worth of a job; it does not say that it is wrong to value jobs hierarchically. Under pay equity every group of employees has a short-term interest in attempting to ensure that they have a higher position in the ranking of jobs than other groups or employees. For this reason some commentators fear that pay equity as it is currently conceived will deepen existing conflicts in the labour force along racial, gender, and status lines (Lewis 1988; Brenner 1987; Warskett 1990).

It is important, however, to be clear that pay equity does not *cause* the conflicts between men and women or visible-minority and white workers in the labour market, although it may be *used* by employers to exacerbate them. Pay equity is simply a procedural reform, the goal of which is to neutralize the systemic undervaluation of women's work. Pay equity techniques can be extended to address the systemic undervaluation of work associated with visible-minority workers. Moreover, Malveaux (1985b) contends that even pay equity initiatives that are addressed exclusively to the systemic undervaluation of women's work would benefit black women and black men employed in female-dominated jobs. By contrast, Brenner (1987, 459) argues that because pay equity legitimizes large-earnings differentials, 'large inequalities by race will remain, but appear to be reflections of differential merit and thus ultimately difficult to challenge.'

The extent to which pay equity challenges gender-biased or racist ideologies and practices that are deeply embedded in workplace hierarchies depends upon the ability of pay equity advocates and unions to mobilize women and visible-minority workers for a concerted attack against entrenched managerial power. The emphasis on technique, expertise, and litigation in pay equity processes tends to undermine the radical potential of pay equity to challenge existing power differentials. Advocates of mechanisms to redress systemic racial discrimination in the workplace can build upon the experience of pay equity in order to develop strategies that avoid its pitfalls. Ultimately, strategies that unite workers, whether they be people of colour, women, or men, will have the greatest potential to challenge the power of employers to establish and maintain wage differentials and discriminatory pay and employment practices.

The Crisis of Distribution and the Polarization of the Labour Market

Pay equity's dominant meaning will be determined through political struggle that is shaped by the current process of economic restructuring. The post-war compromise, which was based on the linkage between mass production and consumption and supported a social consensus premised on a minimum standard of economic welfare for the majority of people, has been broken by the assaults launched by multinational capital and the policies of the new right. What capital is seeking to do in this time of economic restructuring is to exploit flexible labour through out-sourcing, the casualization of work, and union busting (Standing 1989). The new flexible worker differs from the old paradigm of the full-time employee, typically male, in a unionized job for she is ever more likely to be female, part-time, temporary, and non-unionized. But flexibility does not simply characterize the change in the employment relationship, it also refers to capital's attempt to fragment production through the use of out-sourcing, homework, own-account workers, and privatization. Thus, the conditions for solidarity at the point of production no longer exist. Workers tend to work in small workplaces, away from each other, and are typically paid on incentive rates, which further enhances the competition they experience.

This restructuring of the labour market has resulted not only in the fragmentation of production, but also in the vast polarization of the working class. One-third of the society consists of both the new flexible workers who receive virtually nothing and anyone who falls outside the labour market. The remaining two-thirds is comprised of the old traditional working class, the new professional and technology class, and the owning classes (Tilly 1990; Economic Council of Canada 1990). What we have here is an increased polarization within the proletariat and saleriat, a situation that undermines the experience of solidarity and increases the apprehension of fragmentation (Tilly 1990).

Moreover, the process of restructuring is concurrent with and expressed through the feminization of the labour force (Jenson et al. 1987). Women are entering the labour force in ever greater numbers and they are staying in the labour market longer. However, women still work in predominantly female occupations and receive much less pay than men. Moreover, women tend to experience inequality on an individual basis, mediated through a family, rather than collectively as women (Acker 1988). In the United States, where studies on ethnic and racial polarization have been conducted, the labour market is polarized on racial lines more than ever before such that the living standards of Latinos and Blacks has declined in the part fifteen years (Tilly 1990).

Pay equity is being implemented as the crisis of distribution deepens. On the positive side, pay equity may be an important opportunity to mobilize women workers collectively in order to begin to break down the isolating barriers of the home. In addition, it may delegitimize the ideological appeal and material incentives of the family wage that helped to keep women dependent upon men (Acker 1989). The redistribution of wages from men to women may chip away at women's economic dependence upon men and the state and help to alleviate female poverty. On the negative side, pay equity ignores the central element of the current crisis of distribution – the flexibilization of work and the polarization of the labour market. Pay equity is unlikely to help the growing contingent workforce employed in their homes, in small establishments, or on a temporary basis. Because pay equity is limited to remedying discrimination that takes place in a single employer's establishment, it does not directly challenge the existing fragmentation of the labour market, which undermines the conditions for solidarity between workers.

Achieving Equity

No single policy initiative can hope to address the range of factors that contribute to the economic subordination of women. The challenge is to develop a series of related policies devised to help those workers who are at the bottom of the labour market – many, if not most, of whom are women. Moreover, the advantage of this kind of strategy is that it will directly address the crisis of distribution without pitting workers against each other on the basis of gender or race.

Central to any strategy to address the current crisis of distribution and exploitation of flexible labour should be a revised employment-standards policy. A living minimum wage, protection from exploitation and discriminatory treatment, the flexibility to balance work with one's domestic responsibilities and personal aspirations, basic income and job-security protection, inhibitions on the ability of employers to exploit labour through flexible work forms, and the effective enforcement of substantive employment standards are the minimum requirements for industrial citizenship in a democratic society. A revised employment-standards policy would force employers to internalize the costs of doing business as well as increase wages and improve working conditions throughout the labour market. Statutory domestic-responsibility leave would provide women (and men) with the flexibility to combine paid work with the care of children or the elderly. Amendments to collective-bargaining legislation that would break down the present highly fragmented bargaining structure, which takes place on an establishment basis and is the norm in North America, would undermine one of the major impediments to pay equity – the fact that job comparison must take place within, rather than between, establishments.

But the problem is that while it is relatively easy to develop a wish list of labour-market policies that would improve the conditions of women workers, it is much more difficult to attain it. For this reason it may be useful to build upon the momentum behind pay equity. Pay equity employs the language of justice and equity to challenge the fact that women are paid less than men for the work they do simply because they are women. As such, it questions the norm of the neutral market as the only means of distributing wages. However, the development of unbiased job evaluations and gender-neutral compensation schemes is only the first step in the political struggle over how wages are distributed. Feminists must be vigilant to ensure that the many technical issues in pay equity implementation do not obscure what is essentially a struggle for greater power in the workplace. While pay equity can be implemented in ways that exacerbate conflicts between workers, this is not an inevitable outcome of the pay equity process. Rather than simply dividing women and men workers in the struggle over the distribution of wages, pay equity may provide the material basis upon which political solidarity rests.

Pay equity brings women's issues into trade unions and establishes them as central working issues (Acker 1989, 225). Whether unions use their collective power to resist pay equity on behalf of their male members, to try to secure the highest ranking relative to other workers for their women members, or to articulate a demand for wage solidarity that they will reinforce by organizing women workers depends upon both their political vision and their estimate of their chance of success. As union membership declines and more women enter the paid labour force, the labour movement must attempt to organize the growing numbers of women workers employed in the service sector if they are going to survive this century as a political and economic force to be reckoned with. But why should women workers join with men in their struggle against the employer, if men not only continue to refuse to help women in their workplace struggles, but also continue to use their relatively better labour-market positions to exploit women in the home? A commitment to improving women's wages may improve the traditional labour movement's ability to develop and implement strategies for recruiting women members. Women's demand for pay equity may be a rallying symbol similar to the male industrial workers' demand for a living wage throughout the nineteenth and early twentieth centuries (Acker, 252). Whether it develops such resonance will depend, in part, upon the ability of the women's and labour movements to articulate a vision of pay equity that bridges interests shaped by gender and racial segregation in the labour force and challenges the hierarchical ranking of jobs as the basis of compensation.

Bibliography

Aaron, Henry, and Cameran Lougy. 1986. *The Comparable Worth Controversy.* Washington, DC

Ackelsberg, Martha. 1988. 'Communities, Resistance, and Women's Activism: Some Implications for a Democratic Polity.' In A. Bookman and S. Morgen, eds., *Women and the Politics of Empowerment*

Acker, Joan. 1988. 'Class, Gender and the Relations of Distribution.' *Signs* 13/3 (June): 473

– 1987. 'Sex Bias in Job Evaluation: A Comparable Worth Issue.' In Christine Bose and Glenna Spitze, eds., *Ingredients for Women's Employment Policy.* New York

– 1989. *Doing Comparable Worth: Gender, Class and Pay Equity.* Philadelphia

– 1990. 'Hierarchies, Job, Bodies: A Theory of Gendered Organizations.' *Gender and Society* 4/2 (June): 139

– (Forthcoming). 'Thinking about Wages: The Gendered Wage Gap in Swedish Banks.' *Gender and Society*

Acker, Joan, and Ann-Marie Ask. 1989. *Wage Differences between Men and Women and the Structure of Work and Wage Determination in Swedish Banks: A Report of a Preliminary Study* (A Working Paper)

Adamson, Nancy, Linda Briskin, and Margaret McPhail. 1988. *Feminist Organizing for Chance: The Contemporary Women's Movement in Canada.* Toronto

American Association of University Women. 1987. 'Pay Equity Action Guide.' Washington, DC: June

Archibald, Kathleen. 1970. *Sex and the Public Service: A Report to the Public Service Commission of Canada.* Ottawa

Armstrong, Pat. 1988a. 'Where Have All the Nurses Gone?' *Healthsharing* 9/3 (June): 17–19

- 1988b. *Pay Equity in Predominantly Female Establishments: Health Care Sector* (Report to the Minister of Labour by the Ontario Pay Equity Commission). Toronto: September
Armstrong, Pat, and Hugh Armstrong. 1983a. 'Beyond Numbers: Problems with Quantitative Analysis.' *Alternate Routes* 6: 1–40
- 1983b. *A Working Majority: What Women Must Do for Pay* (Canadian Advisory Council on the Status of Women). Ottawa
- 1984. *The Double Ghetto: Canadian Women and Their Segregated Work.* Revised edition. Toronto
- 1990a. 'Lessons from Pay Equity.' *Studies in Political Economy* 32 (Summer): 29–54
- 1990b. *Theorizing Women's Work.* Toronto
Arrowsmith, David. 1986. *Pay Equity: Legislative Framework and Cases.* Kingston
Atherton, L.E. 1952. 'Mercantile Education in the Ante-Bellum South.' *Mississippi Valley Historical Review* 39: 623–40
Bakker, Isabella 1988a. 'Women's Employment in Comparative Perspective.' In Jensen et al., eds., *Feminization of the Labour Force: Paradoxes and Promises.* New York
- 1988b. *Status Report on Ontario Women.* Prepared for the Ministry of Citizenship Working Group on Employment Equity. October
- ed. 1989. *Economic Policy Review: Issues for Discussion and Debate.* Prepared for the Ontario NDP Caucus, Planning and Priorities Committees, Economic Policy Review. August
Balkin, David, and Luis Gomez-Mejia, eds. 1987. *New Perspective on Compensation.* Englewood Cliffs, NJ
Ballantyne, Morna. 1988. 'A Critical Approach to Pay Equity.' Presented to *Canadian Institute for the Advancement of Women,* Quebec City
Barnsley, Jan. 1988. 'Feminist Action, Institutional Reform.' *Resources for Feminist Research* 17/3: 18–21
Barrett, Michele. 1980. *Women's Oppression Today.* London
Berg. I. 1970. *Education and Jobs: The Great Training Robbery.* New York
Blum, Linda. 1987. 'Possibilities and Limits of the Comparable Worth Movement.' *Gender and Society* 1/4: 380–99
- 1991. *Between Feminism and Labor: The Significance of the Comparable Worth Movement.* Berkeley
Bose, Christine, and Glenna Spitze. 1987. *Ingredients for Women's Employment Policy.* New York
Braverman, Harry. 1974. *Labor and Monopoly Capitalism.* New York
Brenner, Johanna. 1987. 'Feminist Political Discourses: Radical versus Liberal

Approaches to Feminization of Poverty and Comparable Worth.' *Gender and Society* 1/4: 447–65

Bridges, William, and Robert Nelson. 1989. 'Organizational and Market Influences on Gender Inequality in a State Pay System.' *American Journal of Sociology* 95/3: 616–58

Briskin, Linda. 1989. 'Socialist Feminism from the Standpoint of Practice.' *Studies in Political Economy* 30 (Autumn): 87–114

Briskin, Linda, and Lynda Yanz. 1983a. *Union Sisters: Women in the Labour Movement.* Toronto

Brown, C., and J. Medoff. 1988. 'The Employer Size Wage Effect.' Unpublished paper Cambridge, MA

Browning, Rufus, Dale Robers, and David H. Tabb. 1981. *Protest Is Not Enough: The Struggle of Blacks and Hispanics for Equality in Urban Politics.* Berkeley

Burtless, Gary. 1990. 'Earnings Inequality over the Business and Demographic Cycles.' *The Future of Lousy Jobs.* Washington

Burton, Clare, Raven Hag, and Gay Thompson. 1987. *Women's Worth: Pay Equity and Job Evaluation in Australia.* Canberra

Canadian Classification and Dictionary of Occupations, Vol. I: *Classifications and Definitions*; Vol. II: *Occupational Qualification Requirements* (Department of Manpower and Immigration). Ottawa, 1971

Canadian Employment and Immigration Union (CEIU). 1982. *The Clerical Workers' Strike.* Ottawa

Canadian Labour Congress. 1976. 'Equality of Opportunity and Treatment for Women Workers.' Policy statement approved by the 11th CLC Constitutional Convention

– 1990. 'Developing Our Strength ... and Sharing It: Union Women's Vision for the Year 2000'

Cassell, Frank, and Jean Baron. 1975. *Collective Bargaining in the Public Sector: Cases in the Public Policy.* Columbus

Chaykowski, Richard P., ed. 1989. *Pay Equity Legislation: Linking Economic Issues and Policy Concerns.* Kingston

Clark, David, Gail Cook, and William Dimma. 1986. *The Report of the Consultation Panel on Pay Equity.* Toronto

Coates, Marilou, David Arrowsmith, and Melanie Courchene. 1989. *The Current Industrial Relations Scene in Canada, 1989.* Kingston

Cohen, Majorie. 1988. *Free Trade and the Future of Women's Work.* Ottawa

Collins. Randall. 1979. *The Credential Society.* New York

Commission on the Economic Status of Women. 1988. *Pay Equity: The Minnesota Experience.* St Paul

Connelly, Patricia, and Martha MacDonald. 1990. *Women and the Labour Force*. Ottawa

Conway, Healther. 1987. *Equal Pay for Work of Equal Value Legislation in Canada: An Analysis*. Ottawa

Cook, Alice. 1983. *Comparable Worth: The Problem and States' Approaches to Wage Equity*. Honolulu, Hawaii

– 1985. *Comparable Worth: A Case Book of Experience in States and Localities*. Ithaca

Coombs, D.C. 1980. 'The Emergence of a White Collar Labour Force in Toronto, 1895–1911.' PhD thesis, York University

Cornish, Mary. 1986. *Equal Pay: Collective Bargaining and the Law* (Women's Bureau). Ottawa

Coneo, Carl. 1990. *Pay Equity: The Labour-Feminist Challenge*. Toronto

Cuthbertson, Wendy. 1978. 'Fleck: The Unionization of Women.' *Canadian Women Studies* 1/2 (Winter): 71–72

Davies, Margery. 1982. *Women's Place Is at the Typewriter: Office Work and Office Workers 1870–1930*. Philadelphia

Day, Tannis 1987. *Pay Equity: Some Issues in the Debate* (Canadian Advisory Council on the Status of Women). Ottawa

Economic Council of Canada. 1990. *Good Jobs, Bad Jobs: Employment in the Service Economy*. Ottawa

– 1991. *Employment in the Service Economy*. Ottawa

Egri, Carolyn P., and W.T. Stanbury. 1989. 'How Pay Equity Legislation Came to Ontario.' *Canadian Public Administration* 32/2 (Summer): 274

Ehrenberg, R.G. 1989. 'Econometric Analysis of the Empirical Consequences of Comparable Worth: What Have We Learned? In M. Anne Hill and Mark Killingsworth, eds., *Comparable Worth: Analysis of Evidence*. Ithaca, NY

Eisenstein, Zillah. 1981. *The Radical Future of Liberal Feminism*. New York

Elizur, Dov. 1980. *Job Evaluation: A Systematic Approach*. Aldershot

– 1987. *Systematic Job Evaluation and Comparable Worth*. Aldershot

Elliot, Cheryl, and Stewart D. Saxe. 1987. *Pay Equity Handbook*. Toronto

Ellis, Evelyn. 1988. *Sex Discrimination Law*. Aldershot

Ellis-Grunfeld, Roberta. 1987. 'Pay Equity in Manitoba.' *Manitoba Law Journal* 16/3: 227–36

Employment and Immigration Canada. 1990. *Employment Equity Act, 1990 Annual Report*. Ottawa

England, Paula. 1982. 'The Failure of Human Capital Theory to Explain Occupational Sex Segregation.' *Journal of Human Resources* 17: 358–70

England, Paula, Marilyn Chassic, and Linda McConnock. 1982. 'Skill Demands and Earnings in Female and Male Occupations.' *Sociology and Social Research* 66: 147–68

England, Paula, G. Farkas, B. Kilbourne, and T. Dau. 1988. 'Explaining Sex Segregation and Wages: Findings from a Model with Fixed Effects.' *American Sociological Review* 53/4: 544–58

England, Paula, and Steven McLaughlin. 1979. 'Sex Segregation of Jobs and Male-Female Income Differences.' In Rodolfo Alverez, Kenneth Lutterman, and Assoc., eds., *Discrimination in Organizations*. San Francisco

England, Paula, and Norris. 1985. 'Comparable Worth: A New Doctrine of Sex Discrimination.' *Social Science Quarterly* 66: 627–43

Epsing-Anderson, Gosta, and Walter Korpi. 1984. 'Social Policy as Class Politics in Post-war Capitalism: Scandinavia, Austria, and Germany.' In R. Goldthorpe, ed., *Order and Conflict in Contemporary Capitalism*. Oxford

Equal Pay: Collective Bargaining and the Law. Ottawa (Labour Canada), 1987

Equal Pay Coalition. 1988. 'Bringing Pay Equity to Those Presently Excluded from Ontario's Pay Equity Act.' Submission to the Pay Equity Commission, Toronto, 13 December

Evans, Sara, and Barbara Nelson. 1989a. *Wage Justice: Comparable Worth and the Paradox of Technocratic Reform*. Chicago

– 1986b. 'Comparable Worth: The Paradox of Technocratic Reform.' *Feminist Studies* 15/1 (Spring): 178

Eyestone, Robert. 1977. 'Confusion, Diffusion and Innovation.' *American Political Science Review* 71 (June): 441–7

Farnquist, Robert, David Armstrong, and Russell Strausbaugh. 1983. 'Pandora's Worth: The San Jose Experience.' *Public Personnel Management* 12/4: 358–68

Feldberg, Roslyn L. 1984. 'Comparable Worth: Toward Theory and Practice in the United States.' *Signs* 10: 311–28

Field, Debbie. 1983. 'Coercion of Male Culture: A New Look at Co-worker Harassment.' In Linda Briskin and Lynda Yanza, eds., *Union Sisters: Women in the Labour Movement*. Toronto

Findlay, Sue. 1987a. 'Facing the State: The Politics of the Women's Movement Reconsidered.' In Heather Jon Maroney and Meg Luxton, eds., *Feminism and Political Economy: Women's Work, Women's Struggles*. Toronto

– 1987b. 'Why No Debate?' *Cayenne* Spring/Summer: 36–40

Flamming, Janet. 1986. 'Effective Implementation: The Case of Comparable Worth in San Jose.' *Policy Studies Review* 5/: 815–37

– 1987. 'Women Made a Difference: Comparable Worth in San Jose.' In Mary Katzenstein and Carol Mueller, eds., *The Women's Movements of the United States and Western Europe*. Philadelphia

– 1991. 'The Politics of Pay Equity in California: Acceptance of Innovation.' In Ronnie Steinberg, ed., *The Politics of Pay Equity*. Philadelphia

Forrest, Anne. 1986. 'Bargaining Units and Bargaining Power.' *Relations In-dustrielles/Industrial Relations* 41/4: 840–50

Franzway, Suzanne, Dianne Court, and Robert Connell. 1989. *Staking a Claim: Feminism, Bureaucracy and the State.* Cambridge

Friedman, Dana. 1988. *Pay Equity* (Conference Board). New York

Gaskell, Jane. 1985. 'Women and Education: Branching Out.' In *Towards Equity* (Economic Council of Canada). Ottawa

Gelb, Joyce, and Marian Palley. 1982. *Women and Public Policies* (revised and expanded ed.). Princeton

Gold, Michael. 1983. *A Dialogue on Comparable Worth.* Ithaca, NY

Gorrie, Peter. 1990. 'Cases Swamp Pay Equity Panel.' *The Toronto Star* 23 June, C-1

Gram, R., and D. Schwab. 1982. 'Systematic Sex-Related Error in Job Evaluation.' Paper presented at the Midwest Academy of Management Meetings, Kalamazoo, Michigan, 14–16 April

Gray, Virginia. 1973. 'Innovations in the States: A Diffusion Study.' *American Science Review* 67 (December): 1174–85

Grocery Products Manufacturers of Canada. 1980. 'Bill 3: "Equal Pay for Work of Equal Value": A Brief to the Standing General Government Committee, Legislative Assembly of Ontario,' 28 January

Gunderson, Morley. 1989. 'Male and Female Wage Differentials and Policy Responses.' *Journal of Economic Literature* 27/1 (March): 46–72

Gunderson, Morley, Leon Muszynski, and Jennifer Keck. 1990. *Women and Labour Market Poverty* (Canadian Advisory Council on the Status of Women). Ottawa

Gustafsson, Siv. 1988. 'Loneskillnader mellan kvinnor och man-gapet okar igen.' *Ekonomiska Debatt* 3: 209–15

Haignere, Lois. 1990. 'Pay Equity Update.' Paper delivered to the Canadian Bar Association, Toronto, April

Hall, O., and R. Carlton. 1977. *Basic Skills at School and Work* (Occasional Paper No. 1, Ontario Economic Council). Toronto

Harrison, Rachel, and Frank Mort. 1980. 'Patriarchal Aspects of Nineteenth-Century State Formation: Property Relations, Marriage and Divorce and Sexuality.' In P. Corrigan, *Capitalism, State Formation and Marxist Theory.* London

Hartmann, Heidi. 1981. 'The Unhappy Marriage of Marxism and Feminism: Towards a More Progressive Union.' In Lydia Sargent, ed., *Women and Revolution.* Boston

– ed. 1985. *Comparable Worth: New Directions for Research.* Washington

Hartmann, Heidi, and Anne Markusen. 1990. 'Contemporary Marxist Theory and Practice: A Feminist Critique.' *Review of Radical Political Economis* 12 (Summer)

Hartmann, Heidi, Patricia Roos, and Donald Treiman. 1985. 'An Agenda for Basic Research on Comparable Worth.' In Heidi Hartmann, ed., *Comparable Worth: New Direction for Research*. Washington, DC

Hill, Anne, and Mark Killingsworth, eds. 1989. *Comparable Worth: Analyses and Evidence*. New York

Hochschild, Jennifer. 1984. *The American Dilemma: Liberal Democracy and School Desegregation*. New Haven

Hodgetts, J.E., and D.C. Corbett, eds. 1960. *Canadian Public Administration*. Toronto

Hubbared & Revo-Cohen, Inc. 1989a. *Draft Final Report to the City of Philadelphia Mayor's Commission for Women*. Philadelphia: February

– 1989b. *City of Ann Arbor Position Classification and Pay Equity Study: Draft Final Report*. Ann Arbor: 2 March

Humphreys, Jane. 1977. 'The Working Class Family, Women's Liberation and Class Struggle: The Case of Nineteenth Century British History.' *Review of Radical Political Economics* 9 (Fall): 25

Hutner, Frances. 1986. *Equal Pay for Comparable Worth: The Working Women's Issue of the Eighties*. New York

Hyman, Richard. 1974. 'Inequality, Ideology and Industrial Relations.' *British Journal of Industrial Relations* 12/2 (July): 171–90

Jacobs, Jerry, and Ronnie Steinberg. (Forthcoming). 'Compensating Differentials and the Male-Female Wage Gap: Evidence from the New York State Comparable Worth Study.' *Social Forces*

Jain, Harish, and Rick Hackett. 1989. 'Measuring Effectiveness of Employment Equity Programs in Canada: Public Policy and a Survey.' *Canadian Public Policy* 15/2: 189–204

Jensen, Jane. 1986. 'Gender and Reproduction: Or, Babies and the State.' *Studies in Political Economy* 20 (Summer): 9–46

Jensen, Jane, Elisabeth Hagen, and Ceallaigh Reddy, eds. 1988. *Feminization of the Labour Force: Paradoxes and Promises*. New York

Johansen, Elaine. 1984. *Comparable Worth: The Myth and the Movement*. Boulder

Jones, Jacqueline. 1985. *Labor of Love, Labor of Sorrow: Black Women, Work and the Family from Slavery to the Present*. New York

Jones, Kathleen, and Anna Jonasdottir, eds., 1988. *The Political Interest of Gender*. Newbury Park, CA

Kahn, Peggy. 1990. 'Wage Wars,' *Women's Review of Books* 8/12: 21–2

Kaufman, Lorna. 1986. *Job Evaluation Systems: Concepts and Issues*. Kingston

Kealey, Gregory. 1980. *Toronto Workers Respond to Industrial Capitalism, 1867–1892.* Toronto

Kelly, Rita Mae, and Jane Baynes, eds. 1988. *Comparable Worth, Pay Equity and Public Policy.* Westport, CT

Kessler-Harris, Alice. 1988. 'The Just Price, the Free Market and the Value of Women.' *Feminist Studies* 14/2 (Summer): 235–50

Kettler, David, James Struthers, and Christopher Huxley. 1990. 'Unionization and Labour Regimes in Canada and the United States: Considerations for Comparative Research.' *Labour/Le Travail* 25 (Spring) 161

Korpi, Walter. 1978. *The Working Class in Welfare Capitalism.* London

Labour Canada. 1986. *Equal Pay: Collective Bargaining and the Law.* Ottawa

Lewis, Debra. 1988. *Just Give Us the Money.* Vancouver

Lewis, Debra, and Jan Barnsley. 1990. *Strategies for Change: From Women's Experience to a Plan for Action* (Women's Research Centre). Vancouver

Lipietz, Alain. 1989. 'The Debt Problem, European Integration and the New Phases of World Crisis.' *New Left Review* No. 178: 37–50

Livernash, Robert, ed. 1984. *Comparable Worth: Issues and Alternatives* (Equal Employment Advisory Council). Washington

Lockwood, David. 1958. *The Blackcoated Worker: A Study in Class Consciousness.* London

Lorde, Audre. 1981. 'The Master's Tools Will Never Dismantle the Master's House.' In Cherrie Moraga and Gloria Anzaldua, eds., *This Bridge Called My Back.* Watertown, MA

Lowe, Graham. 1980. 'Women, Work and the Office: The Feminization of Clerical Occupations in Canada, 1901–1931.' *Canadian Journal of Sociology* 5/4: 361–81

– 1982. 'Class Job and Gender in the Canadian Office. *Labour/Le Travail* 10: 11–37

Mackenzie, Elizabeth. 1988. *The Ontario Pay Equity Act and Its Effect on Collective Bargaining.* Kingston

Mahon, Rianne. 1977. 'Canadian Public Policy: The Unequal Structure of Representation.' In Leo Panitch, ed., *The Canadian State.* Toronto

Malveaux, Julianne. 1985a. 'The Economic Interests of Black and White Women: Are They Similar?' *Review of Black Political Economy* 14: 4–27

– 1985b. 'Comparable Worth and Its Impact on Black Women.' *Review of Black Political Economy* 14: 47–62

Manitoba Civil Service Commission. 1988. *Pay Equity Implementation in the Manitoba Civil Service.* Winnipeg

Mansbridge, Jane. 1986. *Why We Lost the ERA.* Chicago

Marcotte, Marilee. 1987. *Equal Pay for Work of Equal Value.* Kingston

Marks, Lynne. 1984. 'New Opportunities within the Separate Sphere: A Preliminary Exploration of Certain Neglected Questions Relating to Female
Clerical Work, Focusing on Stenography in Canada, 1890–1930.' MA Re-
search Paper (unpublished), York University
Maroney, Heather Jon. 1987. 'Feminism at Work.' In H.J. Maroney and M.
Luxton, eds., Feminism and Political Economy: Women's Work, Women's Strug-
gles. Toronto
– 1988. 'Using Gramsci for Women: Feminism and the Quebec State,
1960–1980.' Resources for Feminist Research 17/3: 26–30
Maroney, Heather Jon, and Meg Luxton, eds. 1987. Feminism and Political
Economy: Women's Work Women's Struggles. Toronto
Marsden, Lorna. 1980. 'The Role of the National Action Committee on the
Status of Women in Facilitating Equal Pay Policy in Canada.' In R.S.
Rather, ed., Equal Employment Policy for Women, Strategies for Implementa-
tion in the United States, Canada and Western Europe. Philadelphia
Mazamanian, David, and Paul Sabtier. 1983. Implementation and Public Policy.
Glenview, IL
McArthur, Leslie Zebrowitz. 1985. 'Social Judgement Biases in Comparable
Worth Analysis.' Comparable Worth New Directions for Research. Washing-
ton, DC
McCrudden, Christopher, ed. 1987. Women, Employment and European Equality
Law. London
McDermott, Patricia C. 1987. 'Pay Equity in Ontario: Coalition Politics.' Cay-
enne Fall: 5–8
– 1990. 'Pay Equity in Ontario: A Critical Legal Analysis.' Osgoode Hall Law
Journal 28/2 (Summer): 381–407
Meidner, Rudolph. 1974. Co-ordination and Solidarity: An Approach to Wages
Policy. Stockhom
Menzies, Heather. 1990. 'Re-thinking the Social Contract: Women, Work and
Technology in the Post-Industrial Era.' Canadian Journal of Women and the
Law 4/1: 205
Milczarek, G.J. 1980. Technical Report: The Willis Factor-Point Position Evalua-
tion System (Norman D. Willis and Associates). Seattle
Mitchell, Lorraine. 1988. 'What Happened on the Way to the Bank: Some
Questions about Pay Equity.' Resources for Feminist Research 17/3: 64–7
Morris, Cerise. 1982. 'Pressuring the Canadian State for Women's Rights: The
Role of the National Action Committee on the Status of Women.' Alternate
Routes 6: 87–108
Myles, J. 1987. The Expanding Middle: Some Canadian Evidence on the Deskill-
ing Debate. Social and Economic Studies Division, Statistics Canada, Re-
search Paper No. 9. Ottawa

Myles, J., G. Picot, and T. Wannel. 1988. *Wages and Jobs in the 1980's: Changing Youth Wages and the Declining Middle.* Social and Economic Studies Division, Statistics Canada, Research Paper No. 17.

Nelson, Barbara. 1984a. *Making an Issue of Child Abuse: Political Agenda Setting for Social Problems.* Chicago

– 1984b. 'Women's Poverty and Women's Citizenship: Some Political Implications of Economic Marginality.' *Signs* 10 (Winter): 209–31

Ng, Roxanne. 1988. *The Politics of Community Services.* Toronto

Niemann, Lindsay. 1984. 'Equality in the Workplace Wage Discrimination and Women Workers: The Move towards Equal Pay for Work of Equal Value' (Women's Bureau). Ottawa

O'Donovan, Katherine, and Erika Szyszczak. 1988. *Equality and Sex Discrimination Law.* Oxford

Ontario Government. 1985. *Green Paper on Pay Equity.* Attorney General and Minister Responsible for Women's Issues. Toronto

– 1986. *Bill 105. An Act to Provide Pay Equity for Employees in Predominantly Female Groups of Jobs in the Public Service.* Ontario Legislative Assembly. Toronto

– 1987. *Bill 154. An Act to Provide Pay Equity.* Ontario Legislative Assembly. Toronto

– 1988. *Pay Equity Act, 1987.* Statues of Ontario, 1987, Chapter 32 and 34, January (Bill 154). Toronto

Ontario Legislative Assembly (OLA). 1986–7. *Hansard Official Report of Debates.* Toronto

Ontario Ministry of Labour 1990a. *News Release* No. 90–08, 2 March

– 1990b. *Policy Directions: Amending the Pay Equity Act.* Discussion paper. February

Ontario Pay Equity Commission. 1988a. *Pay Equity Implementation Series #3: Calculating the Number of Employees in the Private Sector.* Toronto

– 1988b. *Pay Equity Implementation Series #14: Pay Equity Adjustments.* Toronto

– 1988c. *Questions and Answers: Pay Equity in the Workplace.* Toronto

– 1989a. 'Job Evaluation: An American Way.' *Pay Equity Practitioner.* Toronto: May

– 1989b. *Report to the Minister of Labour on Sectors of the Economy Which Are Predominantly Female as Required under the Pay Equity Act, Section 33(2)(e).* Toronto: 5 January

– 1989c. *Report to the Minister of Labour on Options relating to the Achievement of Pay Equity in Sectors of the Economy Which Are Predominantly Female.* Toronto: 18 October

Ontario Standing Committee on the Administration of Justice (SCAJ). 1986–7. Seven boxes of documents, files and transcripts. Public Archives of Ontario. RG 18 F, Acc. 20499

Oppenheimer, V. 1970. *The Female Labour Force in the U.S.* Berkeley

Ostry, Sylvia. 1990. *Governments and Corporations in a Shrinking World.* New York

Palmer, Bryan. 1979. *A Culture in Conflict: Skilled Workers and Industrial Capitalism in Hamilton, Ontario, 1860–1914.* Toronto

Parent, Madeline. 1989. 'Interview with Madeline Parent.' *Studies in Political Economy* 30 (Autumn) 13–36

Paul, Ellen Frankel. 1989. *Equity and Gender: The Comparable Worth Debate.* Princeton

Perrin, Suzanne. 1985. *Comparable Worth and Public Policy: The Case of Pennsylvania.* Philadelphia

Phillips, Ann, and Barbara Taylor. 1980. 'Sex and Skill: Notes towards a Feminist Economics.' *Feminist Review* 6: 79–88

Picot, G. 1980. *The Changing Education Profile of Canadians 1961 to 2000: Projections of Educational Attainment for the Canadian Population and Labour Force* (Statistics Canada). Ottawa

Pierson, David, Karen Shallcross Koziara, and Russell Johannesson. 1984. 'A Policy-Capturing Application in a Union Setting.' In Helen Remick, ed., *Comparable Worth and Wage Discrimination*, 118–37. Philadelphia.

Pigg, Susan. 1990. 'Nurses and Pay Equity.' *The Toronto Star*, 28 August, E-1

Poulantzas, Nicos. 1978. *Political Power and Social Classes.* London

Pringle, Rosemary. 1988. *Secretaries Talk.* Sydney

Public Service Alliance of Canada. 1979. 'Background Paper 1979 Convention: Equal Pay for Work of Equal Value.' Ottawa

– 1988. *Equal Pay for Work of Equal Value: No Small Change.* Ottawa: November

– 1990a. *Equal Pay It's The Law.* Ottawa

– 1990b. 'Pay Equity Fact Sheet.' Ottawa: January

Ramkhalawansingh, Ceta. 1979. 'Equal Value and Job Evaluation.' *Resources for Feminist Research*, Fall: 137–40

Remick, Helen. 1979. 'Strategies for Creating Sound, Bias Free Job Evaluation Plans.' In *Job Evaluation and EEO: The Emerging Issues.* New York

– 1980. 'Beyond Equal Pay for Equal Work: Comparable Worth in the State of Washington.' In Ronnie Steinberg, ed., *Equal Employment Policy for Women.* Philadelphia

– 1981. 'The Comparable Worth Controversy.' *Public Personnel Management* 10: 371–83

Remick, Helen, ed. 1984a. *Comparable Worth and Wage Discrimination*. Philadelphia
– 1984b. 'Dilemmas of Implementation: The Case of Nursing. In H. Remick, ed., *Comparable Worth and Wage Discrimination*. Philadelphia
– 1984c. 'Major Issues in a priori Application.' In *Comparable Worth and Wage Discrimination*. Philadelphia
Remick, Helen, and Ronnie Steinberg. 1984. 'Technical Possibilities and Political Realities: Concluding Remarks.' In *Comparable Worth and Wage Discrimination*. Philadelphia
Robb, Barrie. 1988. *The Pay Equity Act of Ontario: Implications for Collective Bargaining*. Kingston
Robb, Roberta E. 1989. 'Equal Pay for Work of Equal Value: Issues and Policies.' *Canadian Public Policy* 13: 445–61
Rode Fane, Redaksjonen. 1985. 'Omsorgsfag.' *Rode Fane* 1
Rufus, Browing, Dale Rogers Marshal, and David Tabb. 1984. *Protest Is Not Enough: The Struggle of Blacks and Hispanics for Equality in Urban Politics*. Berkeley
Ruggie, Mary. 1984. *The State and Working Women: A Comparative Study of Britain and Sweden*. Princeton, NJ
Sacouman, James, and Henry Veltmeyer. 1990. 'Canada in the Restructuring of America: Restricted Proletarianism and Its Implications.' Presented at the Conference on Canadian Political Economy in the Era of Free Trade Conference, Carleton University, Ottawa, April
Schwab, Donald. 1985a. 'Job Evaluation and Pay Settings: Concepts and Practices.' In E.R. Livernash, ed., *Comparable Worth: Issues and Practices*. Washington
– 1985b. 'Job Evaluation and Research Needs.' In Heidi Hartmann, ed., *Comparable Worth: New Directions for Research*. Washington
Second Report of the Special Committee on Comparable Worth (Special Committee on Comparable Worth, Massachusetts State Legislature). Boston MA 1986
Sengenberger, W., and G. Loveman. 1988. 'Smaller Units of Employment: A Synthesis Report on Industrial Reorganization in Industrialized Countries.' International Labour Office Discussion Paper, Geneva
Shaw, W.H. 1902. *The Story of a Business School*. Toronto
Shakes, Allan. 1990. 'Selecting a Gender Neutral Compassion System – Bargaining in Good Faith.' In *Pay Equity Update*. Toronto: Canadian Bar Association, Ontario Continuing Legal Education
Simm, Birte. 1988. 'Towards a Feminist Rethinking of the Welfare State.' In

Kathleen Jones and Anna Jonasdottir, eds., *The Political Interests of Gender.* Newbury Park, CA

Simpson, Kieran, ed. 1985. *Canadian Who's Who,* Vol. XX. Toronto

Smith, Dorothy. 1987. *The Everyday World as Problematic.* Toronto

Spence, M. 1973. 'Job Marketing Signalling.' *Quarterly Journal of Ecnomics* 87: 355–74

Spenner, K.I. 1943. 'Temporal Change in the Skill Level of Work.' *American Sociological Review* 48/6: 824–37

Standing, Guy. 1988. *European Unemployment, Insecurity and Flexibility: A Social Dividend Solution.* Working Paper No. 23, World Employment Programme Research. Geneva

– 1989. 'Global Feminization through Flexible Labor.' *World Development* 17/7: 1078–85

Steinberg, Ronnie. 1982. *Wages and Hours: Labor and Reform in Twentieth Century America.* New Brunswick

– 1984. 'Identifying Wage Discrimintation and Implementing Pay Equity Adjustments.' In U.S. Commission on Civil Rights, ed., *Comparable Worth: Issue for the 80's.* Washington

– 1985. 'Implementing Comparable Worth and Pay Equity.' *Transaction/Society* July

– 1986. 'The Debate on Comparable Worth.' *New Politics* 1: 108–26

– 1987a. 'Radical Challenges in a Liberal World: The Mixed Successes of Comparable Worth.' *Gender and Society* 1/4: 466–75

– 1987b. 'From Radical Vision to Minimalist Reform: Pay Equity in New York State: The Limits of Insider Reform Initiatives.' Unpublished paper presented at the Sociological Forum, Penn State University, 10 April

– 1987c. 'Women, Reform, and the State: Comparable Worth.' Presentation at Eastern Sociological Society, 1 May

– 1987d. 'Feminist Critiques and Feminist Politics: The Case of Comparable Worth.' Presented at the Annual Meeting, Sociologists for Women in Society, 19 August

– 1988. 'The Unsubtle Revolution: Women, the State, and Equal Employment.' In Jane Jensen, et al., eds., *Feminization of the Labour Force.* New York

– 1990. 'Mainstreaming Comparable Worth: Re-forming Wage Discrimination to Palatable Pay Equity.' Unpublished paper

– (Forthcoming). 'Equitanble Compensation II: Further Thoughts on Gender Bias.' In Ronnie Steinberg, ed., *The Politics and Practice of Pay Equity.* Philadelphia

– (Forthcoming). 'We Did It Our Way: Pay Equity in New York State.' Steinberg, ed., *The Politics and Practice of Pay Equity*. Philadelphia
Steinberg, Ronnie, and Lois Haignere. 1987. 'Equitable Compensation: Meth-
odological Criteria for Comparable Worth.' In C. Bose and G. Spitze, eds.,
Ingredients for Women's Employment Policy. Albany
– 1987. 'The Undervaluation of Work by Gender and Race: The New York
State Comparable Pay Study.' In Bose and Spitze, eds., *Ingredients for Wom-
en's Employment Policy* Albany
Steinberg, Ronnie, Lois Haignere, Carol Possin, Cynthia Chertos, and Donald
Treiman. 1985. *New York Comparable Pay Study: Final Report* (Center for
Women in Government). Albany
Stratham, Anne, Eleanor Miller, and Hans Mauksch, eds. 1988. *The Worth of
Women's Work*. New York
Thompson, Pat. 1987. *Job Vacancies in the Independent Business Sector (Part 2)*
(Canadian Federation of Independent Business). 9 June
Thomson, David. 1978. 'Eliminating Pay Discrimination by Job Evaluation.'
Personnel 55/5: 11–22
Thurow, Lester. 1987. 'A Surge in Inequality.' *Scientific American* 256/5: 34
Tilly, Chris. 1990. 'Politics of the 'New Inequality.' *Socialist Review* 20:
103–20
Tilly, Chris, and Gary Loveman. 1988. 'Good Jobs or Bad Jobs: What Does
the Evidence Say?' *New England Economic Review* 46 (Feb.)
Todres, Elaine. 1987. 'Managing Pay Equity: A Bureaucrat's View of Bill 154.'
Manitoba Law Journal 16/3: 221–6
Treiman, Donald. 1979. *Job Evaluation: An Analytic Review*. Washington, DC
– 1984. 'Effect of Choice of Factors and Factor Weights in Job Evaluation.' In
H. Remick, ed., *Comparable Worth and Wage Discrimination*. Philadelphia
Treiman, Donald, and Heidi Hartmann. 1981. *Women, Work and Wages: Equal
Pay for Jobs of Equal Value*. Washington, DC
Treiman, Donald, Heidi Hartmann, and Patricia Roos. 1984. 'Assessing Pay
Discrimination using National Data.' In H. Remick, ed., *Comparable Worth
and Wage Discrimination*. Philadelphia
Turner, H.A. 1962. *Trade Union Growth, Structure and Policy*. London
Urban Dimensions Group. 1989. *Growth of the Contingent Workforce in On-
tario: Structural Trends, Statistical Dimensions and Policy Implications*. To-
ronto
Wagman, Barnet, and Nancy Folbre. 1988. 'The Feminization of Inequity:
Some New Patterns.' *Challenge* November: 56–9
Walker, Gillian. 1988. 'Conceptual Practices and the Political Process: Family
Violence as Ideology.' PhD thesis, University of Toronto

Walker, Jack. 1969. 'The Diffusion of Innovations among the American States.' *American Political Science Review* 63 (September): 880–900

Waring, Marilyn. 1988. *If Women Counted.* San Francisco

Warskett, Rosemary. 1990. 'Whither Pay Equity: Or Class and Gender in the Structuring of Workplace Hierarchies.' *Studies in Political Economy* 32 (Summer): 55–83

Watson, Sophie. 1990. *Playing the State: Australian Feminist Interventions.* London

Weiler, Paul. 1986. 'The Wages of Sex: The Uses and Limits of Comparable Worth.' *Harvard Law Review* 99 (June): 1728–1807

Weiner, Nan, and Morely Gunderson. 1990. *Pay Equity: Issues, Options and Experiences.* Toronto

White, Julie. 1980. *Women and Unions* (Canadian Advisory Council on the Status of Women). Ottawa

– 1990. *Mail and Female: Women and the Canadian Union of Postal Workers.* Toronto

Willborn, Steven. 1986. *A Comparable Worth Primer.* Lexington

– 1989. *A Secretary and a Cook: Challenging Women's Wages in the Courts of the United States and Great Britain.* Ithaca

Williams, Robert, and Lorence Kessler. 1984. *A Closer Look at Comparable Worth.* Washington, DC

Wolf, Wendy, and Rachel Rosenfeld. 1978. 'Sex Structure of Occupations and Job Mobility.' *Social Forces* 56/3: 823–44

Wolfe, David. 1990. 'Technology and Trade.' Note Prepared for the Atkinson College/OFL Seminar Series, Ontario and the Global Economy. Toronto

Working Group on Sexual Violence. April 1985. *Feminist Manifesto.* Vancouver

Young, Tasia. 1985. 'Statement of Tasia Young, Executive Director, Status for Women, State of New Mexico.' In *Options for Conducting a Pay Equity Study of Federal Pay and Classification Systems.* Hearings Before the Subcommittee on Compensation and Employee Benefits of the Committee on Post Office and Civil Service, House of Representatives, Ninety-ninth Congress. Washington, DC

Contributors

Joan Acker has taught in the sociology department at the University of Oregon since 1967. From 1987 through 1989 she was the research adviser at the Swedish Centre for Working Life in Stockholm. Her most recent publication in the area of pay equity is *Doing Comparable Worth*.

Hugh Armstrong is Associate Dean, General Studies, at Centennial College in Toronto. He is co-author (with Pat Armstrong) of *The Double Ghetto: Canadian Women and Their Segregated Work* (McClelland and Stewart 1984) and most recently *Theorizing Women's Work*.

Pat Armstrong is Professor of Sociology at York University. She is the author of *Labour Pains: Women's Work in Crisis* (Women's Press 1984) and co-author (with Hugh Armstrong) of *A Working Majority: What Women Must Do for Pay* (CACSW 1983), and most recently *Theorizing Women's Work*.

Isabella Bakker is an Associate Professor of Political Science at York University. She has worked for the Organization of Economic Cooperation and Development (Paris) on a publication entitled *The Integration of Women in the Economy* and has written numerous articles on the political economy of gender.

Carl Cuneo has taught sociology at McMaster University in Hamilton, Ontario, since 1973. His most recent publication in the area of pay equity is *Pay Equity: The Feminist-Labour Challenge*.

Sara M. Evans is Professor of History at the University of Minnesota. She is an editor of *Feminist Studies* and co-author (with Barbara Nelson) of *Wage Justice: Comparable Worth and the Paradox of Technocratic Reform*.

Sue Findlay is completing her PhD in Political Science at the University of Toronto. She has worked as a senior policy adviser to the federal government in Canada and is author of 'Facing the State: The Politics of the Women's Movement Reconsidered,' in *Feminism and Political Economy*, edited by H. Maroney and M. Luxton.

Judy Fudge is Associate Professor of Law at York University. She is co-author (with H. Arthurs, D. Carter, and H. Glasbeek) of *Labour Law and Industrial Relations*.

Jane Gaskell is currently the head of the Department of Social and Educational Studies in the Faculty of Education at the University of British Columbia. She has written extensively in the area of gender and education. She is author of *Education and the Labour Market in Comparative Perspective* (forthcoming).

Lois Haignere is Director of Research of United University Professionals in Albany, New York. She has written extensively in the area of pay equity and has acted as a consultant for numerous pay equity plans throughout Canada and the United States.

Debra J. Lewis is currently a research associate at the Women's Research Centre in Vancouver, British Columbia. She is the author of *Just Give Us the Money: A Discussion of Wage Discrimination and Pay Equity*, and coordinator of *Just Wages: A Bulletin on Wage Discrimination and Pay Equity*, a quarterly publication of the Women's Research Centre in conjunction with the Trade Union Research Bureau.

Patricia McDermott is Associate Professor in the Division of Social Science at York University. She teaches in the area of women and the law and has recently published 'Pay Equity in Ontario: A Critical Legal Analysis' in the *Osgoode Hall Law Journal*.

Barbara J. Nelson is Professor of Public Policy at the University of Minnesota's Hubert Humphrey Institute of Public Affairs. She is co-author (with Sara Evans) of *Wage Justice: Comparable Worth and the Paradox of Technocratic Reform*.

Ronnie J. Steinberg is Associate Professor of Sociology at Temple University in Philadelphia. She has published extensively in the area of pay equity and is currently completing two volumes: *The Politics and Practice of Pay Equity,* an edited collection, and *Radical Changes in a Liberal World.*

Rosemary Warskett is completing her doctorate in sociology at Carleton University in Ottawa. Her thesis is in the area of pay equity and she has recently published 'Wage Solidarity or Equal Value' in *Studies in Political Economy.*